D0787708

English and German Diction for Singers

for Singers

A Comparative Approach

Amanda Johnston

THE SCARECROW PRESS, INC.
Lanham • Toronto • Plymouth, UK
2011

Published by Scarecrow Press, Inc.
A wholly owned subsidiary of The Rowman & Littlefield Publishing Group, Inc.
4501 Forbes Boulevard, Suite 200, Lanham, Maryland 20706
http://www.scarecrowpress.com

Estover Road, Plymouth PL6 7PY, United Kingdom

Copyright © 2011 by Amanda Johnston

All rights reserved. No part of this book may be reproduced in any form or by any
electronic or mechanical means, including information storage and retrieval systems,
without written permission from the publisher, except by a reviewer who may quote
passages in a review.

British Library Cataloguing in Publication Information Available

Library of Congress Cataloging-in-Publication Data

Johnston, Amanda, 1971–
  English and German diction for singers : a comparative approach / Amanda Johnston.
    p. cm.
  Includes bibliographical references and index.
  ISBN 978-0-8108-7766-5 (hardcover : alk. paper)
  1. Singing—Diction. 2. English language—Pronunciation. 3. German language—
Pronunciation. I. Title.
  MT883.J64 2011
  783'.043—dc22   2010037773

♾™ The paper used in this publication meets the minimum requirements of American
National Standard for Information Sciences—Permanence of Paper for Printed Library
Materials, ANSI/NISO Z39.48-1992.

Printed in the United States of America

MT
883
.J64
2011

To my students, who continue to challenge and inspire me

Contents

Preface

Far beyond memorizing the rules of pronunciation, the study of diction involves learning to perceive speech patterns in different languages, practicing their precise articulation, recognizing this in one's singing and that of others, and developing an awareness of the refined, delicate movements of the articulators and the subsequent effect on singing tone. Clear diction is equated with healthy singing, which in turn leads to greater means of expression and communication. The approach of this book is one of a comparative language study focusing on the sung language, as opposed to the spoken language.

This textbook is designed to be a complete resource for classically trained singers, vocal coaches, voice teachers, and collaborative pianists. It offers a thorough analysis of both German and English, as well as a comprehensive comparison of the two languages. As languages evolve, the intricate study of diction also advances. A modernized approach includes using the latest adaptation of the *Deutsche Rechtschreibung* (2009). This book is also suitable for singers who sing in English as a second language, as IPA transcriptions are provided throughout.

The ensuing material is based on my experience collaborating with singers, while experimenting, evaluating, considering, and experiencing. As a language is always in a state of flux, so also is the field of diction.

Lyric diction: portal to powerful performance

Words have their own innate, natural rhythm, which is then set to music. It is important to remember that the text always came first. Composers lived with the words for a long time before finally creating music around them. It is highly recommended to speak the text separately from the music and learn to hear the innate rhythm and indeed music in the actual words. This applies to any language, but especially those closely tied to word stress, like English and German.

It is through lyric diction that singers are able to communicate the wishes and desires of the poet, as well as the composer. The study of the International Phonetic Alphabet makes it possible to attain the skills to sound like a native speaker when performing foreign repertoire. Healthy diction results in a free tone, which in turn communicates to the audience on an emotional level. Personal interpretation based on the union of text and music creates a convincing and communicative performance.

Comparative language study

English and German are related languages and thus have many things in common with regards to lyric diction. In pairing German and English, it not only deepens the singer's understanding that English is a Germanic language, but also succeeds in making German increasingly accessible in the process. Commonalities discussed include healthy glottal onsets, common consonant sounds, variation in diphthongs, lyric double consonants, phrasal consonant clusters, linguistic history, and legato singing.

For whom is this book suitable?

This book is designed for both undergraduate and graduate courses in German and English lyric diction, as taught at a North American university or conservatory. Although these languages are ideally studied concurrently, this book may also be used for separate courses in each language. Advanced chapters are catered to graduate students and advanced singers with non-traditional training.

How to use this book

This book is designed for the study of both English and German lyric diction, either consecutively or simultaneously. It may be used for both undergraduate and graduate courses, offering a variety of levels and depth of knowledge in one volume. This book is divided into three main parts: English, German, and the English/German Comparative. It is advisable to concentrate on each language separately and regularly consult the comparative section for greater explanation. Many chapters include extensive exercises for increased practice in certain concepts. Answers for all supplementary exercises are provided in Appendix D. Further, phonetic and anatomical terms used throughout this book are included in a detailed glossary in Appendix A. At the very end of the book, there is a removable flashcard containing a handy reference guide for the IPA.

Beginning students with little knowledge of IPA should commence with the Introduction (Part I). There are three chapters providing detailed explanation of all English and German phonemes. Exercises for improving facility with written IPA are also included for both languages. Undergraduate courses should begin here.

Advanced students may skip the chapters in the Introduction and proceed to the individual languages (Parts II and III). Each language has a chapter dedicated to Advanced Concepts in Diction. These chapters are intended for the more advanced student, and are suitable for the graduate level. The comparative section (Part IV) will be especially valuable to the advanced learner.

Acknowledgements

This incredible and rewarding endeavor would not have possible without the support of several people. Many thanks to Scarecrow Press, especially Renée Camus and Jayme Bartles Reed. Thanks also to June Sawyers, for her comprehensive copyediting and preparation of the index. All musical examples were painstakingly prepared by Dann Mitton.

Thanks for your tireless patience and helpful observations. All illustrations were hand-drawn by Ashley L. Wilson. Thanks for lending your artistry to this publication. Thanks also to Lynn Wilson for her feedback from a speech pathologist's perspective. I have had the privilege of working with several leading interpreters of German lied and discussing aspects of lyric diction along the way. Thanks to Rudolf Jansen, Martin Isepp, Dalton Baldwin, Malcolm Martineau, and Dr. Wolfgang Lockemann for their invaluable insight into this repertoire.

I would like to thank my dear friend Susanne Soederberg for her continuous support and inspiration. Sincere thanks to my parents, John and Elizabeth Johnston, who raised two fearless, independent children. Last but not least, thanks to the English and German composers and poets whose work motivates singers and pianists the world over.

Credits

I wish to thank the following publishers for the permission to reprint excerpts of their copyrighted work:

Barber THE ENGLISH LANGUAGE: A HISTORICAL INTRODUCTION © 2000 Cambridge University Press. All Rights Reserved. Tables 25.1 and 25.2 reprinted with permission of Cambridge University Press.

HANDBOOK OF THE INTERNATIONAL PHONETIC ASSOCIATION © 1999 International Phonetic Association. All Rights Reserved. Figures 1.1 and 17.1 reprinted with permission of Cambridge University Press.

Hey DER KLEINE HEY: DIE KUNST DES SPRECHENS © 1997 Schott Music GmbH & Co. KG, Mainz. © 1956 and 1971 (revised edition) by Schott Music GmbH and Co. KG, Mainz. All Rights Reserved. Used by permission of European American Music Distributors

LLC, sole U.S. and Canadian agent for Schott Music GmbH & Co. KG, Mainz.

Parkin ANTHOLOGY OF BRITISH TONGUE-TWISTERS
© 1969 Samuel French Ltd. London. All Rights Reserved. Used by permission of Samuel French Ltd. on behalf of the Estate of Ken Parkin.

PART I: INTRODUCTION

Chapter 1: Elementary Concepts

1.1 Phonetics and the International Phonetic Alphabet

A phonetic symbol designates one particular speech sound regardless of how that given sound is spelled. In each chapter, the phonetic symbol will be indicated in brackets with the name of the actual symbol directly beside it, e.g., [a] Lowercase A. The International Phonetic Alphabet (IPA) is clearly defined as a scientific tool. Phonetic symbols are not unlike chemical symbols, representing elements of sound. The International Phonetic Alphabet Association recommends using the simplest possible symbol in transcribing, e.g., all possible symbols for *l* can be transcribed as [l] in English. It is up to the singer to know which allophone of *l* is required at a given moment.

The International Phonetic Association was founded in 1886 in Paris under the name Dhi Fonètik Tîcerz' Asóciécon (FTA). Originally a small group of language teachers, its mandate was to promote the use of phonetic notation to aid schoolchildren in acquiring realistic pronunciation of foreign languages. Danish phonetician Otto Jespersen had the vision to suggest that there be an International Phonetic Association, which would develop an international alphabet instead of using different alphabets specific to particular languages.

Principles of the International Phonetic Association was first published in English in 1904, and until recently has been the primary resource for phoneticians, speech pathologists, and language enthusiasts. This landmark publication explained phonetic notation, along with transcriptions of an English fable in ca. 50 languages. In 1999, the *Handbook of the International Phonetic Association* was published. This resource is intended to be a reference work not only for language teachers and phoneticians, but also for speech technologists, speech pathologists, and others. Expanded sections include a useful section on computer codes for the use of phonetic symbols. This diction textbook is based on the most recent adjustments and research reflected in this publication.

1.2 Vowel classification

When considering the production of vowels and consonants, one must ascertain the necessary vowel shape and the principal tactile work of specific articulators. The space and shape necessary to produce pure vowels is integral to finding the correct phoneme. Specifically, the shape of the open passage above the larynx (including the pharynx and mouth) determines the quality of the vowel. It forms a resonance chamber for the sound produced by the vibration of the vocal folds, resulting in distinct vowels. Moreover, the position of the tongue and the lips may alter the shape of this resonance chamber.

The position of the soft palate (velum) strongly influences vowel quality as well. In the production of all vowels (excluding nasal vowels, commonly found in French), the soft palate must be raised so that air cannot escape through the nose. When the soft palate is lowered, air can escape through the nose as well as the mouth, resulting in an unwanted nasalized vowel.

Generally, vowels are classified according to the position of the tongue. When the tongue is in an intermediate position (not markedly raised or lowered), the resultant sound is a neutral vowel or *schwa*. There are eight pure vowels, known as Cardinal Vowels, which are as far removed as possible from the neutral position. They were developed by phonetician Daniel Jones in 1918 (Jones 1962). The primary Cardinal Vowels are numbered as follows: 1 [i], 2 [e], 3 [ɛ], 4 [a], 5 [ɑ], 6 [ɔ], 7 [o], and 8 [u]. In passing through vowels 1–4, the tongue lowers in rather equal increments. Moreover, when passing through vowels 5–8, the tongue rises up with equal (but smaller) increments. One may divide the Cardinal Vowels into groups of front and back vowels (related to the amount of arch in the tongue). The differing vowel quality for the front vowels is determined solely by the position of the tongue. The varied vowel quality for the back vowels is determined by the position of the lips (in addition to the tongue). In the latter group, the lips are the primary articulator.

When vowels 1–3 add lip rounding, mixed vowels result, e.g., [y:], [ø:], [œ]. These are also known as Secondary Cardinal Vowels.

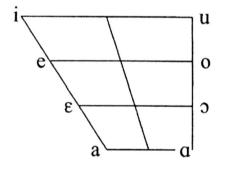

Figure 1.1. Primary cardinal vowels

Source: Daniel Jones, *Handbook of the International Phonetic Association* (Cambridge: Cambridge University Press, 1999), 12.

1.3 Organs of speech

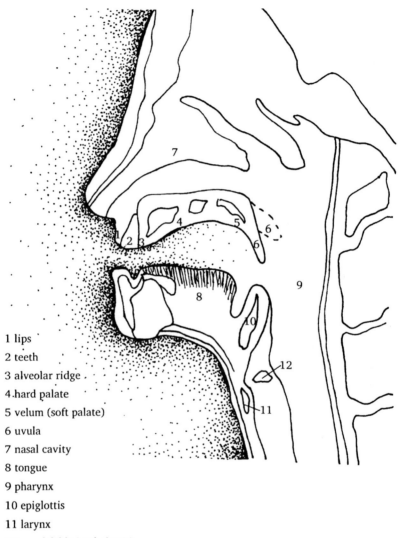

1 lips
2 teeth
3 alveolar ridge
4 hard palate
5 velum (soft palate)
6 uvula
7 nasal cavity
8 tongue
9 pharynx
10 epiglottis
11 larynx
12 vocal folds (and glottis)

Figure 1.2. The primary organs of speech also used in singing

1.4 Points of articulation

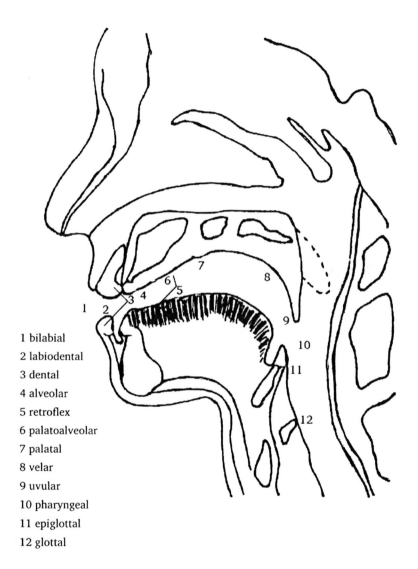

1 bilabial
2 labiodental
3 dental
4 alveolar
5 retroflex
6 palatoalveolar
7 palatal
8 velar
9 uvular
10 pharyngeal
11 epiglottal
12 glottal

Figure 1.3. Concise definitions for all points of articulation may be found in the glossary (Appendix A).

Chapter 2: Proficiency in English IPA

Vowels

English vowels are grouped in three categories: monophthongs, diphthongs, and triphthongs. In the time of one syllable, it is possible to have
one, two, or three vowels. Monophthongs, also known as pure vowels,
are represented by a single IPA symbol. These may be classified according to relative tongue position (close or open), inherent sound quality
(bright, dark), height in the mouth (high, mid, low), or distance from
the opening of the mouth (front, central, back). This text prefers to classify the vowels according to their emotional impact and therefore divides
them into four groups: bright, central, dark, and R-less. Closed vowels
are formed when the tongue is positioned as close as possible to the roof
of the mouth, without creating an obstruction that would result in a
consonant. Open vowels are formed by the opposite position of the
tongue, namely, as far away as possible from the roof of the mouth.

Bright vowels [i][ɪ][ɛ]

[i]   Lowercase I   Bright (tongue), close
Spelling: *ee, ea, ei, i, ie, e*

creek	[kɹik]	machine	[məˈʃin]
dream	[dɹim]	piece	[pis]
receive	[ɹɪˈsiv]	theme	[θim]

8

[ɪ]   Small capital I   Bright (tongue), open
Spelling: *i, ie, ui, y*

| loving | [lʌvɪŋ] | guilt | [gɪlt] |
| cities | [sɪtɪz] | pity | [pɪtɪ] |

[ɛ]   Epsilon   Bright (tongue), open
Spelling: *e, ea, ai, a*

| together | [tə'gɛðə] | again | [ə'gɛn] |
| wealth | [wɛlθ] | many | [mɛnɪ] |

Central vowels [æ][ɑ][ʌ][ə]

[æ]   Lowercase A-E ligature   Central (tongue), open
Spelling: *a, au*

| everlasting | [ɛvə'læstɪŋ] | laugh | [læf] |

[ɑ]   Script A   Central (tongue), open
Spelling: *a, o*

| father | [fɑðə] | rocking | [ɹɑkɪŋ] |

[ʌ]   Turned V   Central (tongue)

This neutral vowel is found in the prefix *un-* and stressed syllables. It is
the stressed counterpart to [ə] and is neither closed nor open.
Spelling: *o, oo, ou, u, un-*

wonderful	[wʌndəfʊl]	but	[bʌt]
flood	[flʌd]	uncouth	[ʌn'kuθ]
trouble	[tɹʌbəl]		

[ə]   Schwa   Central (tongue)

This neutral vowel is only found in unstressed syllables. It is the counterpart to [ʌ] and is neither closed nor open.

Spelling: *a, e, i, o, u, y, ou*

about	[əˈbaʊt]	medium	[midiəm]
heaven	[hɛvən]	syringe	[səˈɹɪndʒ]
pencil	[pɛnsəl]	vicious	[vɪʃəs]
nation	[neɪʃən]		

Spelling: *ar, er, or, -ur, -le, -re* (substitution for *r*)

cougar	[kugə]	murmur	[mɜmə]
persuade	[pəˈsweɪd]	little	[lɪtəl]
factor	[fæktə]	theatre	[θiətə]

Dark vowels [ɔ][o][ʊ][u]

[ɔ]   Open O   Dark (rounded lips), open

Spelling: *a* (before *l* or *ll*), *au, augh, aw, o* (before *rr*), *ough*

almanac	[ɔlmənæk]	law	[lɔ]
all	[ɔl]	sorry	[sɔɹɪ]
fault	[fɔlt]	bought	[bɔt]
caught	[kɔt]		

[o]   Lowercase O   Dark (rounded lips), close

This vowel only occurs in the unstressed prefixes *o-* and *pro-*.

Spelling: *o-, pro-*

omit	[oˈmɪt]	provide	[pɹoˈvaɪd]

[ʊ]   Upsilon   Dark (rounded lips), open
Spelling: *oo, ou, u*

| book | [bʊk] | put | [pʊt] |
| should | [ʃʊd] | | |

[u]   Lowercase U   Dark (rounded lips), close
Spelling: *o, oo, ou, u, ue, ui, ew*

do	[du]	glue	[glu]
food	[fud]	bruise	[bɹuz]
through	[θɹu]	flew	[flu]
ruse	[ɹuz]		

R-less vowels [ɜ][ə]

In everyday speech, one uses the R-colored vowels [ɝ] and [ɚ] in General American English (GA). However, this text strongly recommends the sole use of R-less vowels in lyric diction. In order to keep the soft palate elevated, it is important to avoid the presence of the approximant *r* [ɹ] in the actual vowel sound.

[ɜ]   Reversed epsilon   Central (tongue), open
This R-less vowel is found in stressed syllables only. It is the counterpart to the unstressed *schwa* [ə], but has a greater intensity and focus.
Spelling: *ear, er, ir, or, our, ur, yr*

earth	[ɜθ]	adjourned	[əˈdʒɜnd]
her	[hɜ]	turn	[tɜn]
first	[fɜst]	myrrh	[mɜ]
worms	[wɜmz]		

Diphthongs

When one vowel glides into a successive vowel and produces a smooth, imperceptible blend within one syllable, it is referred to as a diphthong. It is advised to spend 75% of the note value on the first vowel, moving seamlessly through the second vowel for the remaining 25% of the note value. There should be no movement of the lips, tongue, or jaw during this smooth transition between vowels. This text promotes the use of ten diphthongs: five are standard features of General American English (GA) ([aɪ], [aʊ], [oʊ], [ɔɪ], [eɪ]) and five are borrowed from British Received Pronunciation (RP) ([ʊə], [ɛə], [ɔə], [ɑə], [ɪə]).

The use of [a] in English diphthongs
Though not considered a monophthong in GA, the vowel [a] is present in two diphthongs. This bright, open vowel is prevalent in German and the Romance languages. In English lyric diction, its role as the primary vowel increases the sense of vertical space in the mouth and brightens the quality of both [aɪ] and [aʊ].

[aɪ]
Spelling: *ay, i, ie, igh, eigh, ui, y*

bayou	[baɪu]	height	[haɪt]
pride	[pɹaɪd]	guide	[gaɪd]
tie	[taɪ]	my	[maɪ]
right	[ɹaɪt]		

[aʊ]
Spelling: *ou, ough, ow*

| proud | [pɹaʊd] | plow | [plaʊ] |
| bough | [baʊ] | | |

[oʊ]

Spelling: *o, oa, oe, ou, ough, ow*

no	[noʊ]	boulder	[boʊldə]
broach	[bɹoʊtʃ]	although	[ɔlˈðoʊ]
doe	[doʊ]	blow	[bloʊ]

[ɔɪ]

Spelling: *oi, oy*

voice	[vɔɪs]	joy	[dʒɔɪ]

[eɪ]

Spelling: *a, ai, ay, ea, ei, ey*

name	[neɪm]	break	[bɹeɪk]
slain	[sleɪn]	deign	[deɪn]
may	[meɪ]	they	[ðeɪ]

Diphthongs borrowed from Received Pronunciation (with final *r*)

In the following five diphthongs, *r* is replaced by the *schwa* [ə].

[ɑə]

Spelling: *ar, ear*

start	[stɑət]	hearth	[hɑəθ]

[ɛə]

Spelling: *air, are, ear, eir, ere*

flair	[flɛə]	their	[ðɛə]
fare	[fɛə]	there	[ðɛə]
bear	[bɛə]		

[ɪə]
Spelling: *ear, eer, ere, ier*

ear	[ɪə]	here	[hɪə]
leer	[lɪə]	pier	[pɪə]

[ɔə]
Spelling: *oar, oor, our, or, ore, ar*

soar	[sɔə]	or	[ɔə]
door	[dɔə]	core	[kɔə]
pour	[pɔə]	war	[wɔə]

[ʊə]
Spelling: *oor, our, ure*

poor	[pʊə]	pure	[pjʊə]
tour	[tʊə]		

Triphthongs

Triphthongs present the challenge of passing through three vowels within the duration of one syllable. As with diphthongs, the first vowel is sustained for most of the note value. There must be no movement of the lips or the jaw during the smooth transition between vowels.

[aɪə]
Spelling: *ire, yre*

fire	[faɪə]	lyre	[laɪə]

[aʊə]
Spelling: *our, ower*

dour   [daʊə]   flower   [flaʊə]

Consonants

Voiced vs. voiceless
For the purpose of lyric diction, consonants may be divided into two distinct groups: voiced and voiceless. Voiced consonants carry the pitch and when used properly ensure a seamless legato. Voiceless consonants must be articulated in between the notes to certify rhythmic accuracy.

Double consonants
Orthographic double consonants are not pronounced differently from single consonants in English. In general, a double consonant opens the vowel directly preceding it, e.g., hopping [hɑpɪŋ] vs. hoping [hoʊpɪŋ].

Classification of consonants
English consonants may be divided into the following groups: plosives, fricatives, nasals, laterals, and affricates. Please see Appendix A for comprehensive definitions of phonetic terms.

Plosives (Stops) [b][p][d][t][g][k]
[b]   Lowercase B   Voiced bilabial plosive
Spelling: *b, bb*

brown   [bɹaʊn]   rubber   [ɹʌbə]

[p]   Lowercase P   Voiceless bilabial plosive
Spelling: *p, pp*

purple   [pɜpəl]   dapper   [dæpə]

[d]   Lowercase D   Voiced alveolar plosive
Spelling: *d, dd*

diminish   [dəˈmɪnəʃ]   to coddle   [kɑdəl]

[t]   Lowercase T   Voiceless alveolar plosive
Spelling: *t, tt, bt*

triumphant   [tɹaɪˈʌmfənt]   debtor   [dɛtə]
rebuttal   [ɹɪˈbʌtəl]

[g]   Lowercase G   Voiced velar plosive
Spelling: *g, gg, gh, gue*

grape   [gɹeɪp]   ghost   [goʊst]
baggage   [bægədʒ]   catalogue   [kætəlɑg]

[k]   Lowercase K   Voiceless velar plosive
Spelling: *c, cc, ch, ck, k, que*

colorful   [kʌləfʊl]   pocket   [pɑkət]
soccer   [sɑkə]   kindness   [kaɪndnəs]
character   [kæɹəktə]   critique   [kɹəˈtik]

Fricatives [v] [f] [ð] [θ] [z] [s] [ʒ] [ʃ] [h] [ʍ]
[v]   Lowercase V   Voiced labiodental fricative
Spelling: *v, vv*

vivacious   [vəˈveɪʃəs]   savvy   [sævɪ]

[f]   Lowercase F   Voiceless labiodental fricative
Spelling: *f, ff, ph, gh*

foreboding	[fɔəˈboʊdɪŋ]	telephone	[tɛləfoʊn]
baffled	[bæfəld]	laughter	[læftə]

[ð]   Eth   Voiced dental fricative
Spelling: *th*

therefore	[ðɛəfɔə]

[θ]   Theta   Voiceless dental fricative
Spelling: *th*

throughout	[θɹuˈaʊt]

[z]   Lowercase Z   Voiced alveolar fricative
Spelling: *s, z, zz*

hands	[hændz]	dazzling	[dæzlɪŋ]
zephyr	[zɛfə]		

[s]   Lowercase S   Voiceless alveolar fricative
Spelling: *s, ss, ce, ci, cy, sce, sci, ps-*

seminar	[sɛmənɑə]	to recycle	[ɹiˈsaɪkəl]
blossom	[blɑsəm]	scene	[sin]
reception	[ɹɪˈsɛpʃən]	scientific	[saɪənˈtɪfɪk]
circular	[sɔkjələ]	psychology	[saɪˈkɑlədʒɪ]

[ʒ]   Ezh   Voiced postalveolar fricative
Spelling: *si, su, -age*

decision   [dɪˈsɪʒən]   garage   [ɡəˈɹɑʒ]
unusual   [ʌnˈjuʒuəl]

[ʃ]   Esh   Voiceless postalveolar fricative
Spelling: *sh, s, ssi, ce, ch, ci, ti*

shameful   [ʃeɪmfʊl]   chute   [ʃut]
sure   [ʃʊə]   precious   [pɹɛʃəs]
fission   [fɪʃən]   rational   [ɹæʃənəl]
crustacean   [kɹəsˈteɪʃən]

[h]   Lowercase H   Voiceless glottal fricative
Spelling: *h, wh* (before *o*)

headache   [hɛdeɪk]   whom   [hum]

[ʍ]   Turned W   Voiceless labiovelar fricative
Spelling: *wh*

whimper   [ʍɪmpə]

Nasals [m][n][ɲ][ŋ]
[m]   Lowercase M   Voiced bilabial nasal
Spelling: *m, mm, -lm, -mb, -mn*

mother   [mʌðə]   tomb   [tum]
summer   [sʌmə]   column   [kɑləm]
calm   [kɔm]

[n]   Lowercase N   Voiced alveolar nasal
Spelling: *n, nn, gn, kn-*

nobody	[noʊbədɪ]	gnat	[næt]
tunnel	[tʌnəl]	know	[noʊ]

[ɲ]   Left-tail N   Voiced palatal nasal
Spelling: *new, ni, nu*

newspaper	[ɲuzpeɪpə]	nuance	[ɲuɑns]
onion	[ʌɲən]		

[ŋ]   Eng   Voiced velar nasal
Spelling: *n* (before *k* or *x*), *ng*

thankful	[θæŋkfʊl]	something	[sʌmθɪŋ]
lynx	[lɪŋks]		

Laterals [l]

In English speech, one uses two allophones of *l*, depending on where it falls in the word. This text advocates the sole use of the clear *l* in lyric diction. This phoneme is generally associated with initial *l*, e.g., limb, as opposed to the dark *l*, generally associated with final *l*, e.g., call.

[l]   Lowercase L   Voiced alveolar lateral
Spelling: *l, ll*

light	[laɪt]	shallow	[ʃæloʊ]

Affricates [dʒ][tʃ]

[dʒ]   D-Ezh ligature   Voiced postalveolar affricate
Spelling: *dg, ge, gi, gg, gy, ja, je, ji, jo, ju*

badge	[bædʒ]	jalopy	[dʒəˈlɑpɪ]
generation	[dʒɛnəˈɹeɪʃən]	jealous	[dʒɛləs]
gin	[dʒɪn]	jinx	[dʒɪŋks]
suggest	[səˈdʒɛst]	joyous	[dʒɔɪəs]
gymnastic	[dʒɪmˈnæstɪk]	judicious	[dʒuˈdɪʃəs]

[tʃ]   T-Esh ligature   Voiceless postalveolar affricate
Spelling: *ch, tch, -ture*

chariot	[tʃæɹɪət]	picture	[pɪktʃə]
matches	[mætʃəz]		

Glides and approximants [w][j][ɹ]
A glide, also known as a semi-vowel, is a phoneme that begins as a vowel but is ultimately heard as a consonant. It is neither a true vowel, nor a true consonant.

[w]   Lowercase W   Voiced labial-velar approximant
Spelling: *w, qu*

wonder	[wʌndə]	quick	[kwɪk]

[j]   Lowercase J   Voiced palatal approximant
Spelling: *c, d, f, h, l, m, p, s, t* (before *u*), *lli, u-, y* (before vowel)

cute	[kjut]	purify	[pjʊɹəfaɪ]
during	[djʊɹɪŋ]	suitor	[sjutə]

futile	[fjutaɪl]	tune	[tjun]
human	[hjumən]	million	[mɪljən]
lute	[ljut]	use	[juz]
municipal	[mjuˈnɪsəpəl]	your	[jɔə]

[ɹ]   Turned R   Voiced dental or alveolar approximant
Spelling: *r, rh, rr, wr*

| runner | [ɹʌnə] | error | [ɛɹə] |
| rhyme | [ɹaɪm] | wrap | [ɹæp] |

Additional consonants
[ks]
Spelling: *x, cc*

| axe | [æks] | accept | [əkˈsɛpt] |

[gz]
Spelling: *x*

| exalt | [ɪgˈzɔlt] |

Exercises for writing/reading IPA
Vowels: In the following exercises, indicate which vowel is used in the given examples, e.g., queen (Answer: [i]).

1. [i] vs. [ɪ]
bleed, yield, implore, spirit, each, caffeine, mirror, qualities, daisy, achieve, these, routine, citizen, sunny, candies, prestige, reach, guilt

2. [i] vs. [ɛ]

heathen, bread, instead, please, sweater, treachery, leave, teach, threat, dream, breach, weapon, leather, speaking, cream, meadow

3. [ɛ] vs. [æ]

carry, any, shall, answer, anger, adversary, rat, narrow, had, barren, magic, vanish, secretary, says, ask, carrot, capture, annals, sparrow

4. [ʌ] vs. [ə]

patrol, maiden, sadness, pardon, enough, utter, pedal, virus, lament, fun, one, flood, needed, trumpet, untrue, couple, crimson, wonder, supper, unkind

5. [ɑ] vs. [ɔ]

talk, fall, massage, safari, façade, prophets, exhaust, naughty, hawk, hot, father, pawn, horrid, sought, camouflage, altered, sorry, recall, corsage

6. [u] vs. [ʊ]

stood, soot, too, noon, woo, brook, cook, moon, good, food, doom, pool, hook, soon, crook, mistook, foolish, gloom, shook, loose, wool, cool

7. Diphthongs [aɪ][eɪ][aʊ][oʊ][ɔɪ]

widen, load, nation, house, spoil, malign, straight, loincloth, thou, roe, destroy, lie, sigh, boy, soul, steak, neither, dowdy, feign, choice

8. Diphthongs borrowed from RP [ɑə][ɛə][ɪə][ɔə][ʊə]

gargle, moor, pier, stair, heir, appear, poor, quarter, starve, course, gourd, prepare, ore, steer, darkness, force, sincere, hearth, tear, contour

Consonants: Transcribe the following words in their entirety, e.g., talc (Answer: [tælk]).

9. **Plosives (Stops)** [b][p][d][t][g][k]

aghast, behind, shellac, beard, knob, lobby, gallop, occupy, excerpt (n.), nugget, fold, abbess, dialogue, mountain, antique, cheddar, shutter, speed, code, happen, puddle, supper, rattle

10. **Fricatives** [v][f][z][s][ð][θ][ʒ][ʃ][h][ʍ]

theft, barrage, scenario, whisper, parachute, social, designer, why, poverty, psychic, spring, permission, divvy, southern, sugar, confusion, zest, whole, frightening, message, gather, measure, nation, phenomenal, puzzle, giraffe, should, teeth, cough, cedar, home, verbal

11. **Nasals** [m][n][ŋ][ɲ]

think, malign, merry, gnome, Bronx, autumn, summit, knead, ringer, qualm, pinch, newsworthy, aplomb, sinner, union, nubile

12. **Glides and approximants** [w][j][ɹ]

punity, chrome, quart, bewail, phrase, Tuesday, canyon, aware, burr, rhinoceros, cure, wake, lute, wonder, million, wry, musician, quite, Hugh, university, rhapsody, equation, duke, wriggle, quarterly, assume

13. **Affricates** [dʒ][tʃ]

chained, generate, pigeon, search, jasmine, farfetched, lecture, veggie, gymnasium, natural, strategy, justice, majesty, dodge, Fiji, joke, giant, choice, large, jaw

Chapter 3: Proficiency in German IPA

Vowels

German vowels may be divided into two categories: monophthongs and diphthongs. Monophthongs, also known as pure vowels, are represented by a single IPA symbol. These may be classified according to relative length and tongue position (close or open), inherent sound quality (bright, dark), height in the mouth (high, mid, low), or distance from the opening of the mouth (front, central, back). This text prefers to classify the vowels according to their emotional impact and therefore divides them into four groups: bright, central, dark, and mixed. Closed vowels are formed when the tongue is positioned as close as possible to the roof of the mouth, without creating an obstruction that would result in a consonant. Open vowels are formed by the opposite position of the tongue, namely, as far away as possible from the roof of the mouth.

Vowel Length

In German, all closed vowels are *long*. The colon [ː] is used in IPA to illustrate vowel length. This principle does not exist in English and is difficult for non-natives to adopt. In essence, a closed vowel is held almost double the length of an open vowel. This lends a natural rhythm and lilt to the German language. It is possible to have multiple closed vowels within a word. Note that the long closed vowel may fall on an unstressed syllable, e.g., *der Kaffee* [kafeː] vs. *das Café* [kaˈfeː].

Bright vowels [iː][ɪ][eː][ɛ][ɛː]

[iː]   Lowercase I   Bright (tongue), close
Spelling: *i, ih, ie, ieh*

die Augenlider	[aogənliːdɐ]	eyelids
ihr	[iːɐ]	her, to her
die Liebe	[liːbə]	love
ziehen	[tsiːən]	to pull

[ɪ]   Small capital I   Bright (tongue), open
Spelling: *i*

finster	[fɪnstɐ]	gloomy, sinister

[eː]   Lowercase E   Bright (tongue), close
Spelling: *e, ee, eh*

geben	[geːbən]	to give
mehr	[meːɐ]	more
die Seele	[zeːlə]	soul

[ɛ]   Epsilon   Bright (tongue), open
Spelling: *e, ä*

die Schwester	[ʃvɛstɐ]	sister(s)
das Kämmerlein	[kɛmərlaen]	small chamber

[ɛː]   Epsilon   Bright (tongue), near-close
Spelling: *ä, äh*

die Tränen	[trɛːnən]	tears

gähnen   [gɛːnən]   to yawn

Central vowels: [aː][a][ə][ɐ]
[aː]   Lowercase A   Central (tongue), open
Spelling: *a, aa, ah*

der Pfad   [pfaːt]   path
der Saal   [zaːl]   hall, room
fahren   [faːɾən]   to drive

[a]   Lowercase A   Central (tongue), open
Spelling: *a*

das Wasser   [vasɐ]   water

[ə]   Schwa   Central (tongue)
Spelling: *e*

die Tische   [tɪʃə]   tables

[ɐ]   Turned A   Central (tongue), near-open
Spelling: *r, -er, er-, ver-, der-, vor-*

mir   [miːɐ]   to me
später   [ʃpɛːtɐ]   later
erkennen   [ɛɐˈkɛnən]   to recognize
verbergen   [fɛɐˈbɛɾgən]   to hide
dereinst   [deːɐˈ|aenst]   once
die Vorahnung   [ˈfoːɐ|aːnʊŋ]   premonition

Dark vowels: [o:][ɔ][u:][ʊ]

[o:]   Lowercase O   Dark (rounded lips), close
Spelling: *o, oh, oo*

der Mond	[mo:nt]	moon
der Sohn	[zo:n]	son
das Boot	[bo:t]	boat

[ɔ]   Open O   Dark (rounded lips), open
Spelling: *o*

der Hocker	[hɔkɐ]	stool

[u:]   Lowercase U   Dark (rounded lips), close
Spelling: *u, uh*

tun	[tu:n]	to do
der Schuh	[ʃu:]	shoe

[ʊ]   Upsilon   Dark (rounded lips), open
Spelling: *u*

die Mund	[mʊnt]	mouth

Mixed vowels: [y:][ʏ][ø:][œ]

[y:]   Lowercase Y   Mixed (tongue + rounded lips), close
Spelling: *ü, üh, y*

blüten	[bly:tən]	to bloom
die Gefühle	[gə'fy:lə]	feelings
die Lyrik	[ly:ɾɪk]	lyric poetry, verse

[ʏ]   Small capital Y   Mixed (tongue + rounded lips), open
Spelling: *ü, y*

glücklich   [glʏklɪç]   happy
der Amethyst   [ameˈtʏst]   amethyst

[øː]   O-slash   Mixed (tongue + rounded lips), close
Spelling: *ö, öh*

hören   [høːɾən]   to listen/to hear
stöhnen   [ʃtøːnən]   to moan

[œ]   Lowercase O-E ligature   Mixed (tongue + rounded lips), open
Spelling: *ö*

die Wörter   [vœɾtɐ]   words

Diphthongs [ae][ao][ɔø]
When one vowel glides into a successive vowel and produces a smooth, imperceptible blend within one syllable, it is referred to as a diphthong. It is advised to spend 90% of the note value on the first vowel, moving seamlessly through the second vowel for the remaining 10% of the note value. There should be no movement of the lips, tongue, or jaw during this smooth transition between vowels.

[ae]
Spelling: *ei, ey, ai, ay*

die Freizeit   [fɾaetsaet]   freedom
Eyersdorf   [aeəɾsdɔrf]   Eyersdorf (town)
der Hain   [haen]   grove

| Bayern | [baeərn] | Bavaria |

[ao]
Spelling: *au*

| der Raubvogel | [raopfo:gəl] | bird of prey |

[ɔø]
Spelling: *eu, äu*

| erneuern | [ɛɐˈnɔøərn] | to renew, to revive |
| die Räume | [rɔømə] | rooms |

Consonants

Voiced vs. voiceless

As in English lyric diction, consonants may be divided into two distinct groups: voiced and voiceless. Voiced consonants carry the pitch and when used properly secure a seamless legato. Voiceless consonants must be articulated in between the notes to ensure rhythmic accuracy.

Double consonants

Orthographic double consonants are lengthened meaningfully in German compared to single consonants. In essence, a double consonant shortens the vowel directly preceding it, e.g., *bitte* [bɪtə]. Note that this maxim is *not* expressed in written IPA. It is up to the singer to articulate double consonants and thus realize their full expressive potential.

Classification of consonants

German consonants may be divided into six groups: plosives, fricatives, nasals, laterals, trills, and affricates.

Plosives (Stops) [b] [p] [d] [t] [g] [k]

[b]   Lowercase B   Voiced bilabial plosive
Spelling: *b, bb*

| die Blumen | [bluːmən] | flowers |
| die Ebbe | [ɛbə] | ebb tide |

[p]   Lowercase P   Voiceless bilabial plosive
Spelling: *p, pp, b* (latter only at end of word element)

der Papagei	[papaˈgae]	parrot
plappern	[plapərn]	to babble
das Grab	[gɾaːp]	grave

[d]   Lowercase D   Voiced alveolar plosive
Spelling: *d, dd*

| die Demut | [deːmuːt] | humility, humbleness |
| der Widder | [vɪdɐ] | ram |

[t]   Lowercase T   Voiceless alveolar plosive
Spelling: *t, th, tt, dt, d* (latter only at end of word element)

die Tasche	[taʃə]	bag, pocket
das Theater	[teaːtɐ]	theatre
bitte	[bɪtə]	please, you're welcome
die Stadt	[ʃtat]	city
der Tod	[toːt]	death

[g]   Lowercase G   Voiced velar plosive
Spelling: *g, gg*

groß	[gro:s]	tall, big
schmuggeln	[ʃmʊgəln]	to smuggle

[k]   Lowercase K   Voiceless velar plosive
Spelling: *k*, *kk*, *ck*, *g* (latter only at end of word element)

der Kreis	[kraes]	circle
der Akkord	[aˈkɔrt]	chord
blicken	[blɪkən]	to glance, to look
der Tag	[ta:k]	day

Fricatives [v][f][z][s][ʒ][ʃ][h][j][ç][χ]

[v]   Lowercase V   Voiced labiodental fricative
Spelling: *w*, *v*

das Wetter	[vɛtɐ]	weather
das Klavier	[klaˈviːɐ]	piano

[f]   Lowercase F   Voiceless labiodental fricative
Spelling: *f*, *ff*, *v*, *ph* (latter only in borrowed foreign words)

die Freundschaft	[frɔøntʃaft]	friendship
die Waffe	[vafə]	weapon
das Veilchen	[faelçən]	violet
die Phobie	[foˈbiː]	phobia

[z]   Lowercase Z   Voiced alveolar fricative
Spelling: *s*

die Sonne	[zɔnə]	sun

[s]   Lowercase S   Voiceless alveolar fricative
Spelling: *s, ss, ß*

das Glas   [glaːs]   glass

wissen   [vɪsən]   to know

das Schloß   [ʃlɔs]   castle

[ʒ]   Ezh   Voiced postalveolar fricative
Spelling: *g, j*

sich genieren   [ʒeˈniːrən]   to be embarrassed

jonglieren   [ʒɔŋˈliːrən]   to juggle

[ʃ]   Esh   Voiceless postalveolar fricative
Spelling: *sch, s* (before *p, t*)

schimmernd   [ʃɪmərnt]   sparkling

spazieren   [ʃpaˈtsiːrən]   to go for a walk

die Stimme   [ʃtɪmə]   voice

[h]   Lowercase H   Voiceless glottal fricative
Spelling: *h*

die Hochzeit   [hɔχtsaet]   wedding

[j]   Curly-tail J   Voiced palatal fricative
Spelling: *j*

die Jagd   [jakt]   hunt, chase

[ç]   C cedilla   Voiceless palatal fricative
Spelling: *ch* or *-ig* suffix

die Milch   [mɪlç]   milk
der König   [køːnɪç]   king

[χ]   Chi   Voiceless uvular fricative
Spelling: *ch*

die Nacht   [naχt]   night

N.B.: For detailed information regarding Curly-tail J [ʝ], *ich-laut* [ç], and
ach-laut [χ], please see Chapter 16 (Characteristic German Phonemes).

Nasals [m][n][ŋ]
[m]   Lowercase M   Voiced bilabial nasal
Spelling: *m, mm*

der Monat   [moːnaːt]   month
der Himmel   [hɪməl]   heaven

[n]   Lowercase N   Voiced alveolar nasal
Spelling: *n, nn*

nichts   [nɪçts]   nothing
die Wonne   [vɔnə]   rapture

[ŋ]   Eng   Voiced velar nasal
Spelling: *ng, n* (before *k*)

der Finger   [fɪŋɐ]   finger

dunkel   [dʊŋkəl]   dark

Laterals [l]
[l]   Lowercase L   Voiced alveolar lateral
Spelling: *l, ll*

das Licht   [lɪçt]   light
die Stille   [ʃtɪlə]   silence, stillness

Trills [ɾ]
This text advocates the sole use of a one-tapped trill (a.k.a. the flipped *r*)
in lyric diction. One may choose to roll *r* (expressed as [r]) when singing
certain German operatic or oratorio repertoire.

[ɾ]   Fish-hook R   Voiced alveolar tap
Spelling: *r, rr*

der Regen   [reːgən]   rain
klirren   [klɪɾən]   to clang

Affricates [ts][tʃ]
[ts]   T-S ligature   Voiceless dental or alveolar affricate
Spelling: *ts, tz, z, c, ti* (latter two in borrowed foreign words)

rechts   [ɾɛçts]   right
jetzt   [j̊ɛtst]   now
zärtlich   [tsɛːɾtlɪç]   tenderly
Czar   [tsaːɾ]   Tsar
die Funktion   [fʊŋkˈtsioːn]   capacity, function

[tʃ]   T-Esh ligature   Voiceless postalveolar affricate
Spelling: *tsch*

quatschen   [kvatʃən]   to gab, to blather

Additional consonants borrowed from foreign words: *q, x*
[kv]
Spelling: *qu*

die Quelle   [kvɛlə]   source

[ks]
Spelling: *x, chs*

die Hexe   [hɛksə]   witch
der Fuchs   [fʊks]   fox

Exercises for writing/reading IPA
Vowels: In the following exercises, identify the vowel used in the given
example, using the colon as necessary, e.g., *rot* (Answer: [oː]).

1. **[iː] vs. [ɪ]**
studieren, dir, binnen, ihm, die Geschwister, der Delfin, ist, ihnen, die
Maschine, schwimmen, die Biene, das Schiff, der Lindenbaum, legitim,
trinken, wissen, die Beziehung, hilfreich, nichts, das Kind, ihrerseits,
sinken, erziehen, niemals

2. **[eː] vs. [ɛ]**
verstehen, die Hemmung, eben, verschwenden, besser, die Himbeere,
trennbar, gestern, der Klee, drehen, enden, der Weg, das Wetter, er, die
Meerfrau, der Lehrer, rennen, schwer, beleben, sprechen, der Kern

3. [ɛː] vs. [ɛ]

der Lärm, spät, näher, die Gäste, gähnen, die Dämmerung, das Wähnen, die Tränen, mäßig, die Wälder, die Fähigkeit, lästern, die Pläne, älter, gesättigt, gebären, die Gläser, lässig, wärmer, die Universität, die Stätte

4. [aː] vs. [a]

wahnsinnig, der Mann, klagen, die Schlacht, fabelhaft, behaart, backen, die Sachen, die Haarbürste, der Hass, die Fahne, nass, die U-Bahn, die Waage, danke, einladen, der Rand, der Abend, anfangen, angeln

5. [oː] vs. [ɔ]

die Wohnung, locker, toben, der Strom, noch, das Schloß, die Bohnen, froh, oft, das Wort, das Moos, voll, fromm, der Bahnhof, sonderbar, die Krone, doof, gekrochen, das Boot, die Wolken

6. [uː] vs. [ʊ]

das Huhn, die Kuh, munter, die Blumen, der Kunde, die Wut, die Butter, der Thunfisch, muffig, durch, die Armbanduhr, die Furcht, der Durst, und, der Stuhl, der Sonnenhut, der Schlummer, die Kunst, der Zug, der Handschuh

7. [yː] vs. [ʏ]

rhythmisch, die Bemühung, spücken, süß, die Mühle, das Stück, der Typ, berühren, das System, zurück, die Analyse, spüren, füllen, zynisch, syllabisch, die Führung, dynamisch, rückwärts, die Übungen, glücklich

8. [øː] vs. [œ]

verwöhnt, röntgen, die Römer, die Dörfer, der Fön, die Behörde, blöd, die Töpfe, stören, die Stundenlöhne, das Brötchen, der Knöchel, möchte, die Möhren, die Krönung, dröhnen, die Völker, die Götter, die Wörter, der Knödel

9. **Diphthongs** [ae][ao][ɔø]

feiern, der Baum, heute, erscheinen, die Autobahn, betreuen, der Laib, der Papagei, Bayern, das Gebäude, das Zeugnis, der Ausflug, der Kaiser, die Freude, der Wein, blau, auch, arbeiten, neun, die Pause, die Mauer, träumen, der Rauch, häufig

Consonants: Transcribe the following words in their entirety, e.g., *bestimmt* (Answer: [bəʃtɪmt]).

10. **Plosives** [b][p][d][t][g][k]

die Mutter, halb, der Bleistift, dankbar, die Frage, babbeln, die Stadt, der Preis, knuddeln, der Wald, die Grenze, die Puppe, der Betrieb, tanzen, der Baggersee, können, der Akkord, blicken, das Theater, der Schlag, der Brief, der Dienst, die Rückkehr, schmecken

11. **Fricatives** [v][f][z][s][ʒ][ʃ][h]

die Größe, der Neffe, warum, die Sprache, das Visum, aufführen, das Genie, absolvieren, der Student, finden, veranstalten, die Phonetik, das Gras, beweisen, schenken, der Journalismus, die Klarheit, wichtig, müssen, duften, die Haut, der Sommer, der Sprachkurs, gehören

12. **Nasals** [m][n][ŋ]

der Gedanke, das Kinn, manchmal, nächste, sinken, murmeln, anfangen, der Kummer, die Spinne, der Notfall, dringen, kaum, innerhalb, schlank, die Trommel, das Gewimmel, wohnen, anmerken, schwanken, nehmen

13. **[r] vs. [ɐ]**

das Meer, der Unterricht, erzählen, der Vater, die Reihe, das Ohr, weiter, die Sperrung, derselbe, das Fahrrad, der Wirt, rastlos, die Trauer, die Briefmarke, drei, dir, ersehen, verstehen, die Uhr, korrigieren, vorwärts, der Rucksack, vergessen, zerren

14. [ç] vs. [χ]

die Nacht, das Mädchen, die Achtung, nicht, die Milch, durch, doch, die Sehnsucht, brechen, das Bächlein, die Sprüche, das Buch, auch, innig, die Pracht, höher, ewig, manche, gebrochen

15. **Affricates** [ts][tʃ]

der Zahnarzt, kurz, das Celsius, witzig, die Kutsche, aufwärts, reizen, Caesar, lutschen, die Katze, geht's, die Peitsche, die Pflanze, das Rätsel, nichts, rutschen, cyrillisch, sitzen, herzlich, gibt's

16. **Additional consonants** [kv][ks]

das Taxi, die Quelle, die Erwachsene, quietschen, fix, der Quatsch, die Fixierung, sechs, quetschen, die Nixen, das Quadrat, wachsen, das Examen, quasseln, die Qual, der Dachshund, quarren, die Flexibilität, quälen, der Fuchs, das Quartal

PART II: ENGLISH

Chapter 4: Introduction to English Diction
for Singers

In the quest for a beautiful tone, singers sometimes sacrifice the projection of the text. However, singers are the only musicians entrusted with the responsibility to communicate the intentions of both a composer and a poet. Collaborative pianists also share this particular challenge, albeit without the means to truly "taste" the text in the same manner.

4.1 Challenges of singing in English

Perhaps the greatest challenge of singing in English is overcoming preconceived ideas about one's native tongue. When singing in one's mother tongue, laziness and apathy are rather common with respect to IPA. Native speakers of German, French, and Italian also experience this. In order to combat the natural instinct to underarticulate, one must approach the mother language as one would a foreign language, namely with the same degree of preparation. Few singers take the time to analyze the exact vowels they are producing when singing in English. This would be unthinkable in a foreign language. One's spoken facility with a language is not automatically transferred to create clear diction when singing. This can be observed with other languages when a singer speaks a second language at home and brings this fluency to singing. There is no substitute for a clear, distinct vowel in any language, along with the maintenance of the vowel for the entire duration of the note.

Assimilation

There are countless inconsistencies in English spelling, which are a direct result of the many foreign influences on the English language over the past centuries. While this is not problematic for native speakers, it provides a distinct challenge to ESL singers. Assimilation refers to a process whereby a sound disappears or changes based on the adjacent sound. In English, there are two types of assimilation—historical and contextual. The former refers to the development of the language so that a word is now pronounced differently than it was centuries ago (Jones 1962). The latter refers to changes in pronunciation due to surrounding words. Historical assimilation is observable in the high amount of words that are pronounced differently than spelled, as well as the presence of silent letters, e.g., handsome [hænsəm], handkerchief [hæŋkətʃɪf]. Contextual assimilation occurs in such examples as horseshoe [hɔəʃu], whereby [s] is replaced by [ʃ], does she [dʌʒʃi], whereby [z] is replaced by [ʒ], and don't you [doʊntʃu], whereby [tj] is replaced by [tʃ]. As languages evolve, so do regional dialects and accents.

Unless a song or aria is intended to be colloquial in nature, this text does not recommend the observance of contextual assimilation in English. Some words may be pronounced in two different ways, depending on the given poem and/or composition. In the following examples, it is preferable to use the first pronunciation, avoiding assimilation.

situation	[sɪtjuˈeɪʃən]	or	[sɪtʃuˈeɪʃən]
grandeur	[ɡɹændjə]	or	[ɡɹændʒə]
mature	[məˈtjʊə]	or	[məˈtʃʊə]
during	[djʊɹɪŋ]	or	[dʒʊɹɪŋ]

Stress

In English, the meaning of a sentence or group of words may be changed by intonation, word emphases, or punctuation. Conversely, in German punctuation and word order have very little room for variation. English does not have a fixed tonic stress like other languages. There are many noun-verb pairings, whereby pronunciation depends on the individual meaning, e.g., a record, to record; a convict, to convict. Stress may migrate from the first to the penultimate syllable in related words, e.g., 'photograph, pho'tographer, photo'graphic, 'diplomat, di'plomacy, diplo'matic.

4.2 Dialect and accent: General American English (GA) and Received Pronunciation (RP)

Regardless of where English is spoken, there are regional dialects in each country, characterizing one's geographic origin or place of residence. In order to unify a cast, be it on the operatic stage or in the theatre, one must use an English free from regionalisms. In Great Britain, Received Pronunciation (RP) is used by the BBC, which is the standard British English. In the United States and Canada, General American English (GA) is used, though there are some differences in Canadian English.

General American English (GA) is used by trained speakers and performers for public usage. Two standard works integral in the development of GA are *The Pronouncing Dictionary of American English* (Kenyon and Knott), as well as *The NBC Handbook of Pronunciation* (Ehrlich and Hand), although the latter does not have IPA. As singers are required to sing English texts by British, Canadian, American, and Australian composers, GA does not cover all of the necessary phonemes.

This text strongly recommends the use of the *Cambridge English Pronouncing Dictionary (17th edition)* by renowned phonetician Daniel Jones. There are IPA transcriptions throughout and most words are given two possibilities for pronunciation: RP and GA. In lyric diction, it is recommended to take the best of both worlds and use phonemes from both of these standard dialects. Some sources refer to this as a Mid-Atlantic dialect. In essence, lyric diction deals with a standardized version of a language that is created and honed especially for singing.

Each singer's interpretation will be further individualized by his/her expressive use of lyric diction. For example, a conscious choice to pronounce "situation" [sɪtʃu'eɪʃən] instead of [sɪtju'eɪʃən] is perfectly acceptable, as long as one realizes that this renders the text more colloquial in nature. The decisions one makes regarding pronunciation have an immense effect on the overall tone and delivery of any song or aria. Clearly, it is a powerful means of communication in performance.

Chapter 5: English Phonemes

Table 5.1. Overview of English phonemes

IPA Symbol	Spelling	Examples
[ɑ]	*a, o*	father [fɑðə]
		box [bɑks]
[ɑə]	*ar, ear*	charm [tʃɑəm]
		heart [hɑət]
[aɪ]	*ay, i, ie, igh, eigh, ui, y*	cayenne [kaɪɛn]
		tide [taɪd]
		dried [dɹaɪd]
		sigh [saɪ]
		height [haɪt]
		beguile [bɪˈgaɪl]
		thyme [taɪm]
[aɪə]	*ire, yre*	aspire [əˈspaɪə]
		lyre [laɪə]
[aʊ]	*ou, ough, ow*	thou [ðaʊ]
		bough [baʊ]
		clown [klaʊn]
[aʊə]	*our, ower*	hourly [aʊəlɪ]
		flower [flaʊə]
[æ]	*a, au*	lamb [læm]

Continued on next page

Table 5.1—Continued

IPA Symbol	Spelling	Examples
		draught [dɹæft]
[b]	*b, bb*	grab [gɹæb]
		stubble [stʌbəl]
[d]	*d, dd*	dinner [dɪnə]
		plodding [plɑdɪŋ]
[eɪ]	*a, ai, ay, ea, ei, ey*	dazed [deɪzd]
		pain [peɪn]
		array [əˈɹeɪ]
		break [bɹeɪk]
		reign [ɹeɪn]
		convey [kənˈveɪ]
[ɛ]	*e, ea, ai, a*	network [ˈnɛtˌwɜk]
		meant [mɛnt]
		said [sɛd]
		any [ɛnɪ]
[ɛə]	*air, are, ear, eir, ere*	chair [tʃɛə]
		spare [spɛə]
		swear [swɛə]
		heir [ɛə]
		there [ðɛə]
[ə]	*a, e, i, o, u, y, ou,*	above [əˈbʌv]
	ar, er, or, -ur, -le, -re	haven [heɪvən]
		cabinet [kæbənət]
		offend [əˈfɛnd]
		lettuce [lɛtəs]
		syringe [səˈɹɪndʒ]
		raucous [ɹɔkəs]
		altar [ɔltə]

Continued on next page

Table 5.1—Continued

IPA Symbol	Spelling	Examples
		perhaps [pəˈhæps]
		motor [moʊtə]
		measure [mɛʒə]
		ladle [leɪdəl]
		theatre [θiətə]
[ɜ]	*ear, er, ir, or, our, ur, yr*	early [ɜlɪ]
		personal [pɜsənəl]
		birth [bɜθ]
		world [wɜld]
		journey [dʒɜnɪ]
		curl [kɜl]
		myrtle [mɜtəl]
[f]	*f, ff, ph, gh*	flavor [fleɪvə]
		miffed [mɪft]
		telephone [tɛləfoʊn]
		laugh [læf]
[g]	*g, gg, gh, gue*	guess [gɛs]
		gaggle [gægəl]
		ghoul [gul]
		prologue [pɹolɑg]
[dʒ]	*dg, ge, gi, gg, gy,*	badge [bædʒ]
	ja, je, ji, jo, ju	German [dʒɜmən]
		gin [dʒɪn]
		suggestion [səˈdʒɛstʃən]
		gymnast [dʒɪmnəst]
		jalopy [dʒəˈlɑpɪ]
		jealous [dʒɛləs]
		jinx [dʒɪŋks]

Continued on next page

Table 5.1—Continued

IPA Symbol	Spelling	Examples
		joyous [dʒɔɪəs]
		jubilant [dʒubələnt]
[gz]	*x*	exit [ɛgzɪt]
[h]	*h, wh* (before *o*)	house [haʊs]
		whole [hoʊl]
[i]	*ee, ea, ei, i, ie, e*	seemingly [simɪŋlɪ]
		jeans [dʒinz]
		receive [ɹɪˈsiv]
		police [pəˈlis]
		niece [nis]
		obscene [əbˈsin]
[ɪ]	*i, ie, ui, y*	victim [vɪktəm]
		lilies [lɪlɪz]
		built [bɪlt]
		tryst [tɹɪst]
[ɪə]	*ear, eer, ere, ier*	appear [əˈpɪə]
		deer [dɪə]
		severe [sɪˈvɪə]
		pierce [pɪəs]
[j]	*c, d, f, h, l, m, p, s, t* (before *u*), *lli, u-, y* (before vowel)	cube [kjub]
		duke [djuk]
		fuse [fjuz]
		huge [hjudʒ]
		allure [əˈljʊə]
		Munich [mjunɪk]
		purity [pjʊɹətɪ]
		resume [ɹɪˈzjum]
		tumult [tjuməlt]

Continued on next page

Table 5.1—Continued

IPA Symbol	Spelling	Examples
		million [mɪljən]
		unique [juˈnik]
		yesterday [jɛstədeɪ]
[k]	*c, cc, ch, ck, k, que*	coarse [kɔəs]
		accompany [əˈkʌmpənɪ]
		chorus [kɔɹəs]
		package [pækədʒ]
		asking [æskɪŋ]
		plaque [plæk]
[ks]	*x, cc*	oxen [ɑksən]
		accent [æksənt]
[l]	*l, ll*	limber [lɪmbə]
		wall [wɔl]
[m]	*m, mm, -lm, -mb, -mn*	warmth [wɔəmθ]
		summer [sʌmə]
		balm [bɔm]
		womb [wum]
		autumn [ɔtəm]
[n]	*n, nn, gn, kn-*	neptune [nɛptjun]
		banned [bænd]
		feign [feɪn]
		knowledge [nɑlədʒ]
[ŋ]	*n* (before *k* or *x*), *ng*	thankful [θæŋkfʊl]
		minx [mɪŋks]
		singer [sɪŋə]
[ɲ]	*new, ni, nu*	news [ɲuz]
		onion [ʌɲən]

Continued on next page

Table 5.1—Continued

IPA Symbol	Spelling	Examples
		nude [ɲud]
[o]	*o-, pro-* (both unstressed)	obey [oˈbeɪ]
		provide [pɹoˈvaɪd]
[oʊ]	*o, oa, oe, ou, ough, ow*	wrote [ɹoʊt]
		approach [əˈpɹoʊtʃ]
		foe [foʊ]
		shoulder [ʃoʊldə]
		dough [doʊ]
		grown [gɹoʊn]
[ɔ]	*a* (before *l, ll*), *au, augh, aw,*	altered [ɔltəd]
	o (before *rr*), *ough*	ball [bɔl]
		cause [kɔz]
		daughter [dɔtə]
		jaw [dʒɔ]
		horrible [hɔɹəbəl]
		sought [sɔt]
[ɔɪ]	*oi, oy*	joint [dʒɔɪnt]
		employ [ɛmˈplɔɪ]
[ɔə]	*oar, oor, our, or, ore, ar*	boar [bɔə]
		floor [flɔə]
		your [jɔə]
		for [fɔə]
		adore [əˈdɔə]
		quart [kwɔət]
[p]	*p, pp*	maple [meɪpəl]
		happy [hæpɪ]
[ɹ]	*r, rh, rr, wr*	bring [bɹɪŋ]
		rhythm [ɹɪðəm]

Continued on next page

Table 5.1—Continued

IPA Symbol	Spelling	Examples
		narrow [næɹoʊ]
		wrong [ɹɑŋ]
[s]	*s, ss, ce, ci, cy, sce, sci, ps-*	wisp [wɪsp]
		passing [pæsɪŋ]
		cease [sis]
		decision [dɪˈsɪʒən]
		cyber [saɪbə]
		scent [sɛnt]
		science [saɪəns]
		psalm [sɔm]
[ʃ]	*sh, s, ssi, ce, ch, ci, ti*	shout [ʃaʊt]
		sugar [ʃʊgə]
		passion [pæʃən]
		ocean [oʊʃən]
		charade [ʃəˈɹeɪd]
		spacious [speɪʃəs]
		caution [kɔʃən]
[ʒ]	*si, su, -age*	vision [vɪʒən]
		casual [kæʒuəl]
		garage [gəˈɹɑʒ]
[t]	*t, tt, bt*	today [təˈdeɪ]
		attempt [əˈtɛmpt]
		doubt [daʊt]
[ts]	*ts, tz*	warts [wɔəts]
		quartz [kwɔəts]
[tʃ]	*ch, tch, -ture*	chance [tʃæns]
		fetch [fɛtʃ]

Continued on next page

Table 5.1—Continued

IPA Symbol	Spelling	Examples
		lecture [lɛktʃə]
[θ]	*th*	thrifty [θɹɪftɪ]
[ð]	*th*	clothes [kloʊðz]
[u]	*o, oo, ou, u, ue, ui, ew*	prove [pɹuv]
		gloom [glum]
		wound [wund]
		crude [kɹud]
		blue [blu]
		juice [dʒus]
		brew [bɹu]
[ʊ]	*oo, ou, u*	foot [fʊt]
		would [wʊd]
		pull [pʊl]
[ʊə]	*oor, our, ure*	poor [pʊə]
		tour [tʊə]
		sure [ʃʊə]
[ʌ]	*o, oo, ou, u, un-*	love [lʌv]
		blood [blʌd]
		double [dʌbəl]
		cup [kʌp]
		untrue [ʌnˈtɹu]
[v]	*v, vv*	vein [veɪn]
		savvy [sævɪ]
[w]	*w, qu*	winter [wɪntə]
		quiet [kwaɪət]
[ʍ]	*wh*	whether [ʍɛðə]
[z]	*z, zz, s*	zebra [zibɹə]

Continued on next page

Table 5.1—Continued

IPA Symbol	Spelling	Examples
		puzzle [pʌzəl]
		roses [ɹoʊzəz]

Chapter 6: The Structure of English

6.1 Syllabification: sung vs. spoken

The standard division of words into syllables follows distinct rules related to grammatical structure. When a composer sets text, most often these rules are observed and the syllables are separated accordingly. This presents a challenge to singers, who inevitably must divide words alternatively in order to promote legato singing. To treat syllables in an optimal vocal manner is to learn from French, whereby every syllable ends in a vowel. In shifting many consonants over to the next syllable, the vowels are elongated. An exception is the use of certain voiced consonants, e.g., [m], [n], which may be anticipated before the beat. Although the ratio of consonants to vowels is different in Germanic languages compared to Romance languages, it is possible to divide most words with this principle in mind. When reading the poem set underneath the melody, singers must mentally rewrite the words as follows:

Table 6.1. Syllabification in lyric diction

	Conventional	Lyric Diction
reminder	re-mind-er	rem-in-der
seated	seat-ed	sea-ted
difference	dif-fer-ence	di-ffe-rence

Continued on next page

54

Table 6.1—Continued

	Conventional	Lyric Diction
excellent	ex-cel-lent	e-xce-llent
thoughtful	thought-ful	though-tful
province	prov-ince	pro-vince
dancing	danc-ing	dan-cing
fastest	fast-est	fa-stest

6.2 Word stress and "unstress"

In all languages, word stress is an integral component of idiomatic pronunciation. Nothing highlights a well-spoken foreigner quite like an improperly stressed word. Unique national flavors occur in the colors and
stress patterns of different languages. In the Romance languages, stress
is primarily used to illustrate tense. In French, there is said to be an absence of stress. Therefore, it is commonly considered to be the most legato of languages. In English, stress may occur in all syllables and positions in a word. Determining word stress is quite complicated, due to the
mixture of foreign influences in the development of the English language. Primary stress is indicated by ['], while secondary stress is shown
by [ˌ], in each case placed before the stressed syllable.

The ears of a native speaker are attuned to the natural inflection of
his/her language. It is advisable to analyze this sound pattern in order to
transfer it to singing. Syllables within a word exist within a hierarchy,
just as words relate to each other within a sentence. Rarely would one
bring out every word in speech or song. Every language has an innate
cadence, illustrating the beauty of its unique phonetic patterns. There
are peaks of prominence in every spoken or sung line of poetry. In cases
of multiple verb forms in a row, the auxiliaries are never stressed. In

general, articles, prepositions, conjunctions, and pronouns are all unstressed. Further, modifiers should not be stressed over the words that
they qualify, or it becomes difficult to discern the meaning of the sentence. The stress of a given word depends on its relative importance.
Clearly, there is a great deal of room for personal interpretation, which
ensures that language is a viable means of creativity.

How does one show stress within a word? In order to show the difference between strong and weak syllables, one must energize the ac-
cented syllables and de-energize the unstressed syllables. This is accomplished through the use of dynamics, accents, vowel/consonant length,
rhythm, color, articulation, velocity of consonant production, attention
to onomatopoeic possibilities, and alliteration.

A paramount phenomenon in the English language is the concept of
"unstress". The *schwa* is the most common vowel sound in the English
language. The prevalence of this neutral phoneme is not immediately
obvious until one transcribes words into IPA. Unstressing reduces syllables to a weaker intensity and a shorter duration. There may be multiple
unstressed syllables within the same word. If the principle of unstress is
forgotten in singing or orating, one can easily sound pretentious. Moreover, when too many pure vowels exist in polysyllabic words, it results
in a robotic, cold treatment of the words. The natural flow and inflection
of English is lost and the pronunciation becomes stilted and pedantic.

A common error stemming from speech is the substitution of [ɪ] for
[ə], resulting in a colloquial treatment of the text. In the following examples, note that through the use of the *schwa,* the natural word stress is
clearly audible. The neutral quality of the *schwa* easily matches any environment. Please see Chapter 11 (Advanced Concepts in Diction) for a
full explanation of the substitution of [ɪ] in unstressed syllables.

| heaven | [hɛvən] | not | [hɛvɪn] or [hɛvɛn] |
| taken | [teɪkən] | not | [teɪkɪn] or [teɪkɛn] |

motion	[mouʃən]	not	[mouʃɪn] or [mouʃɑn]
melody	[mɛlədɪ]	not	[mɛlodi]
pencil	[pɛnsəl]	not	[pɛnsɪl]

Inflection forms the basis of communication. In the realm of artistic interpretation, the individual artist chooses which words to emphasize, thus personalizing the text. In general, nouns and verbs play a critical role in the intelligibility of a poem. However, there are infinite possibilities for personal expression beyond this. Imagine what one can achieve through the use of vocal color, word-painting, and beautiful tone. Singers are the only musicians entrusted with the task of communicating poetry, which has its own innate expressive possibilities, waiting to be discovered and explored to the fullest.

6.3 Glottal attacks or onsets

Renowned phonetician Daniel Jones does not consider glottal stops or glottal catches to be essential sounds of the English language (Jones 1962). However, in lyric diction, the use of a soft glottal onset greatly aids in clarity. Moreover, glottal onsets may be used for increased dramatic effect. This depends largely on context and interpretation.

In both speaking and singing, there are three methods of vocal onset or attack: breathy, soft, and hard. A breathy onset occurs upon pronouncing an initial *h* [h]. The breath passes through the vocal folds before the glottis has closed. A soft glottal attack occurs when the breath flow begins simultaneously with the closure of the glottis. One uses this attack when pronouncing a word commencing with a stressed vowel. This principle is used when initiating vowels in all Romance languages, and may be applied to Germanic languages as well. A hard glottal attack results from the glottis closing completely before the tone begins and is otherwise known as a glottal stop. The closed glottis causes the air pressure to build up until the vocal folds separate and vibrate upon phonation. A hard glottal onset is commonly heard in popular music and is potentially damaging to the voice.

This text strongly advocates the use of a soft glottal attack in English and German lyric diction. It is considered to be a "healthy" glottal and serves to illustrate where one word ends and another begins. It is represented by the symbol [|], as used in both Duden and Siebs for German. A fresh vocal onset begins with the impulse of the breath and is likened to a lift within the vocal line. It is only truly necessary between a word ending in a consonant and another beginning with a vowel. Glottal onsets should be quick and not detract from the legato line. It follows that comprehension and clarity are the main reasons for the use of glottal attacks. The following examples illustrate resulting differences in text:

| an aim | [ən|eɪm] | a name | [ə neɪm] |
| and I | [ənd|aɪ] | and die | [ən daɪ] |

Occurrence

In English lyric diction it is necessary to use a soft glottal onset on a word beginning with a vowel when the preceding word ends in either a consonant or an identical vowel. When the preceding word ends in a different vowel, it is left to the singer's discretion as to whether a glottal onset is indeed required. Often unintentional words are formed if a glottal onset is omitted.

three easterly winds	[θɹi	istəlɪ wɪndz]	
the eternal plight	[ði	ɪˈtɜnəl plaɪt]	
bright eyes	[bɹaɪt	aɪz]	not "ties"
deaf ears	[dɛf	ɪəz]	not "fears"
some others	[sʌm	ʌðəz]	not "mothers"

There are instances whereby the use of a glottal onset is optional. For example, the presence of an R-colored diphthong often lessens the need for a glottal attack, e.g., their age [ðɛə eɪdʒ]. Leaning on the [eɪ] will illustrate the new word without breaking the legato. Moreover, common combinations such as "it is" or "not at all," do not require the use of glottal separation. Otherwise, this might sound too affected. Further, the rhythmic release and timing of consonants often negates the need for a glottal attack. Please consult Chapter 22 (Legato Singing) for further information.

6.4 Silent letters, alternate spellings

As previously discussed in Chapter 4 (Introduction to English Diction for Singers), inconsistencies in English orthography are a direct result of the many foreign influences on the English language over the past centuries. It is important that one be able to identify letters that are part of the spelling, but not of the sound. This is not problematic for native speakers, but provides a distinct challenge to ESL singers. Here follows a handy list of common words that employ silent letters:

b   debt, doubt, subtle, limb, bomb, womb, tomb, thumb, crumb, dumb, lamb, comb, climb, plumber

c   scene, science, scientific, czar, yacht, reminiscent, descend, indict

d   handsome, sandwich, handkerchief, landslide, grandmother

g   paradigm, resign, benign, sign, malign, phlegm, align, assign, design

gh sigh, thigh, daughter, sleigh, through, though, dough, height, weight

h   hour, honor, heir, herb, honest, hurrah, pharaoh, vehicle, vehement, annihilate, exhaust, exhortation, exhilaration, exhibit, ah, rhetorical, rhyme, rhythmic, rhapsody, rhinoceros, rhotic, oh

k   knowledge, knew, knock, knapsack, knife, knight, knead, knickers

l   colonel, Lincoln, would, should, could, half, calf, halves, calves, salve, balm, calm, psalm, qualm, salmon, palm, chalk, stalk, talk, walked, folk, yolks, polka

n   column, autumn, condemn, solemn, hymn

p   psychology, psychic, pneumonia, pseudonym, psalter, psalm, raspberry, cupboard, psyche

s   isle, aisle, island, corps, debris, viscount, chablis, chassis

t   castle, pestle, thistle, listen, fasten, hasten, chestnut, Christmas, mortgage, often, soften, glisten, rustle, bustle, hustle, christening

th   isthmus, asthma

w   write, wrong, wreak, wretch, wrath, writhe, two, answer, sword, yawn, lawn, awning, dawn, fawn, pawn, tawny, flew, sew, thaw

There are also situations in which a consonant is pronounced, but not spelled. In these cases, semi-consonants and glides are involved, e.g., one, once (begin with [w]), and unite, union (begin with [j]). Words ending in -re or -le often require the insertion of the schwa [ə] in lyric diction. Common examples include metre [mitə], centre [sɛntə] (British spellings of meter and center), theatre [θɪətə], little [lɪtəl], syllable [sɪləbəl], and battle [bætəl].

Homophones are words that are pronounced the same, but spelled differently. There are many alternate spellings to identical phonemes, as outlined in Chapter 5 (English Phonemes). It is suggested that ESL singers become familiar with the following list of common homophones:

affect/effect	[ə'fɛkt]	liar/lyre	[laɪə]
aisle/isle	[aɪl]	made/maid	[meɪd]
allowed/aloud	[ə'laʊd]	mail/male	[meɪl]
ate/eight	[eɪt]	meat/meet	[mit]
ball/bawl	[bɔl]	morning/mourning	[mɔənɪŋ]
base/bass	[beɪs]	none/nun	[nʌn]

bear/bare	[bɛə]	one/won	[wʌn]
beech/beach	[bitʃ]	pail/pale	[peɪl]
billed/build	[bɪld]	pair/pear	[pɛə]
blew/blue	[blu]	peer/pier	[pɪə]
board/bored	[bɔəd]	piece/peace	[pis]
bore/boar	[bɔə]	plain/plane	[pleɪn]
break/brake	[bɹeɪk]	pore/pour	[pɔə]
buy/by/bye	[baɪ]	practice/practise	[pɹæktəs]
capital/capitol	[kæpətəl]	rain/reign	[ɹeɪn]
cell/sell	[sɛl]	read/red	[ɹɛd]
cent/scent/sent	[sɛnt]	right/write	[ɹaɪt]
chews/choose	[tʃuz]	road/rode	[ɹoʊd]
coarse/course	[kɔəs]	rose/rows	[ɹoʊz]
creak/creek	[kɹik]	sail/sale	[seɪl]
days/daze	[deɪz]	scene/seen	[sin]
dear/deer	[dɪə]	sea/see	[si]
dew/due	[dju]	seem/seam	[sim]
fair/fare	[fɛə]	sew/so	[soʊ]
fairy/ferry	[fɛɹi]	soared/sword	[sɔəd]
find/fined	[faɪnd]	sole/soul	[soʊl]
flower/flour	[flaʊə]	son/sun	[sʌn]
for/four	[fɔə]	sore/soar	[sɔə]
foreword/forward	[fɔəwəd]	stair/stare	[stɛə]
gene/jean	[dʒin]	steal/steel	[stil]
grease/Greece	[gɹis]	suite/sweet	[swit]
groan/grown	[gɹoʊn]	tear/tier	[tɪə]
hair/hare	[hɛə]	there/their/they're	[ðɛə]
hay/hey	[heɪ]	threw/through	[θɹu]
heal/heel	[hil]	tire/tyre	[taɪə]
hear/here	[hɪə]	to/too/two	[tu]

hi/high	[haɪ]	vary/very	[vɛɹi]
hoarse/horse	[hɔəs]	waist/waste	[weɪst]
hole/whole	[houl]	wait/weight	[weɪt]
hour/our	[auə]	war/wore	[wɔə]
knight/night	[naɪt]	ware/wear	[wɛə]
knot/not	[nɑt]	weak/week	[wik]
know/no	[nou]	wood/would	[wʊd]
loan/lone	[loun]	yore/your/you're	[jɔə]

Supplementary exercises

1. Transcribe the following into IPA, identifying the silent letters:
fatigue, listening, wretched, critique, psychosis, balk, eight, knee, claw,
written, whose, caulk, comb, salmon, scenic, whom, nigh, rhetoric

2. Transcribe the following into IPA, inserting the *schwa* as necessary:
people, apple, steeple, ripple, simple, trample, able, bubble, bauble,
trouble, riddle, idle, litre (British spelling), cuddle, ogle, coddle

3. Indicate the word whose stress pattern does not match:
   • dictionary, education, automatic, intermission
   • women, button, bottom, begin
   • committee, mechanic, horizon, comedy
   • difficult, agency, department, actual
   • develop, opinion, probable, contribute
   • comfortable, Canada, continue, personal
   • analysis, economy, apology, photographic
   • opportunity, stationary, secretary, vegetable
   • supervisor, necessary, economy, military
   • elevation, acquisition, mediation, admission
   • antelope, catalogue, envelop, beautiful
   • powerful, delusion, secretive, frustrating

4. Which of the following pairs are true homophones?

chants/chance	leased/least	axe/acts
patience/patients	walk/wok	wear/where
missed/mist	marry/merry	rye/wry
close/clothes	flu/flew	cock/caulk

5. Divide the following words into lyric diction syllabification:
governmental, spiritual, accessible, beatitude, concert, intimate, ability, optimistic, anxiety, alternate, recognizable, necessarily, infectious

6. Indicate the primary stress in the following words:
- electric, electronic, electrify, electrolysis, electrician, electrical, electrification
- photograph, photographer, photography, photographic
- analyze, analysis, analytical, analogy
- technique, technology, technological, technician, technical
- medic, medical, medicine, medicinal
- economy, economic, economical
- homogenize, homogeneous, homogeneity
- real, really, realize, reality, realism, realist, realistic, realization
- divide, division, divisible, divisibility, divisional, divisive, divisor
- voluntary, volition, volunteer, voluntarily
- produce (n.), product, production, productive, producible, productiveness, productivity, produce (v.), producer
- relate, relation, relational, relationship, relative, relatively, relativity, relatedness

Chapter 7: Characteristic English Phonemes

7.1 Use of [ɑ] and [æ], but absence of [a]

It is significant that English does not contain the monophthong [a], as this phoneme is prevalent in not only German, but also all of the Romance languages. The only occurrence of this vowel is in the context of two diphthongs: [aɪ] and [aʊ], e.g., crime [kɹaɪm], mouse [maʊs]. The dark, open, central vowel [ɑ] and the bright, open, central vowel [æ] are commonly used for spellings of *a*, e.g., watch [watʃ], man [mæn].

7.2 Importance of the *schwa* [ə]

The term *schwa* comes from a Hebrew word, transliterated as *sheva* or *shewa*, meaning nothingness. The *e* in the transliteration is a short phonetic *schwa* sound, i.e., what is referred to as a neutral, obscure, or indeterminate vowel. Indeed some phoneticians refuse to classify this sound as a vowel, citing that the sound is too indefinite.

Although the same IPA symbol is used, the *schwa* has a distinct sound in each of the languages in which it is represented. This presents the singer with a unique challenge. The English *schwa* is considered to be mid-central and neutral, and is represented by all of our vowels. Common examples include "about," "synthesis," "decimal," "harmony," "medium," "syringe". It is most easily described as sounding like the British English *-er* or the North American English "uh." By contrast, the

German *schwa* is always spelled with the letter *e*. The *schwa* is present in almost every word in the English language. Its ubiquity results in the concept of "unstress", which characterizes the innate rhythm of English.

7.3 Use of Y

When first learning about English vowels in kindergarten, one finds out that *y* is sometimes a vowel and sometimes a consonant. As a result, the letter *y* may be pronounced in three different ways depending on its context and function. These possibilities are outlined as follows:

1. Final: [ɪ] or [aɪ]
Final *y* is pronounced either [ɪ] or [aɪ].

| fantasy | [fæntəsɪ] | mortify | [mɔətəfaɪ] |

N.B.: If final *y* is pronounced [ɪ], the exact phoneme is halfway between closed [i] and open [ɪ]. This may be directly compared to the German word *ich* [ɪç]. Keen aural sensitivity is needed to perfect this vowel.

2. Initial: [j]

| yesterday | [jɛstədeɪ] | youth | [juθ] |

3. Vowel: [ə] or [ɪ]
When *y* is neither final nor initial and functions as a vowel, it is pronounced either as a *schwa* [ə], when unstressed, or as [ɪ], when stressed.

| syrinx | [sə'ɹɪŋks] | synergy | [sɪnədʒɪ] |
| oxygen | [aksədʒən] | myth | [mɪθ] |

Exception: Certain words taken from Greek pronounce *y* as [aɪ].

| gyrate | [dʒaɹeɪt] | rhyme | [ɹaɪm] |

7.4 Allophones of R: [ɾ] [ɹ] [r]

The English language employs many allophones of r: rolled [r], flipped [ɾ], and retroflex [ɹ]. In operatic repertoire both [r] and [ɾ] are used, depending on context and meaning. In art song and oratorio repertoire, this text recommends the sole use of two forms of r: [ɹ] and [ɾ]. Further, the *schwa* is used as a substitute for r in the five diphthongs borrowed from Received Pronunciation. In this case, the r is implied. For detailed information on r substitutes, please consult Chapter 8 (Vowels).

Use of flipped R [ɾ]
Spelling: *cr-, gr-, thr-, r* (intervocalic)

crisp	[kɾɪsp]	thrice	[θɾaɪs]
grief	[gɾif]	spirit	[spɪɾət]

Consonant blends such as *br-, dr-, pr-,* and *tr-* should use the retroflex, or North American r [ɹ]. All of these consonants are strongly plosive. Thus, a simple flip can easily turn into an unwanted roll, sounding affected.

It is recommended to use [ɾ] when singing British art song, such as works by Britten, Finzi, Quilter, or Vaughan Williams. Initial r (especially before [u]) and intervocalic r are good examples of occurrences. The flipped r results in greater cut through an orchestra or thicker accompanying texture. It also possesses greater propulsive power. Therefore, it is better suited to repertoire from opera or oratorio. In particular, high cut-offs and releases often require [ɾ] to be heard over an orchestra. The flipped R may also be used when purposely singing in Received Pronunciation, such as the operettas of Gilbert and Sullivan.

One may use several allophones of r in the same piece or sentence. The varied use of r results in a hierarchy of importance, not unlike the use of the *schwa* to illustrate stress and "unstress". In the following examples, note the choices made regarding the use of *r*. In the Händel excerpt, using [ɾ] for "raging" not only serves as both a word-painting device, but also makes it easier to keep the subsequent diphthong [eɪ] forward and vertical. After starting on a bright [i] with "see", the use of [ɾ] aids in lining up subsequent repetitions of this initial pitch.

"See, the raging flames arise" from *Joshua*, G.F. Händel

"When I am laid in earth" from *Dido and Aeneas*, H. Purcell

Ultimately, the decision as to which *r* to use is primarily based on context and meaning. Above all, one should avoid multiple cases of [ɾ] in succession, especially on words that are neither dramatic nor emotional in quality. All three words using *r* are close together in the above Purcell excerpt. The choice to sing [ɹ] on "wrongs" facilitates the use of straight-tone on this word, which is more effective if the *r* does not distract the listener. Further, an expressive, aspirated [k] and [t] in "create" and "trouble" will propel and center the ensuing vowel.

Supplementary exercise

1. Transcribe the following words into IPA, observing the uses of *y*:
yore, deny, symbol, physics, modify, psyche, you, yearning, tryst, fortify, beautify, yoke, therapy, vilify, yuletide, yield, very, somebody, year, lyric, happily, youth, memory, lovely, quantify, cylinder, psychology

Chapter 8: Vowels

In any language, vowels carry the prime emotional content of a sound. They are also the chief vehicles of intonation. The production of vowels so dominates singing that it often leads to the idea that one can neglect the articulation of consonants. To assert that vowels are more important than consonants would be false. Vowels and consonants must be given the same careful attention. English vowels may be divided into monophthongs, diphthongs, and triphthongs. Each monophthong may be further classified as either closed or open.

Achieving the correct sound for each vowel must be done by ear. The positions of the tongue and lips are addressed, but often the actual vowel shape is achieved by hearing the sound in advance of production.

Vowel length

Closed and open vowels in English are variable in length, depending on context, stress, and overall rhythm of the sentence. For example, the length of the diphthong [aɪ] in nine [naɪn] is much greater than in nineteen [naɪn'tin]. This has to do with the natural word stress. Often composers made the decision as to the length of the vowel in their settings of the words. A closed vowel is formed with the tongue positioned as close as possible to the roof of the mouth without creating an obstruction that would result in a consonant. An open vowel is formed with the opposite position of the tongue, namely, as far as possible away from the roof of the mouth.

8.1 Monophthongs

Monophthongs, also known as pure vowels, consist of a sole phoneme. Their purity is characterized by a clear tone that does not waver or oscillate from the very beginning of the pitch until the very end. The quality of a given vowel is determined by the position of the tongue, jaw, and lips, as these alter the shape of the cavity through which the air passes. Moreover, different shapes create different resonances. A tongue that is raised accidentally will become part of the vowel sound and naturally will impede its production. Sometimes a movement in the articulators will change the quality of a monophthong resulting in an accidental diphthong. Great care must be taken to avoid this common mistake. This may also be regulated by the singer's keen aural sensitivity.

Vowels may be categorized according to relative tongue position (close or open), inherent sound quality (bright, dark), height in the mouth (high, mid, low), or the distance from the opening of the mouth (front, central, back). This text prefers to classify the vowels according to their emotional impact and therefore divides English monophthongs into four categories: bright, central, dark, and R-less.

Bright vowels [i][ɪ][ɛ]
[i]   Lowercase I   Bright (tongue), close
Spelling: *ee, ea, ei, i, ie, e*

reed	[ɹid]	ravine	[ɹəˈvin]
breathe	[bɹið]	thief	[θif]
deceive	[dɪˈsiv]	scheme	[skim]

N.B.: key [ki]

Production: The tongue is arched forward with the back high, the sides lightly touching the upper molars, and the tip resting against the lower teeth. Upon properly positioning the tongue, the jaw will automatically lower slightly and rotate back. The lips are not directly involved in the formation of this vowel and therefore should be relaxed. As the tongue is arched as far as possible, without becoming a consonant, one must be mindful of any tension forming in the tongue. This vowel is slightly less closed than its German counterpart [iː].

[ɪ]   Small capital I   Bright (tongue), open
Spelling: *i, ie, ui, y*

| with | [wɪθ] | biscuit | [bɪskət] |
| deities | [deɪətɪz] | tarry | [tæɹɪ] |

N.B.: hideous [hɪdɪəs], been [bɪn], busy [bɪzɪ]

Production: The tongue is arched forward with the back high, the sides slightly touching the upper molars, and the tip resting against the lower teeth. In comparison to [i], the front of the tongue moves back slightly and depresses. The jaw will automatically lower slightly and rotate back while positioning the tongue. The lips are not directly involved in the formation of this vowel and therefore should be relaxed. Native speakers of Romance languages often have difficulty pronouncing this vowel.

N.B.: When a word ends in final *-y* or *-ies*, the vowel is best described as being halfway between [i] and [ɪ]. This hybrid sound is directly compara-ble to the vowel in the German word *ich*, e.g., [ɪç]. Some sources rec-ognize this phoneme as [i], which is a closed vowel, slightly lower than [i]. This text prefers to use [ɪ] to represent this vowel in both languages.

Practice alternating between [i] and [ɪ], noticing the backwards movement of the tongue for the formation of [ɪ]. The position of the jaw and
lips remains the same for both vowels.

N.B. FOR ESL SINGERS: Most monosyllabic words spelled with *i* are
pronounced [ɪ]. Here are some common examples for quick reference:

brick, bid, big, bill   miss, mince, miffed, mill
chin, chip, crib, clip   pill, prim, pick, pig
drip, dim, drill, did   rich, rid, rim, ripped
fib, frill, flip, fin   still, slip, sing, sick,
give, glib, gin, grin   shin, ship, shift, shit
him, hit, hid, hill   this, thin, think, thick
it, is, in, ill   win, wing, with, wit
kiss, kit, kid, kin   which, whiff, whig, whim
live, lift, lips, lick

[ɛ]   Epsilon   Bright (tongue), open
Spelling: *e, ea, ai, a*

method   [mɛθəd]   said   [sɛd]
heaven   [hɛvən]   anything   [ɛnɪθɪŋ]

N.B.: friend [fɹɛnd], bury [bɛɹɪ], leopard [lɛpəd]

Production: The tip of the tongue is in contact with the lower teeth,
while the back is mid-high (slightly lower than [ɪ]). The sides of the
tongue only slightly touch the sides of the upper molars, while the rest
of the tongue moves backwards slightly and flattens its curvature at the
front. The jaw naturally rotates back slightly, as for [ɪ]. This vowel

should feel bright and vertical, not dark and vague. Take care to ensure that it does not spread laterally and thus lose focus and intensity.

Practice speaking the following words alternating between [ɪ] and [ɛ], noticing the slight backwards movement and flattening of the tongue for the formation of [ɛ]. The position of the jaw and lips remains the same for both vowels.

[ɛ]	[ɪ]	[ɛ]	[ɪ]
hem	him	meant	mint
sense	since	slept	slipped
crept	crypt	left	lift
send	sinned	head	hid
dead	did	bet	bit
mess	miss	petty	pity
sell	sill	well	will

Central vowels [æ][ɑ][ʌ][ə]

[æ]   Lowercase A-E ligature   Central (tongue), open

Spelling: *a, au*

lamb   [læm]   laugh   [læf]

N.B.: plaid [plæd]

Production: The back of the tongue is mid-low, while the tip remains in contact with the lower teeth. As the jaw naturally opens, the front of the tongue flattens. The sides no longer have contact with the upper molars. There is a feeling of greater vertical height at the back of the mouth, as compared to [ɛ]. The proper production of this phoneme results in a vowel that is in between [a] and [ɛ]. One's ear is the best guide for this sound, as it does not exist in German, French, or Italian.

> Practice alternating between [ɪ], [ɛ], and [æ], noticing the slight back-wards movement and flattening of the tongue with each successive vowel. Then practice the same in reverse, feeling the tongue gradually rise. The position of the jaw and lips remains the same for all vowels.

N.B.: A common pitfall is to spread the lips laterally to form [æ]. It is crucial that all vowels be pronounced within an inner vertical space.

[ɑ]   Script A   Central (tongue), open
Spelling: *a, o*

watch   [watʃ]   gospel   [gɑspəl]

N.B.: broad [bɹɑd]

Production: The jaw rotates back and drops naturally to a low, comfort-able position. It should not be dropped by force or with any tension whatsoever. The back of the tongue is low, while the tip lightly touches the lower teeth. The lips are relaxed and open wide. It is important to avoid labial tension by ensuring that the jaw is not open too far. This vowel does not exist in German or Italian, both of which use [a] or [aː].

[ʌ]   Turned V   Central (tongue)
Spelling: *o, oo, ou, u, un-*

son   [sʌn]   luck   [lʌk]
blood   [blʌd]   unbelievable   [ʌnbɪˈlivəbəl]
double   [dʌbəl]

N.B.: was [wʌz], dost [dʌst], does [dʌz]

Production: This neutral vowel is the stressed counterpart to the *schwa* [ə]. It is neither closed nor open and does not exist in German or the Romance languages. The tongue-tip is in contact with the lower teeth, while the middle and back move backward and downward. The exact position of the tongue determines this vowel and distinguishes it from [ae]. The jaw rotates back and falls open naturally. The lips are relaxed in a neutral position.

Exception: The prefix *un-* is commonly used to reverse and deny the original meaning of a word. Although this prefix is unstressed, it is always expressed as [ʌn].

unworthy   [ʌnˈwɜði]   to untie   [ʌnˈtaɪ]

[ə]   Schwa   Central (tongue)
Spelling: *a, e, i, o, u, y, ou*

about   [əˈbaʊt]   upon   [əˈpɑn]
seven   [sɛvən]   syrinx   [səˈɹɪŋks]
lentil   [lɛntəl]   porous   [pɔɹəs]
offensive   [əˈfɛnsəv]

Exception: The unstressed prefixes *dis-, in-, im-* and suffixes *-ing, -ic* are always pronounced [ɪ] and never reduced to the *schwa*.

Spelling: *ar, er, or, -ur, -le, -re*
cellar   [sɛlə]   pleasure   [plɛʒə]
cover   [kʌvə]   addle   [ædəl]
doctor   [dɑktə]   theatre   [θiətə]

N.B.: porpoise [pɔəpəs], tortoise [tɔətəs]

For the above spellings with *r*, British singers use [ɐ] instead of [ə]. The main difference is that there is greater R-color in [ɐ]. For further information, please consult Chapter 16 (Characteristic German Phonemes).

Production: This neutral vowel is the unstressed counterpart to [ʌ]. It is neither closed nor open and does not exist in the Romance languages. Since English is not a phonetic language, the decision as to when to use the *schwa* must be determined by word stress. This may be challenging to non-native speakers, who often substitute pure vowels instead.

As discussed in Chapter 6 (The Structure of English), the *schwa* is an important element of "unstress" in English. However, in choral singing the use of the *schwa* is often discouraged due to its indefinite quality. The inconsistency in its exact pronunciation results in chaos and a lack of clarity when singing in a larger group. In this case, it is best to use a vowel with greater definition, e.g., [ʌ], [ɪ], or [ɛ].

Dark vowels [ɔ][o][ʊ][u]

[ɔ]   Open O   Dark (rounded lips), open
Spelling: *a* (before *l* or *ll*), *au*, *augh*, *aw*, *o* (before *rr*), *ough*

exalted	[ɪgˈzɔltəd]	draw	[dɹɔ]
wall	[wɔl]	sorrow	[sɔɹou]
autumn	[ɔtəm]	fought	[fɔt]
taught	[tɔt]		

Production: The tip of the tongue remains in contact with the lower teeth, though it feels slightly retracted. The back of the tongue is raised while the middle and front lie quite flat. In fact, the tongue retracts as far as possible, without becoming a fricative consonant, e.g., [ʁ] or [χ].

The lips are rounded and protruded, forming a small, oval aperture, while maintaining a sense of vertical space inside the mouth. The jaw is rotated back and relaxed. It is not advisable to drop the jaw very much.

N.B.: This vowel does not truly exist in General American English (GA). It is best acquired through imitation or the relation to a foreign language, e.g., *farò, die Wolke,* or a British accent, e.g., bought. The most common error is interchanging [ɑ] with [ɔ]. Indeed in the vernacular, these vowels are regularly exchanged in North America. However, in singing greater attention to the difference in quality between these vowels allows for greater precision and expression. In general, [ɔ] is shorter in time value as compared to [ɑ]. It is a more focused sound, requiring a significant lip protrusion and a sense of inner vertical space. This alone is foreign to native speakers of English, who are used to very little lip movement. It is easy for [ɔ] to decay by moving the lips out of position.

Practice alternating between [ʌ] and [ɔ]. Note that the main difference is in the rounding and protrusion of the lips.

---

[o]   Lowercase O   Dark (rounded lips), close
Spelling: *o-, pro-*

obey   [oˈbeɪ]   protect   [pɹoˈtɛkt]

Production: The tip of the tongue is in contact with the lower teeth and the lips are protruded and rounded without any labial tension. The middle of the tongue is high, while the back of the tongue is lower. The back of the tongue is slightly higher than for [u]. One must imagine a high vertical space at the back of the mouth, although the front forms a small, round aperture. This pure vowel is also found in German, French, and Italian. It is slightly less closed than its German counterpart [o:].

N.B.: Closed [o] only occurs in the unstressed prefixes *o-* and *pro-*. All other instances of unstressed *o* are pronounced [ə] or [oʊ], e.g., desolate [dɛsələt], pillow [pɪloʊ].

[ʊ]   Upsilon   Dark (rounded lips), open
Spelling: *oo, ou, u*

look   [lʊk]   cushion   [kʊʃən]
could   [kʊd]

N.B.: bosom [bʊzəm], woman [wʊmən], wolf [wʊlf]
Note that the suffix *-ful* is never neutralized to [ə], e.g., woeful [woʊfʊl].

Production: The tongue-tip remains in contact with the lower teeth and feels slightly retracted. The front and middle of the tongue arch forward as for [ɪ], while the back is also raised. The lips are relaxed and neutral. It is not advisable to drop the jaw to form this vowel. It is important to note that this vowel is *not* exactly the same as its German counterpart and is not found in the Romance languages. Compared to German, the English [ʊ] is much more open and uses far less lip rounding.

[u]   Lowercase U   Dark (rounded lips), close
Spelling: *o, oo, ou, u, ue, ui, ew*

move   [muv]   blue   [blu]
droop   [dɹup]   cruise   [kɹuz]
ghoul   [gul]   drew   [dɹu]
flute   [flut]

Production: The lips are protruded and rounded, but without any labial tension. The middle of the tongue is high, while the tip touches the lower teeth and the back is low. One must imagine a high vertical space at the back of the mouth, although the front forms a small, round aperture. Great care must be taken not to add a *schwa* [ə] or a glide [w] upon the release. This phoneme is often mispronounced as a diphthong in everyday speech [uə], especially before *l* and when final, e.g., school, shoe. N.B.: This vowel is not as closed as its German counterpart [uː].

Practice intoning the following words, mindful of the slight movements of the articulators, when passing from vowel to vowel:

bead → bid → bade → bed → bad

read → rid → raid → red → rad

feast → fist → faced → fest → fast

least → list → laced → lest → last

peat → pit → pate → pet → pat

beat → bit → bait → bet → bat

R-colored vs. R-less vowels

There are two pairs of vowels that are defined as R-colored or R-less according to the presence of the approximant *r* in the actual vowel sound, e.g., [ɜ] and [ɝ], [ə] and [ɚ]. This text recommends the sole use of R-less vowels in lyric diction. An R-colored vowel is also called a retroflex vowel, due to the position of the tongue during production (Jones 1962). When forming an R-colored vowel, the soft palate falls, closing off any vertical space in the mouth. They are characteristic features of both GA and Irish. It is difficult to achieve a beautiful tone when singing R-colored vowels. They may be used for North American songs that demand a colloquial setting, but must be used with care and moderation.

Use of R-less vowels

The decision to use either [ɜ] or [ə] depends on whether or not the syllable in question is stressed or unstressed.

[3]   Reversed epsilon   Central (tongue), open

Spelling: *ear, er, ir, or, our, ur, yr*

learn	[lɜn]	journey	[dʒɜnɪ]
mercy	[mɜsɪ]	murmur	[mɜmə]
birch	[bɜtʃ]	myrtle	[mɜtəl]
word	[wɜd]		

N.B.: worry [wɜɹɪ]

Production: The back of the tongue is arched toward the front of the mouth, as for [ɛ]. The tip of the tongue remains in contact with the lower teeth. The lips protrude and round slightly. Care must be taken to avoid any labial tension. It is also important to keep the soft palate raised at the back of the mouth. This vowel is used solely for stressed syllables. It is helpful to imagine a British accent when finding this vowel. This phoneme is similar to the German mixed vowel [œ], the main difference being the production of [3] uses far less lip rounding. Both [3] and [ə] may occur in the same word, e.g., learned (adj.) [lɜnəd], merger [mɜdʒə].

R-Colored vowels

[ɝ]   Right-hook reversed epsilon   Central (tongue), open

Production: This is the R-colored version of [3], whereby the retroflex *r* is part of the vowel. It is not advisable to use this vowel in singing.

[ɚ]   Right-hook schwa   Central (tongue), open

Production: This is the R-colored version of [ə], whereby the retroflex *r* is part of the vowel. It is not advisable to use this vowel in singing.

8.2 Diphthongs

When one speech sound glides into another successive speech sound, producing a smooth, imperceptible blend within one syllable, it is referred to as a diphthong. This text promotes the use of ten English diphthongs. Five are standard features of GA ([aɪ], [aʊ], [oʊ], [ɔɪ], [eɪ]) and five are borrowed from RP ([ʊə], [ɛə], [ɔə], [ɑə], [ɪə]). Note that a diphthong refers to the *sound* of two vowels, not the spelling. This is especially important in English, as it is not a phonetic language.

Some phoneticians arrange diphthongs according to the perceived direction of movement, e.g., rising, falling, or centering. It is imperative that all diphthongs finish with either the lips or the tongue. It is common error to move the jaw to end a diphthong, resulting in a distorted tone and chewed vowel.

The primary vowel in each diphthong is sustained for most of the value of the note. One moves smoothly through the second vowel (a.k.a. vanish vowel) while passing on to the next consonant or vowel. This text recommends spending 75% of the note value on the first vowel and the remaining 25% on the second vowel. In practice, the actual length of the second vowel is determined by the tempo and setting of the given word. A common mistake is to begin the second vowel too early, resulting in improper word stress. Further, it is imperative that the second vowel maintain the identical pitch and intensity of the first vowel.

In everyday speech, English diphthongs beginning with *a* are often pronounced with [ɑ]. However, the use of [a] as the primary vowel serves to increase the sense of vertical space in the mouth and encourage a brighter quality of tone. This has been intentionally modified for the purpose of lyric diction. When singing in English, it is imperative that all vowels and diphthongs remain distinct, and not swallowed.

[aɪ]

Spelling: *ay, i, ie, igh, eigh, ui, y*

aye	[aɪ]	sleight	[slaɪt]
trite	[tɹaɪt]	beguile	[bɪˈgaɪl]
compiled	[kəmˈpaɪld]	defy	[dɪˈfaɪ]
high	[haɪ]		

N.B.: geyser [gaɪzə], stein [staɪn], kaleidoscope [kəˈlaɪdəskoʊp], eye [aɪ], aisle [aɪl], buy [baɪ], choir [kwaɪə]

Production: After spending 75% of the note value on [a], lift the middle of the tongue quickly to distinctly form [ɪ] for the remaining 25% of the note. There should be no movement of the lips or the jaw during this smooth transition between vowels, as everything happens internally.

[aʊ]

Spelling: *ou, ough, ow*

ground	[gɹaʊnd]	vowed	[vaʊd]
bough	[baʊ]		

N.B.: sauerkraut [saʊəkɹaʊt], umlaut [ʊmlaʊt]

Production: After spending 75% of the note value on [a], round the lips slightly and quickly to distinctly form [ʊ] for the remaining 25% of the note. There should be no movement of the jaw during this smooth transition between vowels. Great care must be taken to ensure that the first vowel is truly [a], and not [æ] or [ɑ], as is common in everyday speech.

[oʊ]
Spelling: *o, oa, oe, ou, ough, ow*

stole	[stoʊl]	shoulder	[ʃoʊldə]
coach	[koʊtʃ]	though	[ðoʊ]
foe	[foʊ]	pillow	[pɪloʊ]

N.B.: chauffeur [ʃoʊ'fɜ], chauvinist [ʃoʊvənəst], mauve [moʊv], brooch [bɹoʊtʃ], sew [soʊ]

Production: After spending 75% of the note value on [o], lift the middle of the tongue and slightly protrude the lips to distinctly form [ʊ] for the remaining 25% of the note. There should be no movement of the jaw during this smooth transition between vowels.

[ɔɪ]
Spelling: *oi, oy*

rejoice	[ɹɪ'dʒɔɪs]	oyster	[ɔɪstə]

Production: After spending 75% of the note value on [ɔ], lift the middle of the tongue slightly and quickly to distinctly form [ɪ] for the remaining 25% of the note. There is no movement of the lips or the jaw during this smooth transition between vowels, as everything happens internally.

[eɪ]
Spelling: *a, ai, ay, ea, ei, ey*

angel	[eɪndʒəl]	great	[gɹeɪt]
afraid	[ə'fɹeɪd]	freight	[fɹeɪt]
display	[dɪs'pleɪ]	abeyance	[ə'beɪəns]

N.B.: gauge [geɪdʒ]

Production: After spending 75% of the note value on [e], allow the tongue to flatten and fall back slightly and quickly to distinctly form [ɪ] for the remaining 25% of the note. There should be no movement of the lips or the jaw during this smooth transition between vowels, as everything happens internally. Take great care to ensure that the first vowel is truly [e], and not [ɛ], in order to avoid a spread and indistinct sound.

Diphthongs borrowed from RP (with final r)
When a vowel is followed by r, it forms a diphthong whereby r is replaced by the *schwa* [ə] and effectively implied. The initial vowels are open to allow for less movement of the articulators. This differs slightly from common speech and is better suited to singing. Economy of movement is paramount to healthy, clean, lyric diction. In replacing r with [ə], it allows for a clearer vowel preceding the consonant, since the tongue is not curling up and obscuring the space. For singers who tend to "chew" their words, this is most helpful. The use of [ə] does not result in an affected English accent.

These five diphthongs do not follow the previous pattern. Namely, it is recommended that one remain on the first vowel for 90% of the duration of the note. For the remaining 10%, one moves smoothly through [ə]. This is directly comparable to the German approach to diphthongs.

Occurrence
1. r followed by a consonant (either within one word or in the context of a sentence)

charm   [tʃɑəm]   for me   [fɔə mi]

2. r followed by a silent letter
farewell   [fɛə'wɛl]   foretold   [fɔə'toʊld]

It is crucial that one passes through the *schwa* in order to imply the written *r* sound. Otherwise, lark [lɑək] could easily resemble lock [lɑk].

N.B.: If a diphthong borrowed from RP is followed by a vowel, it is imperative that *r* be pronounced to link the sounds in a legato manner. In this case, the *schwa* is no longer necessary, e.g., dairy [dɛɹɪ] not [dɛəɹɪ]. For more information, please see Chapter 9 (Glides and Approximants).

[ɑə]
Spelling: *ar, ear*

ardent	[ɑədənt]	heart	[hɑət]

N.B.: sergeant [sɑədʒənt], are [ɑə]

[ɛə]
Spelling: *air, are, ear, eir, erc*

chair	[tʃɛə]	heirloom	[ɛəlum]
warfare	[wɔəfɛə]	where	[ʍɛə]
pear	[pɛə]		

N.B.: err [ɛə], they're [ðɛə], ne'er [nɛə], e'er [ɛə], prayer [pɹɛə]

[ɪə]
Spelling: *ear, eer, ere, ier*

fear	[fɪə]	revere	[ɹɪˈvɪə]
peer	[pɪə]	tier	[tɪə]

N.B.: we're [wɪə], weir [wɪə], weird [wɪəd]

[ɔə]
Spelling: *oar, our, oor, or, ore, ar*

boar	[bɔə]	horse	[hɔəs]
four	[fɔə]	implore	[ɪmˈplɔə]
indoors	[ɪnˈdɔəz]	quart	[kwɔət]

N.B.: o'er [ɔə], drawer [dɹɔə], you're [jɔə]

[ʊə]
Spelling: *oor, our, ur*

boor	[bʊə]	demure	[dɪˈmjʊə]
tour	[tʊə]		

Exception: When a word ends in an unstressed *-ure*, it is pronounced [ə], e.g., pleasure [plɛʒə].

8.3 Triphthongs

The triphthong presents the unique challenge of passing through three vowels within the duration of one note. There are two triphthongs in the English language. As with the diphthong, the first vowel is sustained for most of the note value. In context, the actual length of the first vowel is dependent on the word setting by the given composer. This is left to the singer's discretion. It is sometimes useful to group the last two vowels as one unit. One must take great care to avoid extraneous, unnecessary movement of the articulators when passing through the three vowels. It is recommended to think of the triphthong as being *one gesture*, containing three distinct vowel sounds. It is important to note that neither triphthong employs the glide [j]. This is a common mispronunciation that often involves movement of the jaw on the third phoneme.

When a word is set over two syllables, it is not considered to be a true triphthong, but rather a sequence of vowels. If a word normally pronounced with two syllables is set on only one note, it becomes a triphthong, e.g., power (to rhyme with flour).

[aɪə]
Spelling: *ire, yre*

aspire   [əˈspaɪə]   pyre   [paɪə]

N.B.: choir [kwaɪə]

[aʊə]
Spelling: *our, ower*

flour   [flaʊə]   power   [paʊə]

N.B.: As with diphthongs, if a triphthong precedes an *r* followed by a vowel, *r* is pronounced, removing the need for the *schwa*, e.g., devouring [dɪvaʊɹɪŋ] not [dɪvaʊəɹɪŋ].

Supplementary exercises
In the following exercises, transcribe all words into IPA:

1. [ʌ] vs. [ə]
above, humble, double, mother, unfortunate, tussle, husband, shovel, bubble, judgment, loveliest, covet, other, crumble, among, rubble, younger, unhappiness, rustle, trouble, sudden, brother, onion, asunder

2. [ɔ] vs. [ɑ]

father, lost, caught, fought, cross, altogether, gone, swatches, flaw, install, glossy, tomorrow, hopping, haunt, lawyer, bond, plodding, torrid, wander, although

3. [ɜ] vs. [ə]

rehearse, surge, journey, verse, misery, master, perhaps, actor, iron, girl, Herbert, server, learner, curtail, burner, never, bird, ever, sever, tether, another, burden, fervor, worker, murmur, murder, perverted, shepherd, neighbor, curtsey, perform, measure, hurt

4. [u] vs. [ʊ]

tooth, wooded, brook, spoon, soothe, took, goon, shook, moon, good, cool, pool, forsook, soon, looked, loose, crooked, fool, wooed, book, soot, loon, food, swooned, balloon

5. [ʌ] vs. [ə]

until, mediant, dialect, underneath, liter, unless, sofa, unreal, center, underworld, roses, dove, presence, come, tough, hopeless, kingdom, attempt, done, glove, riot, none, treble, someone, sun, purpose, touch, pebble, dull, rifle, quiet, untie

6. [ʊə] vs. [ə]

measure, censure, verdure, cure, obscure, leisure, nature, surely, pure, rapture, stature, security, capture, treasure, tenure, lure, assure, sure, enclosure, composure, endure, furniture, venture, future, lecture, creature, feature, insurance

7. [o] [oʊ] [ə]

desolate, protect, pope, prolific, ago, roamed, profound, omit, smolder, protest (v.), follow, doe, toad, November, globe, hoe, frivolous, molest, provide, mediocre, mold, erode, pronounce, melody, borough, window, thorough, obey, arrow, prohibit, boast, proclaim, police

8. Diphthongs: use of [ɹ]

very, dire, pure, dare, dairy, hear, mere, diary, sincerely, fare, veer, ear, fairy, fairly, secure, devour, devouring, tiring, purity, eerie, queer, teary, query, yearly, weary, poorer, curious, airy, vary, rarest, cheery, cheerful, care, dearly, hereby, nearly, revere, sincere, tired, security, verily, carry

9. [ɜ] vs. [ə]

learn, mercy, heard, collar, yearning, remember, birch, proctor, favorite, treasure, virtue, journey, pursue, worry, murmur, labor, myrtle, verge, brother, encourage, flourish, leisure, surge, nectar, perplex, defer, differ, word, girth, castor, comfort, humor, colourful, purport, courageous, curt

10. Diphthongs

woeful, neighborly, allow, voice, smoke, sleigh, broil, road, sublime, gray, furlough, annoy, thousand, coma, royal, silence, frown, fable, bellow, resign, decade, thou, pillow, painful, cried, height, rainy, foamy, break, deny

11. Diphthongs borrowed from RP

carefully, sphere, before, sure, beer, hoarse, war, allure, star, endearing, your, obscure, card, where, beard, court, hair, pure, alarm, floor, leer, their, outdoor, carve, reindeer, adorn, paired, beware, storm, elsewhere, explore, soared

12. [ɜ] [ə] [ʌ]

firmly, love, infer, homeward, rough, woodland, never, thirst, undone, menace, surpass, hum, work, peruse, unhappy, nourish, dearest, traitor, purpose, shove, trouble, myrrh, tumor, phantom, earthly, clung, noble, surprise, determine, under, pearl, much, inference

13. [æ] [ɑ] [ɔ]
pop, aunt, potholder, applaud, walk, comma, fawn, draught, bonding, thought, alternate (n.), claw, gone, barrage, borrow, not, caution, garage, wand, small, mirage, sorrow, sabotage, enthrall

14. Indicate which words contain true triphthongs:
employer, lawyer, desire, slower, conspire, lower, admire, tower, player, sour, slayer, devour, layer, our, purveyer, conveyer, inspire, mayor, wires, coward, dire, towel, lyre, vowels, fire, higher, liar, trial, denial, cower, showered

Chapter 9: Glides and Approximants

A glide is a phoneme that begins as a vowel but is ultimately heard as a consonant, e.g., [w], [j]. The weakly articulated initial vowel rapidly glides into a consonantal sound of greater prominence. It is also known as a semi-vowel or semi-consonant, as this phoneme is neither a true vowel nor a true consonant.

9.1 Use of [w] and [ʍ]

[w]   Lowercase W   Voiced labial-velar approximant
Spelling: *w, qu*

award   [əˈwɔəd]   squirrel   [skwɜl]

N.B.: choir [kwaɪə], suave [swɑv], persuade [pəˈsweɪd], suite [swit]

Description: The tongue and lips form the vowel [u] with the back of the tongue raised and the lips rounded and protruded. Upon commencing the production of [u], the lips immediately move to the position of the subsequent vowel. This occurs swiftly and energetically. Note that the fleeting, initial [u] is not expressed in IPA. The semi-consonant [w] is a direct result of both sounds formed in rapid succession. This phoneme releases in a forward direction.

Alternate between [u] and [ə], at first slowly, then gradually increasing the speed. The lips move slightly laterally, but never extend to a horizontal position. Practice speaking and intoning the following: "We would work if we were wise," maintaining the intensity of the vowels.

N.B.: Not all words spelled with *w* use [w]. If set over one syllable, the triphthong [auə] is formed, e.g., flower [flauə]. Alternatively, if a word is polysyllabic, it does not form a true triphthong, e.g., coward [kauəd].

"The Blessed Virgin's Expostulation," H. Purcell/N. Tate

In the above excerpt, notice how the glide [w] always precedes the rhythmic beat in the IPA. Taking time from the previous note value, the lips prepare [u] and the glide is executed directly on the beat. Since [w] is voiced, it is not prudent to sing it before the beat, as a scoop will result. Further, one must be conscious of the release into the succeeding vowel. The faster the glide, the longer one is on the following vowel, anchoring the higher pitches with ease. It is critical that the lips remain relaxed when many glides appear in a row.

[ʍ]   Turned W   Voiceless labial-velar fricative
Spelling: *wh*

whenever   [ʍən'ɛvə]   whither   [ʍɪðə]

Description: This phoneme begins with [h] and is considered to be an aspirant (air sound). Both [w] and [ʍ] are produced using the same lip formation and action. It is imperative that one prepare the position for [u] prior to producing [h]. This limits the amount of movement and increases efficiency. Note that [h] is not expressed in IPA. This phoneme releases in a forward direction.

9.2 Use of [j]

In English, the glide [j] is most commonly used before the vowel [u]. In everyday speech, the use of [j] is often limited. However, it does belong to proper English and thus should be observed when singing art song or opera. An exception would be if a song required a colloquial, less-formal manner of delivery. This is left to the singer's discretion.

[j]   Lowercase J   Voiced palatal approximant
Spelling: c, d, f, h, l, m, p, s, t (before u), lli, u- y (before vowel)

secure	[sɪˈkjʊə]	pure	[pjʊə]
due	[dju]	suit	[sjut]
refute	[ɹɪˈfjut]	gratitude	[gɹætətjud]
huge	[hjudʒ]	billion	[bɪljən]
value	[vælju]	usually	[juʒuəlɪ]
mule	[mjul]	yesterday	[jɛstədeɪ]

Description: The tip of the tongue remains in contact with the lower teeth. The lips are relaxed and only slightly open. The tongue prepares [i], then releases forward, as the sides of the tongue lightly contact the inner surface of the upper teeth. This occurs swiftly and energetically. It is crucial that one does not form a true [i]. The glide proceeds directly into [u]. One must imagine a high vertical space at the back of the mouth, although the front forms a small, round aperture. This phoneme is not identical to its German counterpart [j̟].

Occurrence: Please memorize this handy phrase: **FeLiCiTY HaD SPaM**. When the consonants (and semi-consonant *y*) in this phrase occur before *u*, one must use [j]. This is particularly useful, if the regular use of [j] is not part of the singer's regional dialect. The only exception to this rule is if one of the above consonants is paired with *l*. In this case, they do *not* use [j]: clue, exclude, include, flew, flue, flute, plew, plume, slew, slue.

Additional Common Occurrences of [j] :

askew, dew, ewe, feudal, few, lewd, pew, pewter, spew, view, ebullient, beautiful, beauty, bugle, butane, imbued, argue, queue, behavior, savior

---

N.B.: If *n* is followed by [u], use the consonant [ɲ], e.g., new [ɲu]. The combination [nj] does not exist. Please consult Chapter 10 (Consonants) for further information.

9.3 Use of retroflex R: [ɹ]

The term *retroflex* refers to how the tip of the tongue curls up towards the hard palate with a lateral contraction. In English, the retroflex R [ɹ] is an approximant, whereby the articulators approach one another, but not closely enough to form either a fricative or a stop/plosive consonant.

[ɹ]   Turned R   Voiced dental or alveolar approximant
Spelling: *r, rh, rr, wr*

brace	[bɹeɪs]	hurry	[hɜɹɪ]
rhythm	[ɹɪðəm]	written	[ɹɪtən]

Description: The tongue-tip approaches the alveolar ridge as if forming [d], but instead of making contact, it curls slightly backward with a raised tip. It is helpful to imagine that this phoneme is preceded by [ə], allowing there to be a greater sense of space at the back of the mouth.

Occurrence: *r* before a vowel or *y* (within a word or a sentence)

spirit	[spɪɹət]	arise	[əˈɹaɪz]
crave	[kɹeɪv]	for us	[fɔ ɹʌs]
very	[vɛɹɪ]	forever	[fɔ ɹɛvə]
far away	[fɑ ɹəˈweɪ]	exaggerate	[ɪgˈzædʒəɹeɪt]

All other occurrences of *r* are expressed through diphthongs borrowed from RP. This includes 1) *r* followed by a consonant (either within a word or in the context of a sentence), 2) final *r*, and 3) *r* followed by a silent letter. Note that when a word ends in an R-colored diphthong or *schwa*, one may form [ɹ] at the beginning of the next word, in order to avoid a glottal onset, e.g., before us [bɪˈfɔ ɹʌs]. Naturally, this depends on context and clarity. One should avoid the formation of other words, e.g., slumber on [slʌmbə |ɑn] vs. [slʌmbə ɹɑn]. The former example is preferable, as it is not desirable to form the word "Ron". Please consult Chapter 22 (Legato Singing) for further information.

Common examples

care	[kɛə]	carry	[kæɹɪ]
mare	[mɛə]	marry	[mæɹɪ]
bear	[bɛə]	berry	[bɛɹɪ]
sore	[sɔə]	sorry	[sɔɹɪ]
were	[w3]	worry	[w3ɹɪ]
bore	[bɔə]	borrow	[bɔɹoʊ]
spire	[spaɪə]	spiral	[spaɪɹəl]
pore	[pɔə]	porous	[pɔɹəs]

tire	[taɪə]	tirade	[taɹeɪd]
tear	[tɪə]	teary	[tɪɹɪ]
more	[mɔə]	moral	[mɔɹəl]

N.B.: As previously discussed in Chapter 7 (Characteristic English Phonemes), when performing oratorio or operatic repertoire, a flipped *r* [ɾ]
may also be used for an intervocalic *r*, e.g., spirit [spɪɾət]. This is left to
the singer's discretion and is dependent on both style and setting.

Supplementary exercises
Transcribe all of the following words into IPA:

1. [w] vs. [ʍ]
whet, wet, whether, weather, witch, which, wear, where, whiff, whine,
why, while, wail, whale, wake, wonder, woe, whatever, watch, whisper,
weary, weird, wine, wasp

2. [ju] vs. [u]
duplicate, two, Cuba, induce, duke, duly, duty, elude, prelude, interlude,
pursuit, assume, plume, consume, slue, resume (v.), coo, tumult, student, allude, stupid, multitude, astute, stoop, who, flute, choose, flew,
June, fruit, lose, recruit, blew, Tuesday, inclusion, illusion, clues, pewter

3. Use of [ɹ]
your own, the other end, far away, slumber on, stare at me, star and
moon, a pair of shoes, more and more, fire engine, nearer and nearer

4. Use of [j]
blue, few, trillion, grew, view, clue, beyond, pew, include, dew, exclude,
askew, use (v.), glue, feud, ewe, beautiful, delude, suitor, beauty, future,
imbued, bugle, butane, music, argue, queue, presume, humor, lewd

Chapter 10: Consonants

10.1 Efficiency in production

Clear, well-articulated consonants provide clarity to the text, deliver rhythmic precision, support tone production, eliminate excessive tension, assist in the correct pronunciation of vowels, aid in overcoming pitch problems, and enable the voice to cut through a thick orchestral texture. Many factors may influence a singer's ability to articulate consonants. These include the size and agility of the tongue, the condition of the teeth and gums, and the control of the labial muscles.

Although good tone production is dependent on proper vowel formation, the duration and dynamic level of the tone is greatly determined by the consonant. Consonants can propel a tone when initial and keep a held tone from sagging in the middle of a phrase. Many singers are unaware of the benefits of voiced consonants. Indeed the initial, medial and even final consonants play an enormous role in good intonation. All neighboring consonants should be merged to achieve true legato. One consonant flows into the next on a supported breath stream without any gaps or stoppages. It is important to avoid the insertion of an intrusive vowel. This is often the result of releasing a voiced consonant too strongly or anticipating a voiced consonant too early, e.g., [n]. In colloquial speech, medial and final consonants tend to be minimally pronounced or even dropped altogether. Great care must be taken to ensure that final consonants are clearly articulated and projected, especially final *d*. A gentle word deserves a strong consonant, just as a slower tempo requires fast consonants. These are not mutually exclusive!

Much of vocal tension may be attributed to the improper articulation of consonants. A tensely produced consonant will result in a tight, pinched vowel. All phonemes must be prepared and executed with care and thought. It is imperative that the singer only use the articulators required to make the sound, and not engage extra muscles in the process. It is a common fallacy that correct enunciation is somehow more work. In fact, the clear, precise pronunciation of consonants is much more efficient and provides a superior tone instantly. Once a singer experiences this phenomenon, there is no turning back!

All consonants have the ability to either help or hinder vocal production. It depends on whether or not they are formed in an efficient, healthy manner. This principle applies to all languages but is especially useful in Germanic languages, as consonants exist in a higher ratio. Analogy: Imagine that a vocal phrase is in the form of long sheets hanging on a clothesline. In this scenario, the melodic line is horizontal and dominated by vowels, as represented by the sheets. The consonants are vertical, much like the clothespins used to keep laundry from falling off the line. The ratio of sheets to clothespins is what must be kept in mind when singing. One must not give the impression that there are several single socks hanging on the line! The continuants are an integral part of the horizontal vocal line, e.g., [s], [z], [f], [v], [m], [n], [l], [ð], and [θ]. All other consonants enter in a vertical manner, with a quick precise point of entry and an equally swift release.

10.2 Voiced vs. voiceless

In lyric diction, consonants may be divided into two distinct groups: voiced and voiceless. Voiced consonants carry the pitch and ensure a seamless legato when sung to their full potential. The pitch essentially never stops when singing through a voiced consonant. By contrast, voiceless consonants must be articulated in between the notes. If their production is labored, the singer is inevitably rhythmically late.

As in German, the timing of voiced and voiceless consonants differs. In general, voiced consonants are to be sung *on the beat*, while voiceless consonants are to be sung *before the beat*. This ensures that the singer does not lag behind the musical pulse and the vowel is always securely on the beat. As voiced consonants carry the pitch, they do not delay the vowel. One must allow enough time to articulate voiceless consonants, always "taking time" from the previous phoneme. In the following examples, take note of the timing for voiced and voiceless consonants.

"Come all ye songsters" from *The Fairy Queen*, H. Purcell

"The Timely Admonition," T. Arne

It is a common but unfounded fear that producing aspirated consonants robs the singer of the breath needed for the completion of a successful phrase. In fact, aspirated consonants use residual air; in other words, air that is already present in the mouth. One need not inhale to produce a highly aspirated consonant. As a result, strong aspirates do not use the air required for singing. In fact, their clean release allows the singer to have *more* air at the end of the phrase. This is due to the fact that one is not holding on to air in an effort to conserve, but rather releasing it. As the adage says, "One must spend money to make money." The same may be said of air: "One must release air in order to have air."

Another erroneous concern is that voiceless consonants prevent a legato singing line. Nothing could be further from the truth. A properly formed and released voiceless consonant keeps the air flowing, bridges the gaps between words, and forges a fluid legato line. When there is an absence of legato, this is due to a space or a hole in the vocal line.

> Method of identifying voiced and voiceless consonants: Cover the ears firmly while intoning [v], followed by [f]. When uttering or singing [v], a vibration will be felt in the head. The same may be tried with one finger on the Adam's apple or larynx. When producing a voiceless consonant, no vibration will be felt in the finger or head.

Table 10.1. Cognates

Voiceless	Voiced
[p]	[b]
[t]	[d]
[k]	[g]
[f]	[v]
[s]	[z]
[θ]	[ð]
[ʃ]	[ʒ]
[tʃ]	[dʒ]
[ʍ]	[w]

All English voiceless consonants, except *h*, have a corresponding voiced consonant formed with the exact same articulation process. These pairs are called *cognates*. By contrast, several voiced consonants do not have a voiceless partner, e.g., [l], [m], [n], [ɲ], [ŋ].

10.3 Double consonants

In English, orthographic double consonants are not pronounced any differently from single consonants, e.g., hopping [hɑpɪŋ], hoping [hoʊpɪŋ]. However, as many English words are onomatopoeic in nature, e.g., hiss, the expressive lengthening of certain consonants is strongly encouraged.

10.4 Individual consonants

Plosives (Stops) [b][p][d][t][g][k]

[b]   Lowercase B   Voiced bilabial plosive
Spelling: *b, bb*

begin   [bɪ'gɪn]   cabbage   [kæbədʒ]

[p]   Lowercase P   Voiceless bilabial plosive
Spelling: *p, pp*

plough   [plaʊ]   copper   [kɑpə]

Production: The cognates [b] and [p] require the same lip formation and action. The lips are relaxed and gently closed in a slight pout during inhalation. As the air is released, the lips bounce energetically apart. Often, as with [m], too much force is involved in this process, resulting in a consonant that pokes out of the melodic line. The lips should never purse or roll inwards in an effort to make a stronger consonant. Note that the tongue is not active. Both [b] and [p] release in a forward motion, leading smoothly into the following vowel or consonant. The exact sound produced depends on the speed of the release.

Practice singing "bumblebee" on any pitches, varying the tempo until it is fluid, maintaining relaxed lips at all times.

N.B.: It is a common error to sing [m] before [b]. This results in a lowered soft palate at the beginning of the phrase and a slow onset. Singers tend to do this as a means of "softening" the [b], or testing out the note first. A plosive [b] will not poke out of the melodic line if the surrounding phonemes are similar in intensity. A consonant must match its environment.

[d]   Lowercase D   Voiced alveolar plosive
Spelling: *d, dd*

dismal   [dɪzməl]   addicted   [əˈdɪktəd]

[t]   Lowercase T   Voiceless alveolar plosive
Spelling: *t, tt, bt*

taken   [teɪkən]   debt   [dɛt]
button   [bʌtən]

N.B.: thyme [taɪm], receipt [ɹɪˈsit], Thames [tɛmz]

Production: The cognates [d] and [t] are formed by the same action of the tongue toward or against the alveolar ridge. It is imperative that the tongue be independent from the jaw when articulating these phonemes. The tongue-tip raises to cleanly touch the alveolar ridge at the juncture of the upper teeth and gums. Before producing [d], the tongue-tip must already be in contact with the alveolar ridge; however, it is possible to form [t] as the tip of the tongue moves toward it. Then, the tip breaks contact with the ridge, moving swiftly and directly to the position of the subsequent vowel or consonant. A speedy tongue-tip results in a clean, crisp consonant, which supports a long, pure vowel (unimpeded by the tongue). A small release of air occurs, resulting in an aspirated consonant. Although [t] is aspirated in English, it is not as strongly aspirated as its German counterpart.

These cognates are called *stop consonants*, as the airflow is interrupted. They cannot be sustained for a sizable amount of time. The exact sound produced depends on the speed of the release. Note that the lips are not active for the production of these consonants.

N.B.: It is a common error to sing [n] before [d]. This results in a lowered soft palate at the beginning of the phrase and a slow onset. Singers tend to do this as a means of "softening" the [d], or testing out the note first. A plosive [d] will not poke out of the melodic line if the surrounding phonemes are similar in intensity. A consonant must match its environment.

[g]   Lowercase G   Voiced velar plosive
Spelling: *g, gg, gh, gue*

glide	[glaɪd]	ghastly	[gæstlɪ]
luggage	[lʌgədʒ]	rogue	[ɹoʊg]

[k]   Lowercase K   Voiceless velar plosive
Spelling: *c, cc, ch, ck, k, que*

picnic	[pɪknɪk]	clock	[klɑk]
broccoli	[bɹɑkəlɪ]	kangaroo	[kæŋgə'ɹu]

orchid   [ɔəkɪd]   plaque   [plæk]

N.B.: khaki [kækɪ]

Production: The cognates [g] and [k] require the same action of the tongue, but the force of exhalation is greater to produce [k]. The tongue-tip is in constant contact with the lower teeth while the middle of the tongue contacts the hard palate. The air releases in a swift, forward motion away from the hard palate. These consonants are considered to be velar, as the soft palate briefly touches the back of the tongue. It is recommended to imagine these consonants as being palatal to ensure that both consonants are not produced too far back in the mouth. In forming [k] and [g], variations in the exact point of articulation exist, depending on the nature of the following vowel (Jones 1962). Note that the lips are not active for the production of these cognates.

> Practice speaking and intoning "gone" and "Guy" [gi], noting how the position of the tongue affects the exact point of articulation for [g].

N.B.: It is a common error to sing [ŋ] before [g]. This results in a lowered soft palate at the beginning of the phrase and a slow onset. Singers tend to do this as a means of "softening" the [g], or testing out the note first. A plosive [g] will not poke out of the melodic line if the surrounding phonemes are similar in intensity. A consonant must match its environment.

Fricatives [v][f][ð][θ][z][s][ʒ][ʃ][h][ʍ]
All fricatives may be pronounced with varying degrees of audible friction. They are formed as a result of a narrowing of the air passage using the lips, teeth, and/or tongue. The length of the actual fricative depends on both context and meaning, giving the singer great expressive control.

All English fricatives, with the exception of [ʍ], are classified as *continuants* and therefore may last as long as there is breath supply.

[v]   Lowercase V   Voiced labiodental fricative
Spelling: *v, vv*

vine   [vaɪn]   navvy   [nævɪ]

[f]   Lowercase F   Voiceless labiodental fricative
Spelling: *f, ff, ph, gh*

forward   [fɔəwəd]   phony   [founɪ]
coffee   [kɑfɪ]   tough   [tʌf]

Production: The continuant cognates [v] and [f] are produced with the same articulation process. The lower lip recedes slightly and lifts to touch the outside edge of the upper teeth. However, the lower lip should not be inside of the upper teeth. These consonants are referred to as labiodental consonants, as they are formed by the lips and involve contact with the upper teeth. The outward flow of air is partially impeded through light contact between the lower lip and upper teeth. It is imperative that the lips be relaxed. Any tension in the labia will result in a tight consonant that is very difficult to sustain.

N.B.: Singers often neglect to sing through [v]. In fact, it may be anticipated for expressive use. This is left to the singer's discretion.

[ð]   Eth   Voiced dental fricative
Spelling: *th*

northern   [nɔəðən]   soothe   [suð]

[θ]   Theta   Voiceless dental fricative
Spelling: *th*
thumb   [θʌm]   breath   [bɹɛθ]

Production: The cognates [ð] and [θ] are produced with the same action of the tongue. The tongue-tip gently contacts both the upper and lower teeth, resting lightly in between. The outward flow of air is partially impeded as it passes through the narrow opening between the tongue and the teeth. One should feel a light tingling sensation in the tongue. Great care must be taken to sing through [ð], keeping the air in constant motion. Neither of these cognates exists in German, French, or Italian.

Occurrence: The rules for when to use [ð] and [θ] correspond to the position of *th* in a given word. Generally, final *th* is pronounced [θ], while medial *th* is pronounced [ð]. Initial *th* may be either voiced or voiceless. When in doubt, ESL singers should consult a dictionary.

Practice speaking the following, mindful of whether to use [ð] or [θ]
bath/bathes, cloth/clothes, moth/moths, mouth/mouths, death/deaths,
oath/oaths, path/paths, breath/breathes, swath/swathes, teeth/teethes,
birth/births, south/southern, worth/worthy, youth/youths

[z]   Lowercase Z   Voiced alveolar fricative
Spelling: *s, z, zz*

resolve   [ɹɪˈzɑlv]   blizzard   [blɪzəd]
zone   [zoʊn]

N.B.: dissolve [dɪˈzɑlv], dessert [dɪˈzɜt], possess [pəˈzɛs], scissors [sɪzəs], to house [haʊz], to use [juz], to close [kloʊz], xenophobe [zinəfoʊb], xerox [zɹɹɑks], xylophone [zaɪləfoʊn]

[s]   Lowercase S   Voiceless alveolar fricative
Spelling: *s, ss, ce, ci, cy, sce, sci, ps-*

scream	[skɹim]	cynical	[sɪnəkəl]
gossip	[gɑsəp]	scenic	[sinək]
center	[sɛntə]	scientific	[saɪənˈtɪfɪk]
lyricism	[lɪɹəsɪzm]	psalm	[sɔm]

Production: The cognates [z] and [s] are produced with the exact same articulation process. They are referred to as *sibilants*, due to their hissing quality. While the tip of the tongue is pointed toward the front teeth, the blade lightly touches the alveolar ridge. The sides of the tongue gently contact the upper back teeth while the lips are relaxed and close together. The vibration for these consonants is centralized between the tongue-tip and the alveolar ridge. Great care must be taken to sing through [z], keeping the air in constant motion.

Pronunciation rules for ESL singers
Final *s* may be pronounced [s] or [z] depending on the preceding sound.

1. Preceded by an unvoiced consonant, final *s* is pronounced [s]

lasts	[læsts]	trips	[tɹɪps]
Hubert's	[hjubəts]		

2. Preceded by a voiced consonant or a vowel, final *s* is pronounced [z]

frowns	[fɹaʊnz]	Herb's	[hɜbz]
Mary's	[mɛɹɪz]	companies	[kʌmpənɪz]
finishes	[fɪnəʃəz]		

[ʒ]   Ezh   Voiced postalveolar fricative
Spelling: *si, su, age*

aversion   [ə'vɜʒən]   corsage   [kɔə'sɑʒ]
visual   [vɪʒuəl]

N.B.: luxurious [ləg'ʒʊɹɪəs], bourgeois [bʊəʒ'wɑ], regime [ɹɪ'ʒim], beige [beɪʒ], seizure [siʒə], prestige [pɹɛs'tiʒ]

[ʃ]   Esh   Voiceless postalveolar fricative
Spelling: *sh, s, ssi, ce, ch, ci, ti*

shoe   [ʃu]   chagrin   [ʃə'gɹɪn]
censure   [sɛnʃə]   special   [spɛʃəl]
mission   [mɪʃən]   nation   [neɪʃən]
ocean   [oʊʃən]

N.B.: luscious [lʌʃəs], conscious [kɑnʃəs], fascism [fæʃɪzm], mansion [mænʃən]

Production: The sibilant cognates [ʒ] and [ʃ] are produced with the exact same articulation process. The tongue-tip points toward the alveolar ridge, while the middle arches toward the hard palate, forming a groove through which the breath is drawn. The sides of the tongue lightly contact the upper molars, as the breath is released. The aperture between the upper and lower teeth is very narrow. Compared to the other sibilants [s] and [z], the tongue is further back, with the surface being quite flat. Great care must be taken not to involve the lower jaw, ensuring it does not jut forward. The lips are rounded and relaxed.

[h]   Lowercase H   Voiceless glottal fricative
Spelling: *h, wh* (before *o*)

harmony   [hɑəmənɪ]   whose   [huz]

Production: Neither the tongue nor the lips is active in the production of this consonant. The glottis is open as the breath passes through freely, and then closes with the ensuing vowel. It is important to prepare the shape of the forthcoming vowel with the necessary articulators prior to producing [h]. In general, [h] tends to be formed too far back in the mouth, which wastes air and delays the onset of the vowel. As with [k], it is advantageous to produce [h] slightly further forward in the mouth.

[ʍ]   Turned W   Voiceless labiovelar fricative
Spelling: *wh*

white   [ʍaɪt]   which   [ʍɪtʃ]

Production: As with the semi-consonant [w], the lips must round in preparation for the phoneme [u]. However, instead of producing [u], [h] is formed. As soon as [h] is produced, the lips move swiftly to the position for the succeeding vowel sound. This occurs in a forward direction and uses residual air that is already present in the mouth. It is not necessary to inhale before producing this consonant. For further examples of the use of [ʍ], please see Chapter 9 (Glides and Approximants). Note that the fricatives [h] and [ʍ] are also considered to be *aspirants*, as they represent air sounds.

Nasals [m][n][ɲ][ŋ]
[m]   Lowercase M   Voiced bilabial nasal
Spelling: *m, mm, -lm, -mb, -mn*

mercy   [mɜsɪ]   numb   [nʌm]
comment   [kɑmənt]   condemn   [kən'dɛm]
salmon   [sæmən]

Production: The lips come together lightly (as when the mouth is gently closed) and separate in a bouncing, forward movement. This motion may be likened to the act of blotting lipstick. It is not nearly as energetic as for [b]. The soft palate is lowered so that air may escape through the nose. During pitch production, [m] resembles a hum and is accompanied by a slight tickling sensation. It is crucial that the lips be relaxed or a pressed tone will result. The tongue is flat and inactive, moving directly to the position of the succeeding vowel or consonant upon release.

Rhythmic timing: Before or on the beat, depending on melodic context

A leap in the vocal line is often facilitated by an early [m], i.e., before the beat. This enhances legato and aids in singing through the ensuing interval. In the following musical example, it is recommended to sing [m] before the beat in the words "remember me". When properly voiced, an early [m] will ensure a seamless legato. The sense of spin never ceases during the production of this continuant. Great care must be taken not to suck the lips inward, but rather to allow them to gently bounce apart, spinning the air directly into the following vowel.

"When I am laid in earth" from *Dido and Aeneas*, H. Purcell

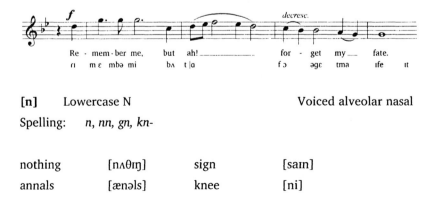

| [n] | Lowercase N | | Voiced alveolar nasal |
Spelling: *n, nn, gn, kn-*

| nothing | [nʌθɪŋ] | sign | [saɪn] |
| annals | [ænəls] | knee | [ni] |

N.B.: ignore [ɪgˈnɔə], ignoble [ɪgˈnoʊbəl], ignorance [ɪgnəɹəns]

Production: As with [d], the tongue-tip cleanly touches the alveolar ridge, while the sides are in contact with the upper teeth. The soft palate is lowered so that air may escape through the nose. Upon release, the tongue moves directly to the position of the succeeding phoneme. The lips are relaxed and inactive. The jaw is not connected to the production of [n]. It is imperative that singers have jaw/tongue independence for the proper, efficient production of this phoneme.

Rhythmic timing: Before or on the beat, depending on melodic context

[ɲ]   Left-tail N   Voiced palatal nasal
Spelling: *new, ni, nu*

newcomer   [ɲukəmə]   numerous   [ɲuməɹəs]
minion   [mɪɲən]

N.B.: nuisance [ɲusəns], knew [ɲu], pneumonia [ɲuˈmoʊnɪə], pneumatic [ɲuˈmætɪk]

Production: The tip of the tongue begins in contact with the alveolar ridge and releases in a swift downward motion. The soft palate is lowered so that air may escape through the nose. Upon release, the tongue and/or lips move swiftly and directly to the position of the next vowel. It is especially important to prepare the space and shape needed for [u].

[ŋ]   Eng   Voiced velar nasal
Spelling: *n* (before *k* or *x*), *ng*
drink   [dɹɪŋk]   anything   [ɛnɪθɪŋ]
pharynx   [fɛɹɪŋks]

Production: This nasal consonant is classified as velar since the middle of the tongue rises toward the soft palate. However, it is helpful to imagine producing [ŋ] slightly more forward and directed toward the hard palate. The soft palate is lowered so that air may escape through the nose. The tongue-tip lightly contacts the lower teeth, while the sides touch the upper molars. The lips are relaxed and inactive throughout.

N.B.: Three of the nasal consonants ([m], [n], [ŋ]) are considered to be continuants, lasting as long as there is breath supply. One must sing and spin through nasal consonants, in order to avoid a stoppage of air and a subsequent break in the vocal line. Since the soft palate is lowered to allow the breath to escape through the nose, it is crucial that singers employ greater breath energy in order to remain perfectly in tune.

Special situation: [ŋ] vs. [ŋg]
Occurrence of [ŋ]:
1. When a word is monosyllabic, or is formed from an existing verb

| thing | [θɪŋ] | longing | [lɑŋɪŋ] |

Occurrence of [ŋg]:
1. When the first syllable of the word does *not* form a word

| finger | [fɪŋgə] | anger | [æŋgə] |

2. When the first syllable of the word means something completely different from the full word

| single | [sɪŋgəl] | hunger | [hʌŋgə] |

3. When an adjective is in the comparative or superlative form

| younger | [jʌŋgə] | strongest | [stɹɑŋgəst] |

Laterals: allophones of [l]

In colloquial English speech, one uses two allophones of *l*, depending on where *l* falls in the word: clear *l* (before vowels and [j]) and dark *l* (before consonants and when final). The dark *l*, e.g., call, welcome, is not used in lyric diction. Regardless of where *l* falls in a word, the clear *l* is recommended. One must be careful that the tongue does not curl back when pronouncing a medial or final *l*. This ensures that [l] is formed at the front of the mouth and a swallowed sound is avoided.

[l]   Lowercase L   Voiced alveolar lateral
Spelling: *l, ll*

limp   [lɪmp]   hollow   [hɑloʊ]

Production: The tip of the tongue begins in contact with the alveolar ridge and releases in a swift downward motion. As the tongue moves forward and down, it directly prepares the next vowel or consonant. The lips are relaxed and inactive. The jaw is not connected to the production of [l]. It is imperative that singers have jaw/tongue independence for the proper, efficient production of this phoneme.

N.B.: When found in combination with another voiced consonant, it is imperative that [l] be considered the primary consonant and be pitched on the beat. If the first voiced consonant is emphasized, a shadow vowel inevitably occurs. This principle also exists in German. Examples include blind, blame, blend, blubber, glow, glass, gleam, glimmer.

Practice singing the following, taking care to use a clean, light [l]:
ball, poll, roll, troll, bell, fell, fill, bill, bull, gull, child, mild, wild, bold, jolt, molten, scold, told, cellar, wealth, calling, double, middle, full, doll, settle, pulpit, nails, cold, owls, health, fulfilled

---

Affricates [dʒ] [tʃ]

[dʒ]   D-Ezh ligature   Voiced postalveolar affricate

Spelling: *ge, gi, gg, gy, dg, ja, je, ji, jo, ju*

gender	[dʒɛndə]	jazz	[dʒæz]
gin	[dʒɪn]	deject	[dɪˈdʒɛkt]
exaggerate	[ɪgˈzædʒəɹeɪt]	jingle	[dʒɪŋgəl]
dingy	[dɪndʒɪ]	cajole	[kəˈdʒoʊl]
badge	[bædʒ]	June	[dʒun]

N.B.: soldier [soʊldʒə], verdure [vɜdʒə]

[tʃ]   T-Esh ligature   Voiceless postalveolar affricate

Spelling: *ch, tch, -ture*

chair	[tʃɛə]	picture	[pɪktʃə]
kitchen	[kɪtʃən]		

N.B.: cello [tʃɛloʊ], concerto [kənˈtʃɛətoʊ], cappuccino [kæpəˈtʃinoʊ], question [kwɛstʃən], combustion [kəmˈbʌstʃən], righteous [ɹaɪtʃəs]

Production: The affricate cognates [dʒ] and [tʃ] are produced with the exact same articulation process. The tongue-tip lightly contacts the alveolar ridge, forming [d] or [t], respectively. Both sides of the tongue touch the upper molars, preventing air from escaping through the side of the mouth. The tip of the tongue releases in a quick, forward and downward motion while air escapes to form a fricative. This results in the production of either [ʒ] or [ʃ]. The lips are relaxed and inactive throughout. It is imperative that the affricate be formed as one gesture and not two separate phonemes.

N.B.: Some words may be pronounced two different ways, depending on the ease of production and context, using either [tʃ]/[dʒ] or [tj]/[dj].

during	[djʊɹɪŋ] or [dʒʊɹɪŋ]	not	[dʊɹɪŋ] or [dʒɹɪŋ]
mature	[məˈtjʊə] or [məˈtʃʊə]	not	[məˈtʊə]

Additional consonants: [ks][gz]

[ks]

Spelling: *x*, *cc*

oxen	[ɑksən]	accede	[əkˈsid]

N.B.: facsimile [fækˈsɪməlɪ]

[gz]

Spelling: *x*

exhume	[ɪgˈzjum]	exam	[ɪgˈzæm]

Occurrence of [ks] vs. [gz]

If *ex-* is followed by *h* or a vowel, [gz] is used, e.g., exhaust [ɪgˈzɔst], exempt [ɪgˈzɛmpt]. Conversely, [ks] is used if *ex-* is followed by any consonant (except *h*), or *x* is followed by a consonant or vowel, e.g., exclaim [ɪksˈkleɪm], fixture [fɪkstʃə], galaxy [gæləksɪ].

10.5 Consonant blends, contractions

The term *consonant blend* refers to two adjacent consonants pronounced in a single gesture within one syllable. Adjacent consonants within a word or phrase should always be merged without the occurrence of an extra, intrusive vowel (a.k.a. shadow vowel), resulting from a drop or movement of the articulators. As a result, consonants are sometimes imploded/exploded. Please see Chapter 11 (Advanced Concepts in Diction) for further information. When both consonants in the blend are voiced, it is important that one treat the second consonant as the primary consonant, voicing it on the beat, e.g., *gl, bl, dr, gr, br.*

Common blends

bl black, blade, bless, blister, blind, block, blue, blown, blush, blood

br braces, brain, brake, brand, breakfast, bridal, brown, brother, brush

cl clean, clear, claim, classic, claw, cloy, client, close, clumsy, clouds

cr crawl, creep, Christmas, crown, crime, crumble, crass, creation

ct abduct, depict, distinct, actor, actress, perfect, conductor, conflict

dr dream, drifter, dread, kindred, bedroom, laundry, drag, drought

ds reads, fields, woods, needs, yields, maids, bonds, sleds, hounds

dw dwell, dweeb, dwarf, dwelling, dwarves, dwindle

fl floor, flare, fly, flower, fleck, flag, flamboyant, flavor, fling, florist

fr fright, frame, fresh, frost, frantic, frenetic, frenzy, from, frustrated

gl gleaming, glum, gloom, glue, glamour, glimmer, glass, global, glory

gn ignore, ignorance, ignoble, ignite, ignition, ignorant, igneous

gr grand, great, grime, gross, grunt, greenery, ground, gruesome, gripe

ks thanks, links, minx, Bronx, lynx, larynx, succeed, accentuate, thinks

ld mild, child, wild, bold, old, fold, hold, mold, scold, sold, told, weld

mb slumber, September, mumble, tremble, number, remember, crumble

nd behind, ponder, grind, ending, kind, find, lend, remind, stand, spend

ng young, sing, strong, long, hung, bang, cling, slang, fling, ring, wrong

ng younger, single, linger, tingle, strongest, longer, hunger, anger

nk sunk, drank, sink, think, bank, blink, wink, shank, cranky, shrunk

pl employ, player, pliable, explain, placid, pleasing, pledge, plight

pr princess, prance, premonition, priest, prodding, praise, premium

ps soups, doorstops, snaps, courtships, perhaps, treetops, turnips, cups

qu question, quality, quite, quick, quote, quorum, quarter, quietly

sc scream, scary, scallop, school, scotch, scull, scratch, screw, scalding
sh share, shoe, lashes, splash, shiny, shoulder, shocker, ashes, crush
sl slow, sleepy, slander, slime, slumber, slender, slope, sliver, sleeve
sp spacious, sport, clasp, grasp, crisp, speech, spill, spiral, splendour
st steam, street, stand, stringent, storm, started, stood, stage, starlet
tr trick, treasure, travel, tradition, trout, poultry, actress, symmetry
ts cats, curtsey, adopts, impacts, credits, awaits, parts, attests, nuts
tz chintz, quartz, waltz, blitz, ersatz, kibbutz, ritz, klutz, putz

Supplementary exercises
In the following exercises, transcribe all words into IPA.
1. **[ŋ] vs. [ŋg]**
long, wrong, young, elongate, elongation, prolong, tingle, monger, jingle, strongest, congress, king, winged, tongue, longing, bang, swing, single, hunger, angle, language, linger, languid, ringer, prolongation

2. **[ð] vs. [θ]**
thwart, teethe, truth, north, worthy, south, breathe, tooth, clothe, both, mouths, mother, though, worth, method, thus, there, thin, that, paths, thy, theme, death, smooth, berth, thirst, father, throw, loathe, author

3. **[dʒ] vs. [g]**
vogue, germ, job, grow, turgid, eager, gyration, gown, fridge, jet, jalopy, jester, beggar, jig, banjo, gherkin, catalogue, juniper, binge, gill, wriggle, spaghetti, epilogue, tiger, regimen, ghetto, edge, giggle, jump, toboggan

4. **[ks] vs. [gz]**
lox, exam, extrapolate, exit, succinct, exhaust, accent, experiment, oxen, boxes, exaltation, extinguish, accident, extreme, affix, examples, exempt, exactitude, exemplary, succeed, access, experience, hexagon, exhume, exaggerate, accentuate, exonerate, axe

Chapter 11: Advanced Concepts in Diction

The following chapter addresses advanced concepts in lyric diction that promote the idiomatic treatment of English, without compromising clarity. This includes the use of implosion/explosion in incidental words, as well as the use of [ɪ] in specific unstressed prefixes. As in German, consonants should always be merged without the occurrence of an intrusive vowel (a.k.a. shadow vowel), resulting from a drop or movement of the articulators. Further, the expressive doubling of certain consonants is highly encouraged as a means of word-painting.

11.1 Treatment of monosyllabic, incidental words

In every language, a grammatical hierarchy exists within a given sentence or thought. An incidental word refers to a small word of weak grammatical importance, usually composed of only one syllable, e.g., conjunction, preposition, article, or auxiliary verb. If all words were weighted equally, it would give the sentence a vertical quality similar to a computerized voice or how one intones chant. It is imperative that a musical phrase be horizontal to evoke direction and flow. For example, a modifier (a word which describes or qualifies another), e.g., adjective and adverb, is always "moving" to a stronger word in the sentence. This creates a natural, idiomatic inflection, which is indispensable for the conveyance and communication of a poem.

Implosion/explosion

In English, stop consonants (plosives) are often imploded and then exploded in rapid succession. A consonant is imploded when its production is stopped prior to becoming aspirated (for a voiceless consonant) or fully voiced (for a voiced consonant). A consonant is exploded when the air pressure is suddenly released. In English, this combination is the closest thing to an Italianate double consonant, e.g., *tutto* [tut:to]. In this example, two individual dental *t's* are articulated, resulting in a moment of suspension after the first *t*. The tongue-tip is firmly attached to the upper teeth, while a light pressure builds up. The second *t* then quickly releases into the final vowel. An imploded English *t* will sound more like its Italian counterpart (dental, unaspirated). Moreover, an imploded English *b* will resemble an Italian *p* (unaspirated).

In everyday speech, when articulating the words "want to", the first *t* is said to be imploded, while the second *t* is exploded. It begins as in the Italian example, but since the English *t* is aspirated, an explosion of air occurs when pronouncing the second *t*. Note that the moment of suspension after forming the first consonant is very slight. Thus, it is not truly a double consonant. Practice saying "want to" as one would in Italian (two dental *t's*) and then as one would in English (imploded initial *t*, and an exploded aspirated *t*). Without implosion/explosion, both *t's* would be aspirated, sounding artificial and over-mannered. The only exception to this rule occurs in the case whereby a particular word is purposely emphasized for artistic, interpretive purposes. Please note that implosion/explosion is *not* expressed in IPA transcriptions.

Occurrence of implosion/explosion of consonants

1. Within a word:

midday, hotdog, sadly, handful, Agnes, napkin, submit, abnormal, obtain, eighth, bedtime, width, admire, dogma, picture, empty, bookcase, apt, ebbed, suitcase, scrapbook, subpoena, lecture, mindful, submarine

2. Adjacent words, same consonant:

crab box, deep prayer, sad dream, what tragedy, dig gold, speak quietly, that time, red deer, lamp post, drab boy, big goblet, quick cars

3. Adjacent words, cognates:

deep beauty, ripe banana, had to, sit down, break ground, not done, egg cup, black gown, soap bubble, that day, used to, accustomed to

4. Auxiliary verbs followed by consonant:

could be, should tell, had found, would go, did find

5. "Good," "bad," and "glad" followed by consonant:

goodbye, good night, good luck, bad therapist, gladness, glad moments

Exception: When final [dʒ] or [tʃ] is followed by the same consonant or cognate starting the adjacent word, one must pronounce both affricates fully. Implosion/explosion is not possible in this instance, due to reasons of clarity and comprehension.

such charm	[sʌtʃ tʃɑɑm]	large jury	[lɑədʒ dʒʊɹɪ]
which journey	[ʍɪtʃ dʒɜnɪ]	watch Gerald	[wɑtʃ dʒɛɹəld]
each chance	[itʃ tʃæns]	orange jam	[ɔɹəndʒ dʒæm]

Special circumstances

-ed (grammatical ending)

When a monosyllabic word ends in -*ed*, the final *d* may be voiced [d] or voiceless [t]. The quality depends on and directly corresponds to the preceding consonant. In other words, it matches its environment.

| troubled | [tɹʌbəld] | crowned | [kɹaʊnd] |
| kissed | [kɪst] | dashed | [dæʃt] |

When a polysyllabic word ends in -ed, the final d is always voiced, e.g., waited [weɪtəd], blessed (adjective) [blɛsəd] vs. blessed (verb) [blɛst].

N.B.: Implosion/explosion does *not* apply to words ending in -ed, as it would change the meaning of the sentence. Specifically, the tense would not be clear. For example, "talked to" would sound like "talk to" if the d were imploded. Both *t's* must be exploded and aspirated, e.g., [tɔkt tu].

with

Similarly, the *th* in "with" may be voiced [ð] or voiceless [θ], depending on its context. Matching this incidental word to its surroundings promotes increased legato and ensures that this word remains unstressed.

with me	[wɪð mi]	with you	[wɪð ju]
with her	[wɪθ hɜ]	with him	[wɪθ hɪm]

Recommended elision:

with thoughts   [wɪ θɔts]   with thee   [wɪ ði]

N.B.: In cases where "with" is part of a longer word, the *th* may be either voiced or voiceless, e.g., without [wɪθaʊt], within [wɪðɪn].

and, at

The final consonants in both "and" as well as "at" should be imploded in all circumstances. If the tempo is slow, it allows one to emphasize the consonant beginning the next word in the sentence, be it voiced or voiceless. Since neither word is ever stressed, a final exploded d (or an energetically aspirated t) would sound unnatural and thus foreign. In some cases, elision may occur, whereby the final consonant is omitted completely, e.g., at times [ə taɪmz], and dream [ən dɹim]. For more information, please consult Chapter 22 (Legato Singing).

In the following example, note that elision occurs with the words "heart to". As a result, there is no breakage in the melodic line. If implosion/explosion were used instead, there would be a brief moment of suspension on the peak of the phrase. By merging the consonants and effectively only singing one [t], a beautiful legato is ensured.

"What if I never speed?" J. Dowland

| Come, | come, | come | while I have a heart | to | de-sire | thee, |
| kʌ m | kʌ m | kʌ m | ʍ a ɪl\|a ɪhæ v\|ə hɑ | ətu | dɪ za | ɪəði |

Vowel changes: strong and weak forms

Monosyllabic, incidental words may be "strong" or "weak" depending on the musical context. This phenomenon is known as *gradation* and is ubiquitous in English. The principle of whether a word is strong or weak is related to its role in the sentence or musical phrase. Generally, when an incidental word is in its weak form, it is formed with the *schwa*. Conversely, when in its strong form, it uses a true, pure vowel. Sometimes the composer has already determined which form of the word one is to use, i.e., if the note value is short it is fitting to use the *schwa*, whereas the pure vowel should be used for longer note values. As previously discussed in Chapter 6 (The Structure of English), one must adhere to the appropriate use of the *schwa* in English. The overuse of pure vowels results in a pedantic, stilted performance, since the natural word stress is negatively affected.

The proper use of weak forms in English is integral to lyric diction, as it keeps the language from sounding too contrived or artificial. Many foreign speakers of English tend to use pure vowels in incidental words. Consequently, words that are less important grammatically are given too much prominence, and words having greater meaning are often lost.

In everyday speech, most conjunctions, prepositions, articles, and auxiliary verbs are subject to gradation. This frequent use is highly colloquial and thus not recommended in lyric diction. Hence, gradation is restricted to the following words: **am, and, as, at, can, for, from, has, have, of.** All other incidental words use the strong form at all times, e.g., are, but, by, some, than, that, then, them, there.

Strong form		**Weak form**	
What do you hope **for**?	[fɔə]	He waits **for** love	[fə]
Here I **am**	[æm]	I **am** wondering	[əm]
Stay—if you **can**	[kæn]	I **can** do that	[kən]
Who **has** it?	[hæz]	He **has** vanished	[həz]
Certainly, I **have**	[hæv]	They **have** gone	[həv]
What do you dream **of**?	[ʌv]	A friend **of** mine	[əv]
Where is he **from**?	[fɹʌm]	Far away **from** here	[fɹəm]

N.B.: For the words "from" and "of," the vowel is identical in sound, but is expressed as stressed [ʌ] or unstressed [ə] in the written form.

Special circumstances
the
This common article exists in both strong and weak forms, depending on its context. It is never stressed and rarely prolonged musically.

the owl	[ði aʊl]	before a vowel
the day	[ðə deɪ]	before a consonant

a
This word precedes an initial consonant and is always pronounced [ə].

a time	[ə taɪm]	a day	[ə deɪ]

an

This word precedes an initial vowel and is primarily pronounced [ə].

an enemy   [ən |ɛnəmɪ]   an opportunity [ən |ɑpə'tjunətɪ]

Exception: When "an" precedes a word beginning in *a*, it is recommended that the singer prepare the space for the succeeding vowel in advance. This provides greater efficiency vocally, as one maintains the identical vowel shape.

an apple   [æn |æpəl]   an anchor   [æn |æŋkə]

could/should/would

These auxiliary verbs are always pronounced [ʊ], regardless of context.

I should finish it.   [ʃʊd]
I would not go, even if I could.   [wʊd], [kʊd]

to

In everyday speech, this preposition exists in both strong and weak forms. However, this is not advocated in singing, as the weak form sounds highly colloquial. It is preferable to use the strong form [tu] in all circumstances, e.g., to do [tu du] vs. [tə du].

11.2 Unstressed syllables: use of [ɪ] in prefixes

Some unstressed prefixes are pronounced differently than one would expect orthographically. They are divided into the following two groups:

1. Unstressed prefixes that *always* require the use of [ɪ]: *e-, be-, se-*
electric   [ɪ'lɛktɹɪk]   emotion   [ɪ'moʊʃən]

| beloved | [bɪˈlʌvəd] | become | [bɪˈkʌm] |
| seduce | [sɪˈdjus] | serene | [sɪˈɹin] |

2. Unstressed prefixes that *sometimes* require the use of [ɪ]: *de-*, *re-*, *pre-*

deliver	[dɪˈlɪvə]	despise	[dɪˈspaɪz]
respond	[ɹɪˈspɑnd]	remorse	[ɹɪˈmɔəs]
prepare	[pɹɪˈpɛə]	pretend	[pɹɪˈtɛnd]

If the *de-* prefix serves to mean "the opposite," then [i] is used.

| defrost | [diˈfɹɑst] | decompose | [dikəmˈpoʊz] |

If the *re-* prefix serves to mean "to do again," then [i] is used.

| redo | [ɹiˈdu] | restart | [ɹiˈstɑət] |

If the *pre-* prefix serves to mean "in advance," then [i] is used.

| preheat | [pɹiˈhit] | prepay | [pɹiˈpeɪ] |

Special circumstance

ex-

This prefix may be pronounced [ɪ] or [ɛ], depending on word stress.

| extract (verb) | [ɪkˈstɹækt] | extract (noun) | [ɛkstɹækt] |
| exploit (verb) | [ɪkˈsplɔɪt] | exploit (noun) | [ɛksplɔɪt] |

Supplementary exercises

1. Transcribe the following into IPA, observing incidental words and the context:

with thee, forever and a day, without a care, with Charles, I have tried to go, "Sure, I have!", at a loss, she enjoys being looked at, all for them, the occasion, all the while, "What are you waiting for?", hard of hearing, the burning heart, with beauty, with thorns, with thanks, with thine

2. Transcribe the following words into IPA:
locked, dreamed, touched, walked, grounded, laughed, founded, liked, worked, grasped, loved, sagged, missed, rushed, packed, composed, vanished, asked, feigned, attached, pledged, stopped, rubbed, cracked, dragged, talked, hoped, blessed, watched, dropped, heaped, evoked, wrecked, fibbed, fulfilled, coughed, seemed, mounted

3. Transcribe the following into IPA, mindful of the words' meaning:
deserving, reminder, delightful, restore, devotion, desist, prefer, resist, prepay, receive, return, demotivate, debug, decode, remember, desire, decipher, defrost, rejoice, despite, preamble, present (verb), deliberate, revere, predate, decision, resplendent, predict, despair, prevent, destroy

4. Transcribe the following words into IPA, mindful of word stress:
belittle, seclusion, example, benign, ecstatic, beknownst, excrete, equip, secure, elect, serene, equitable, severe, exit, elastic, semantics, excrement, elaborate, exalted, sequester, expletive, evade, begin, exile, behavior, exactitude, believe, expat, bespeak, beside, eventual, because, before, between, ebullient, secretion, exist, ecstasy, series

5. Indicate which of the following would use implosion/explosion:
could be, thou art kind, greatly, let no one, sweet dreams, bright vision, great triumph, lest I lose you, drop down, leap forth, weep not, gladness, help them, keep peace, help proudly, take courage, walk quickly, invoke crime, rich choice, bad thoughts, good luck, glad tidings, big girl, dog growls, fond dreams, huge joke, urge justice, each child

Chapter 12: Common Pitfalls

When singing in English, there are many common errors that befall singers. Some correspond to mistakes made in everyday speech, including mispronunciations, omissions of phonemes, and speech impediments. An improperly produced consonant in speech will directly transfer to singing. This chapter addresses various common pitfalls that one encounters in English lyric diction, and it may be used as a reference guide.

1. Improper word stress
- Words are stressed equally within a sentence, resulting in a syllabic, pedantic performance. Similarly, syllables are weighted equally within a word.
- Unintentional stressing of monosyllabic, incidental words by using pure vowels instead of the *schwa* [ə].
- Complete absence of stress (common in French native singers), resulting in an English that is unclear and indefinite.

2. Lisps
- Frontal lisp caused by the tongue touching the alveolar ridge, when it should remain between the teeth, e.g., substituting [θ] for [s], or [ð] for [z]. This may also occur if the upper and lower teeth are too close together or the tongue groove is too narrow.
- Whistling [s] or [ʃ] due to the tip of the tongue being either too far back or against the lower teeth.

126

3. Use of spoken regionalisms

This is especially important for American English speakers. Common regional differences occur in the following examples:

- Vowel substitutions: substitution of [ε] for [ɪ], e.g., him, pin, been; substitution of [ɪ] for [ε], e.g., enter, empty; substitution of [ε] for [æ], e.g., marry, carry, tarry, embarrass, arrow
- Addition of intrusive glides: use of [j] before [l]: reveal, wield, deal, field, steel; use of [w] before [l]: fool, school, pool, rule; use of [ə] before [l]: pale, fail, hail, veil
- Omission of glottal onsets: I am [aɪjæm] vs. [aɪ |æm]; some others [sʌ mʌðəs] vs. [sʌm |ʌðəs]

4. Omission of consonants

Final consonants: kept, gift, I must go
Medial consonants: youths, texts, myths

5. Unvoicing of final consonants

This is a challenge for German native speakers (hand [hænd] vs. *Hand* [hant]), especially in words borrowed from German. However, this error is rampant among English native speakers as well, and often is a result of simple carelessness or thinking of the next word. It is imperative to fully finish the word one is on before moving on to the next word.

6. Common mispronunciations

often	[afən]	not	[aftən]
soften	[safən]	not	[saftən]
chestnut	[tʃɛsnʌt]	not	[tʃɛstnʌt]
prescription	[pɹəˈskɹɪpʃən]	not	[pəɹˈskɹɪpʃən]
pronunciation	[pɹoˈnʌnsɪeɪʃən]	not	[pɹoˈnaʊnsɪeɪʃən]
experiment	[ɪkˈspɛɹəmənt]	not	[ɪkˈspɹɪəmənt]
mischievous	[mɪstʃəvəs]	not	[mɪsˈtʃivɪəs]

accompanist	[əˈkʌmpənəst]	not	[əˈkʌmpənɪəst]
sail	[seɪl]	not	[seɪəl]
meal	[mil]	not	[mijəl]
film	[fɪlm]	not	[fɪləm]
wheel	[ʌil]	not	[ʌijəl]
clothes	[kloʊðz]	not	[kloʊz]
song	[sɑŋ]	not	[sɑŋg]
children	[tʃɪldɹən]	not	[tʃʊldɹən]
acts	[ækts]	not	[æks]
neglects	[nəˈglɛkts]	not	[nəˈglɛks]
predicts	[pɹɪˈdɪkts]	not	[pɹɪˈdɪks]
calm	[kɔm]	not	[kɑlm]
woman	[wʊmən]	not	[wʊmæn]
women	[wɪmən]	not	[wʊmɛn]
gentleman	[dʒɛntəlmən]	not	[dʒɛntəlmæn]
gentlemen	[dʒɛntəlmən]	not	[dʒɛntəlmɛn]

7. Using jaw as an active articulator

The lips, teeth, tongue, hard and soft palates are considered to be articulators. Active articulators, e.g., lips, tongue, soft palate, move in precise movements to form consonants and vowels. Conversely, passive articulators are approached or contacted, e.g., teeth, hard palate. Although the jaw falls open naturally to allow for enough space to form certain phonemes, it is *not* directly involved in the production or maintenance of any vowels or consonants. Similarly, the jaw is never involved in supporting the breath while singing.

8. Tongue tension

The base of the tongue attaches just above the larynx. If the tongue is curled back and held, it results in a swallowed, tense sound. If the tongue is lifted at the back, it becomes too close to the soft palate, resulting in a fuzzy tone. Similarly, the tongue is never involved in supporting the breath while singing.

9. Use of hard glottal attacks

This is a bad habit borrowed from colloquial speech. Unfortunately, the use of hard onsets is widespread in the genre of popular music by artists such as Enrique Iglesias and Britney Spears. Some voice teachers advocate producing [h] before a vowel to get the air flowing. However, as long as one always is aware of initiating every vowel with the breath, the glottal attack should be minimized and softened. All glottal onsets should be *soft* in nature (not breathy), initiated in the position of the impending vowel. This limits any unnecessary movement.

10. Nasalization

Hypernasality: When vowels are adjacent to nasal consonants, sometimes they become unintentionally nasalized. Practice the following words with a prolonged initial vowel, maintaining a raised soft palate and a sense of vertical space at the back of the mouth. One should delay the production of [n], [m], or [ŋ] until the last minute. Otherwise, the result is the occurrence of what could be called *N-colored* vowels (similar to R-colored vowels). Place a mirror in front of the nose while pronouncing the following words (there should be no fog/mist evident):

hand	man	sang	dance	tense	won't
wine	want	stem	limb	come	long
seen	then	length	can't	alone	rain
town	coin	end	tomb	pond	under
home	find	found	joined	finger	time

Denasality: This is caused by insufficient nasal resonance and resembles the feeling of having a bad head cold. In these cases, [m] becomes [b], [n] becomes [d], and [n] becomes [g]. Nasality may be removed when the nose is held while singing or speaking.

11. Production of shadow vowels

Consonants should be merged without allowing any space in between phonemes, or a drop in the articulators. Shadow vowels may be avoided by certifying that a given consonant is completely finished production before the articulators move to form the next sound. For example, when singing [v], vibration must cease prior to any movement of the teeth or lips. Consonant blends must be pronounced in a single gesture, while keeping the integrity of the individual consonant. Further, one must remember to sing through voiced blends and keep releasing the air during voiceless blends.

PART III: GERMAN

Chapter 13: Introduction to German Diction
for Singers

13.1 *Hochdeutsch* and *Bühnendeutsch*

In lyric diction, one strives to sing in the "high form" of each language. For example, in English there is Received Pronunciation (RP) for Great Britain and General American English (GA) for the United States and Canada; in French one uses Parisian French; in German one uses *Hochdeutsch*. The term *Hochdeutsch* translates as "high German" and refers to the dialect from the province Niedersachsen. The city of Hannover is the center for *Hochdeutsch*. Indeed, few people speak in this manner, but it is the standardized language used in media broadcasting. Foreigners studying the German language learn *Hochdeutsch* and can be understood regardless of geographic location. By contrast, it can be highly difficult to understand certain German dialects, which often differ greatly from *Hochdeutsch* in both pronunciation and vocabulary.

Also known as Stage German, *Bühnendeutsch* was developed by German linguist Theodor Siebs. A standardized pronunciation intended for the stage arose from the need for clear enunciation and strong projection. This differs from the requirements of everyday speech. For example, Siebs does not distinguish between the use of flipped [ɾ], rolled [r], and uvular [ʁ], weighting all three equally. Moreover, the vowel substitute for *r* [ɐ] is not used. His standard reference work is still widely used today, the first edition of which was published in 1898.

13.2 Reference books

This text uses extensive information provided by the two leading reference books on German pronunciation, grammar, and orthography: Siebs' *Deutsche Aussprache, 19th edition* (1969), and Duden's *Das Aussprachewörterbuch* (2006). These books differ on a few fronts, namely, slight variations in diphthongs and the treatment of syllabic consonants. Generally, Duden depicts how modern German is pronounced in everyday life, and has the most current information with respect to the *Neue Rechtschreibung*. Conversely, Siebs outlines a pronunciation best suited to the speech or theatre arts. Many decisions in Siebs do not support optimal vocal production and thus are not desired for singing. As a result, this text promotes a combination of the best offerings from both of these invaluable resources. It is highly recommended to purchase Duden and to use it in combination with a German dictionary, e.g., *Langenscheidt*.

13.3 *Neue Rechtschreibung*

The German language has undergone many changes with regards to spelling in the past decade. In 2006, the *Neue Rechtschreibung* came into effect, the result of a complete overhaul of the German language. This language reform began and developed in Switzerland and has since been adopted by all German-speaking countries. The main changes involve the separation of compound words (becoming more similar to English), the reduced use of the *Eszett (ß)*, the abolition of consonant assimilation in compound words, the Germanization of foreign loan words (no longer showing the word origin via the spelling), and changes related to syllabification rules. In singing, one deals with centuries-old texts that will continue to be published with older spellings. It is not necessary to know the rules of the *Neue Rechtschreibung*, but it is valuable to be able to recognize the changes in German orthography, especially when singing modern texts by contemporary poets.

13.4 Orthographic features: Umlaut and *Eszett (ß)*

The three umlauts *ä, ö,* and *ü* are notable orthographic features in German. These three letters represent the following six phonemes:

ä	[ɛ:]	das Mädchen	[mɛːtçən]	girl, maiden
	[ɛ]	die Dämmerung	[dɛmərʊŋ]	dusk, twilight
ö	[ø:]	schön	[ʃøːn]	beautiful
	[œ]	die Götter	[gœtɐ]	gods, deities
ü	[y:]	sich fühlen	[fyːlən]	to feel
	[ʏ]	zurück	[tsuːˈrʏk]	back

While umlauts do not exist in English, they are present in other Germanic languages, e.g., Dutch, Swedish, Danish, Finnish, and Norwegian.

The *Eszett (ß)* is also known as the *scharfes s* (hard *s*). It is a functioning double consonant, meaning its preceding vowel is shortened while [s] is elongated. Until recently, the *Eszett* was essentially interchangeable with *ss* in German spelling. Many old German texts use both spellings for the same words, corresponding perhaps to the age of the original text, or the printing press used, e.g., *der Kuß* vs. *der Kuss*. Now, according to Duden's latest *Deutsche Rechtschreibung* (2009), the *Eszett* should only be used when it follows a long, closed vowel or a diphthong. One uses the spelling *ss* exclusively when it follows a short vowel. Modern usage depends solely on vowel length.

schließen	[ʃliːsən]	to close, shut
draußen	[draosən]	outside, outdoors
das Schloss	[ʃlɔs]	castle

Chapter 14: German Phonemes

Table 14.1. Overview of German phonemes

IPA Symbol	Spelling	Examples
[aː]	*a, aa, ah*	sagen [zaːgən]
		der Hörsaal [høːɾzaːl]
		die Fahrt [faːɾt]
[a]	*a*	der Bach [baχ]
[ae]	*ei, ey, ai, ay*	zwei [tsvae]
		Meyer [maeɐ]
		die Saite [zaetə]
		Bayern [baeəɾn]
[ao]	*au*	der Baum [baom]
[ɐ]	*r, -er, er-, ver-, der-, vor-*	dir [diːɐ]
		das Feuer [fɔøɐ]
		der Ersatz [ɛɐˈzats]
		vergessen [fɛɐˈgɛsən]
		dermaßen [ˈdeːɐmaːsən]
		vorbei [foːɐˈbae]
[b]	*b, bb*	bang [baŋ]
		die Ebbe [ɛbə]
[ç]	*ch, -ig*	echt [ɛçt]
		fertig [fɛɾtɪç]

Continued on next page

136

Table 14.1—Continued

IPA Symbol	Spelling	Examples
[d]	*d, dd*	dulden [dʊldən]
		der Widder [vɪdɐ]
[e:]	*e, ee, eh*	regnen [reːgnən]
		das Beet [beːt]
		gehen [geːən]
[ə]	*e*	die Mühe [myːə]
[ɛ]	*e, ä*	das Wetter [vɛtɐ]
		hätten [hɛtən]
[ɛ:]	*ä, äh*	später [ʃpɛːtɐ]
		zäh [tsɛː]
[f]	*f, ff, v, ph*	der Lauf [laof]
		hoffen [hɔfən]
		das Vöglein [føːglaen]
		der Philosoph [filoˈzoːf]
[g]	*g, gg*	neigen [naegən]
		die Flagge [flagə]
[ʒ]	*g, j*	das Genie [ʒeˈniː]
		das Journal [ʒʊrˈnaːl]
[h]	*h*	die Hoheit [hoːhaet]
[i:]	*i, ih, ie, ieh*	wider [viːdɐ]
		ihre [iːrə]
		die Lieder [liːdɐ]
		sieht [ziːt]
[ɪ]	*i*	immer [ɪmɐ]
[j̊]	*j*	jagen [j̊aːgən]
[k]	*k, kk, ck, g*	das Kind [kɪnt]
		der Akkord [aˈkɔrt]

Continued on next page

Table 14.1—Continued

IPA Symbol	Spelling	Examples
		der Wecker [vɛkɐ]
		der Steg [ʃteːk]
[ks]	x, chs	die Hexe [hɛksə]
		der Lachs [laks]
[kv]	qu	die Quelle [kvɛlə]
[l]	l, ll	spielen [ʃpiːlən]
		füllen [fʏlən]
[m]	m, mm	der Mann [man]
		der Sommer [zɔmɐ]
[n]	n, nn	erneuern [ɛɐˈnɔøɐrn]
		die Nonne [nɔnə]
[ŋ]	ng, n (before k)	der Gesang [gəˈzaŋ]
		danke [daŋkə]
[oː]	o, oh, oo	die Botschaft [boːtʃaft]
		der Lohn [loːn]
		das Boot [boːt]
[ɔ]	o	voll [fɔl]
[ɔø]	eu, äu	teuer [tɔøɐ]
		versäumen [fɛɐˈzɔømən]
[øː]	ö, öh	schön [ʃøːn]
		die Söhne [zøːnə]
[œ]	ö	die Götter [gœtɐ]
[p]	p, pp, b	das Papier [paˈpiːɐ]
		die Rippen [rɪpən]
		hinab [hɪˈnap]
[r]	r, rr	die Ehre [eːrə]
		irre [ɪrə]

Continued on next page

Table 14.1—Continued

IPA Symbol	Spelling	Examples
[s]	s, ss, ß	das Los [loːs]
		gerissen [gəˈrɪsən]
		der Fuß [fuːs]
[ʃ]	sch, s (before p, t)	die Schwester [ʃvɛstɐ]
		sportlich [ʃpɔrtlɪç]
		stolz [ʃtɔlts]
[t]	t, th, tt, dt, d	treu [trɔø]
		der Thron [troːn]
		retten [rɛtən]
		die Städte [ʃtɛːtə]
		das Land [lant]
[ts]	ts, tz, z, c, ti	nichts [nɪçts]
		der Platz [plats]
		zehn [tseːn]
		Caesar [tsɛːzaːr]
		die Aktien [aktsiən]
[tʃ]	tsch	der Kitsch [kɪtʃ]
[uː]	u, uh	die Mut [muːt]
		ruhig [ruːɪç]
[ʊ]	u	der Bund [bʊnt]
[v]	w, v	weinen [vaenən]
		das Klavier [klaˈviːɐ]
[χ]	ch	der Lauch [laoχ]
[yː]	ü, üh, y	lügen [lyːgən]
		die Bühne [byːnə]
		das Elysium [eˈlyːziʊm]
[ʏ]	ü, y	künstlerisch [kʏnstlərɪʃ]

Continued on next page

Table 14.1—Continued

IPA Symbol	Spelling	Examples
		die Myrthen [mʏrtən]
[z]	*s*	suchen [zuːχən]

Chapter 15: The Structure of German

The principal or tonic stress of a word usually falls on the first syllable in words of Germanic origin. In polysyllabic words, the tonic stress falls on the root of a given word. This occurs with great regularity. Moreover, the root stem remains the stressed part of the word even after prefixes and suffixes have been added. By contrast, words of non-Germanic origin follow a different stress pattern. Here follows a description of the logical, structured manner with which German is organized.

15.1 Root system and word structure

When studying Italian, one learns quickly that syllabification plays a significant role in determining pronunciation. In German, pronunciation is strongly linked to word structure, especially when determining vowel quality and length. It is crucial that one identify the root (or root stem), in order to know how a word is pronounced and to recognize the addition of various suffixes and prefixes.

The root stem of a word is the fundamental base to which all suffixes, prefixes, and inflectional and grammatical endings are added. Usually the root is monosyllabic, but it may also be polysyllabic, e.g., *arbeit*. For example, in the verb *singen*, the root is *sing*. All subsequent conjugations are built on the same root. German verbs are divided into two groups: strong and weak. Contrary to many other languages, the

terms "regular" and "irregular" are not used. The major difference between strong and weak verbs is in the formation of the past tense.

Strong verb:

1. singen   [zɪŋən]   to sing

Present tense: ich **singe**, du **singst**, er/sie/es **singt**, wir **singen**, ihr **singt**,
sie/Sie **singen**

Present perfect: ich habe gesungen   I have sung

Simple past: ich sang   I sang

das **Sing**spiel   [zɪŋʃpiːl]   German comic opera

Weak verb:

1. machen   [maχən]   to do, to make

Present tense: ich **mache**, du **mach**st, er/sie/es **macht**, wir **machen**, ihr
macht, sie/Sie **machen**

Present perfect: ich habe **gemacht**   I have done

Simple past: ich **machte**   I did

machbar   [maχbaːɐ]   able to be done, doable
gemach   [gəˈmaχ]   slowly

2. hören   [høːrən]   to hear, to listen

Present tense: ich **höre**, du **hörst**, er/sie/es **hört**, wir **hören**, ihr **höret**,
sie/Sie **hören**

Present perfect: ich habe **gehört**   I have heard

Simple past: ich **hörte**   I heard

das Ver**hör**   [fɛɐˈhøːɐ]   interrogation
hörbar   [høːrbaːɐ]   audible
der **Hör**saal   [høːrzaːl]   lecture hall

Since the root stem *hör* has a closed, long vowel [ø:], the presence of multiple consonants does not change the quality of the vowel, e.g., *hörst* [hø:rst]. This is a common error. In the case of *der Hörsaal*, one must identify this as a compound word in order to recognize that *Hör* is the root. Please consult Chapter 17 (Vowels) for a full explanation as to how to determine the quality of a vowel (closed or open) and thus its length.

15.2 Grammatical and inflective endings

The term *grammatical ending* refers to the addition of one or more letters to the root stem. An ending illustrates grammatical function, e.g., indirect or direct object, or occurs as a result of verb conjugation. Contrary to English, word order does not determine grammatical structure. Rather, German uses different *cases* to show a word's function in the sentence, clarifying its meaning, e.g., accusative (direct object), dative (indirect object), genitive (possessive). In fact, the case is the only indicator of subject vs. object in German. The term *inflective ending* refers to the addition of prefixes and suffixes to change the meaning of a given word. German words may be composed of multiple inflective and grammatical endings. Therefore, it is imperative that one recognize these endings in order to easily find the word in a dictionary.

ein	[aen]	a, one

Grammatical endings: **ein**en, **ein**em, **ein**es, **ein**er, **ein**s, **ein**st

ein Mann	[aen man]	a man, one man
eines Mannes	[aenəs manəs]	a man's (possessive)

The addition of a grammatical ending to an article, conjunction, or preposition illustrates the function of the word or following noun, e.g., a possessive, the subject, direct or indirect object.

N.B.: Certain prepositions commonly contract when used with articles indicating case. For example, *vor dem Haus* becomes *vorm Haus*. The *m* indicates that *Haus* is the indirect object of this sentence. Note that this does not apply to the following prepositions: *auf, aus, bis, für, gegen, mit*.

an dem = am	on, at, by (the)
bei dem = beim	at, by (the)
hinter dem = hinterm	behind (the)
unter den = untern	under (the)
unter dem = unterm	under (the)
von dem = vom	from, of (the)
vor dem = vorm	in front of (the)

15.3 Prefixes, suffixes

The use of inflectional endings is boundless in the German language. In fact, German has a much smaller vocabulary than English. One could describe German as being a building-block language. It is possible to create words once one knows the meaning of various prefixes and suffixes. In this way, German is highly logical. In order to understand the subsequent meaning of a word, one must know the meaning of the inflectional endings involved.

Prefixes may be divided into two groups: separable and inseparable. A separable prefix moves to the end of the sentence in conjugation, while an inseparable prefix does not stray. Further, the word stress falls on a separable prefix, but occurs *directly after* an inseparable prefix.

ausgehen	Ich gehe aus	I am going out
aufgeben	Nun gibt sie auf	Now she gives up
erwarten	Er erwartet mich bald	He expects me soon
vergessen	Ich vergesse das immer	I always forget that

Separable prefixes vs. inseparable prefixes

Separable prefixes

ab-	abnehmen (to take down, to lose)	[apne:mən]
an-	annähern (to get closer to)	[anɛ:ərn]
auf-	aufgehen (to rise, ascend)	[aofge:ən]
aus-	ausmachen (to shut off/down)	[aosmaχən]
bei-	beistehen (to stand by)	[baeʃte:ən]
da-	dabehalten (to keep there)	[da:bəhaltən]
dar-	darstellen (to portray)	[da:rʃtɛlən]
durch-	durchdringen (to penetrate)	[dʊrçdrɪŋən]
ein-	einholen (to catch up to)	[aenho:lən]
empor-	emporkommen (to get on in life)	[ɛm'po:rkɔmən]
entgegen-	entgegennehmen (to receive)	[ɛnt'ge:gəne:mən]
fort-	fortbringen (to get rid of, remove)	[fɔrtbrɪŋən]
heim-	heimkehren (to return home)	[haemke:rən]
her-	herstellen (to produce)	[he:rʃtɛlən]
hin-	sich hingeben (to give in to)	[hɪnge:bən]
mit-	mitbringen (to bring with)	[mɪtbrɪŋən]
nach-	nachmachen (to imitate)	[na:χmaχən]
nieder-	niederschreiben (to write down)	[ni:dərʃraebən]
um-	umziehen (to move (location))	[ʊmtsi:ən]
vor-	vorahnen (to know in advance)	[fo:ɐ|a:nən]
weg-	wegstellen (to set aside)	[vɛkʃtɛlən]
weiter-	weitertreiben (to continue to do)	[vaetərtraebən]
zu-	sich zutrauen (to dare)	[tsu:traoən]
zurück-	zurückgeben (to give back)	[tsu:'rʏkge:bən]
zusammen-	zusammenarbeiten (to collaborate)	[tsu:'zamən|arbaetən]

Exceptions: The following words have inseparable prefixes: *umarmen* [ʊm'\|armən] (to embrace), *durchfressen* [dʊrç'frɛsən] (to eat through)

Inseparable prefixes

be-	beantworten (to answer, to reply)	[bə'	antvɔrtən]
emp-	empfehlen (to recommend)	[ɛm'pfe:lən]
ent-	entschleiern (to unveil)	[ɛnt'ʃlaeərn]
er-	erwarten (to expect)	[ɛɐ'vartən]
ge-	gebrauchen (to use)	[gə'braoχən]
miss-/miß-	mißbrauchen (to abuse, to misuse)	[mɪs'braoχən]
ver-	vergessen (to forget)	[fɛɐ'gɛsən]
zer-	zerschmettern (to destroy)	[tsɛr'ʃmɛtərn]

Special Situation: *über* and *unter*

Prepositions functioning as prefixes are usually separable. However, *über* and *unter* may be either separable or inseparable. They are known as dual prefixes. Since this is impossible to identify without speaking the language, the following list of common occurrences must be memorized:

Separable		
übergehen	[y:bərge:ən]	to go over, to overflow
übererfüllen	[y:bər|ɛɐfʏlən]	to overachieve
untergehen	[ʊntərge:ən]	to go down, to set
unterbringen	[ʊntərbrɪŋən]	to accommodate
Inseparable		
überwinden	[y:bər'vɪndən]	to overcome
überlegen	[y:bər'le:gən]	to think about
übertragen	[y:bər'tra:gən]	to carry over
unterschreiben	[ʊntər'ʃraebən]	to write down
unterrichten	[ʊntə'rɪçtən]	to instruct, to teach
unterbrechen	[ʊntər'brɛçən]	to interrupt

In compound adverbs and similar words, the stress is shifted to the second word element. Further, a glottal onset is not required before an element beginning in a vowel, e.g., *voraus* [fo:ɾaos] not [fo:ɐ|aos].

allein	[a'laen]	unterwegs	[ʊntəɾ've:ks]
allerdings	[aləɾ'dɪŋs]	vorüber	[fo:'ɾy:bɐ]
einander	[ae'nandɐ]	warum	[va:'ɾʊm]
heraus	[hɛ'ɾaos]	worauf	[vo:'ɾaof]
hinweg	[hɪn'vɛk]	zurück	[tsu:'ɾʏk]
sogar	[zo:'ga:ɐ]	zusammen	[tsu:'zamən]
überhaupt	[y:bəɾ'haopt]		

Suffixes

-artig	eigenartig	[aegən|aɾtɪç]	one-of-a-kind
-bar	machbar	[maχba:ɐ]	doable
-chen	das Mädchen	[mɛ:tçən]	maiden
-ei	die Brauerei	[braoə'rae]	brewery
-haft	tugendhaft	[tu:gənthaft]	virtuous
-heit	die Gesundheit	[gə'zʊnthaet]	health
-ig	nebelig	[ne:bəlɪç]	foggy
-in	die Gattin	[gatɪn]	wife
-isch	träumerisch	[trɔømərɪʃ]	dreamy
-keit	die Nutzbarkeit	[nʊtsba:ɾkaet]	usefulness
-lein	das Kämmerlein	[kɛmərlaen]	small chamber
-lich	peinlich	[paenlɪç]	embarrassing
-ling	der Fremdling	[frɛmtlɪŋ]	foreigner
-nis	das Erlebnis	[ɛɐ'le:pnɪs]	experience
-sal	das Schicksal	[ʃɪkza:l]	fate
-sam	heilsam	[haelza:m]	healing
-schaft	die Freundschaft	[frɔøntʃaft]	friendship

| -tum | der Reichtum | [ɾaeçtuːm] | wealth |
| -ung | die Bedeutung | [bə'dɔøtʊŋ] | meaning |

15.4 Compound words

A compound word is comprised of two words, which may exist on their own. In English, one often writes these words separately, whereas in German it is possible to build long words by joining both related and unrelated words. For example, "voice teacher" is written as only one word in German: *der Gesangslehrer* [gə'zaŋsleːɾe]. Creating new compound words that do not exist in the German language is a poetic device often used by Romantic poets such as Heine and Eichendorff. Compound words are always stressed on the first syllable. A common error is allowing for a secondary stress of equal weight. This results in miscomprehension, as it resembles two separate words instead of a compound word.

"An die Nachtigall, op.46. no.4," J. Brahms/L.C.H. Hölty

In the above musical example, the compound words *liebentflammten* (enflamed with love) and *tonreichen* (rich in tone) are spread over an entire measure, or one and a half measures, respectively. At a slower tempo, it is important that the tonic stress on the first syllable be clearly emphasized. When this is achieved on the word *tonreichen*, the metric accent is shifted, leading to a stronger horizontal line and forward movement. The same is true for the next example, whereby one word is extended over eight bars to illustrate the long journey of Elf Queen. She appears to move in slow motion, adding to the eerie quality of this text.

"Neue Liebe, op.19, no.4," F. Mendelssohn/H. Heine

15.5 Word origin and loan words

Knowing the origin of a German word is not necessary but it is helpful in determining its pronunciation. Loan words, or words borrowed from other languages, tend to be stressed irregularly, as they are often pronounced as they would be in their original language. There are two main differences that must be observed in loan words: 1) vowel length and 2) word stress.

There is a preponderance of pure vowels in words of non-Germanic origin. As a result, many closed vowels exist in a shortened state. This is indicated by the absence of the colon in IPA, e.g., *Melodien* [melo'diːən]. Please consult Chapter 17 (Vowels) for further information on vowels in loan words. In general, words of Germanic origin have a tonic stress on the first syllable (including compound words) or root stem. In loan words, the stress falls where it normally would in the original language. For example, in words of Greek origin, the stress often falls on the third syllable, e.g., *Ganymed* [gany'meːt], *psychologisch* [psyço'loːgɪʃ].

15.6 Glottal attacks or onsets

The glottal onset is an important aspect of the German language and thus a distinct component in essaying to sing like a native speaker. It is an essential part of clarity and comprehension, as its absence directly affects both. As in English, glottal onsets may be used for increased dramatic effect. This is left to the discretion of the singer and depends solely on context and interpretation.

In both speaking and singing, there are three methods of vocal onset or attack: breathy, soft, and hard. A breathy onset occurs upon pronouncing an initial *h* [h]. The breath passes through the vocal folds before the glottis has closed. A soft glottal attack occurs when the breath flow begins simultaneously with the closure of the glottis. One uses this attack when pronouncing a word commencing with a stressed vowel. This principle is used when initiating vowels in all Romance languages, and may be applied to Germanic languages as well. There is no need to ever use a hard glottal attack in the German language. A hard attack results from the glottis closing completely before the tone begins and is otherwise known as a *glottal stop*. The closed glottis causes the air pressure to build up until the vocal folds separate and vibrate upon phonation. A hard glottal onset is commonly heard in popular music and is potentially extremely damaging to the voice.

This text strongly advocates the sole use of a soft glottal attack in both English and German lyric diction. It is considered to be a "healthy" glottal and serves to illustrate where one word ends and another begins. It is represented by the symbol [|], as used in both Duden and Siebs. Glottal onsets should be quick and light, supporting the legato line.

Occurrence

In German lyric diction, one is required to use a soft glottal onset at the beginning of a word or word element commencing with a vowel. This is especially important when the preceding word or word element ends in a consonant. Contrary to English, the omission of a glottal onset does not necessarily create unwanted words, but rather makes the word and sentence difficult to understand.

By using the vowel [ɐ] as a substitute for *r*, the strength of the glottal onset is reduced. It greatly aids the legato line and gives German an increased sense of singing vowel-to-vowel. Further, the rhythmic release and timing of consonants often negates the necessity for a strong glottal attack. Please consult Chapter 22 (Legato Singing) for further information, including several musical examples.

die Erinnerung   [diː|ɛɐ'|ınərʊŋ]   memory
eine andere Art   [aenə|andərə|art]   another method

Supplementary exercises
1. Identify the components of the following words, labeling root stem, grammatical (verbal) endings and inflectional endings (prefixes and suffixes). N.B.: Some words may contain multiple elements.

unvergesslich, zerbrechlich, unausweichlich, beeinflussen, vergebens, gebrochen, verwendbar, unbewohnbar, durchdringen, unruhig, langsam, versinnlichen, unglaublich, verführerisch, ungezwungen, unerreichbar, außergewöhnlich, vorenthalten, beenden, ausländisch

2. Identify which words have separable prefixes.
abmachen, darbieten, erweitern, fortpflanzen, bestellen, einladen, sich empfinden, ausbreiten, gebrauchen, dastehen, mißgönnen, verstehen, aufklären, durchlesen, nachbestellen, niederputzen, entfernen, zertrümmern, zurückkehren, hergeben, wegziehen, behalten, mitnehmen, umbauen, anhören, einkaufen, vorbereiten, weitermachen, hinfahren

Chapter 16: Characteristic German Phonemes

This section will describe in detail various speech sounds featured in German. None of these phonemes is found in English, but they do exist in other languages. The *schwa*, although prevalent in English, has a unique quality in German, which will be illustrated in section 16.3.

16.1 The *ich-laut* [ç] , *ach-laut* [χ] , and Curly-tail J [j]

The German word *laut* is a general term meaning sound. The verb *läuten* translates to mean "to ring" or "to resound". The following three phonemes must be mastered in order to achieve authentic German pronunciation and fluid facility with the language.

[ç]   C cedilla   Voiceless palatal fricative
Spelling: *ch* or *-ig* (suffix)

Production: The *ich-laut* is formed by first placing the tongue in the position for [iː] and then energetically expelling residual air centralized on the alveolar ridge. As with [h], one need not inhale to make an effective *ich-laut*. The residual air already floating in the mouth is sufficient for an *ich-laut* that will project with clarity. There should be no escape of air either laterally or along the hard palate. The closest sound to an *ich-laut* in English is an initial *h* before *u*, as in Hubert or Hugo.

152

It is a common error to round the lips when producing [ç]. This results in a sound closer to [ʃ] and is incorrect. It is imperative that singers not move any of the articulators during the formation of the *ich-laut*. This is also crucial in maintaining pure vowels, in passing smoothly through two vowels in a diphthong, and in forming the German *schwa*.

Occurrence

1. *ch* preceded by a vowel (except *a*, *o*, or *u*)

This includes all mixed vowels and two diphthongs ([ae][ɔø]). Note that the *ich-laut* may occur multiple times within one word.

das Lächeln	[lɛçəln]	smile
die Bücher	[byːçɐ]	books
höchste	[høːçstə]	highest
der Becher	[bɛçɐ]	cup, mug
nichts	[nɪçts]	nothing
lächerlich	[lɛçɐlɪç]	ridiculous
fürchterlich	[fʏrçtɐlɪç]	dreadfully
hauptsächlich	[haoptzɛçlɪç]	mainly

2. *ch* preceded by a consonant (except *s*)

die Milch	[mɪlç]	milk
manche	[mançə]	some
durch	[dʊrç]	through
das Mädchen	[mɛːtçən]	girl, maid, lass

3. final *-ig* at end of word, or word element

der König	[køːnɪç]	king
fertig	[fɛrtɪç]	finished
die Ewigkeit	[eːvɪçkaet]	eternity

Exception: If *-ig* precedes either *-lich* or *-reich*, it is pronounced [ɪk].

königlich	[kø:nɪklɪç]	royal
das Königreich	[kø:nɪkɾaeç]	kingdom, realm

Exercise for singers with difficulty pronouncing [ç]

Upon encountering a student who has difficulty achieving a proper *ich-laut*, I suggest making up nonsense words that incorporate the German word, as well as a similar sound in English. This method incorporates visualization, aural, and oral work. By prolonging the first syllable, the student has the necessary time to think about the tongue position and the air required to form the *ich-laut*.

Sample word: das Lächeln   [lɛçəln]   smile

H...ugo (exaggerating and elongating *h*, to feel where air collects on alveolar ridge for *ich-laut*)

Ch...ugo (exact same pronunciation and elongation, but visualizing that it is spelled as *ich-laut*)

Lä...chugo alternating with **Lä...chel** (repeat 5 times)

Lä...cheln (repeat 5 times, mindful that articulators do not move)

Lächeln (normal speech rhythm, no longer prolonging first syllable)

[χ]   Chi   Voiceless uvular fricative
Spelling: *ch*

Production: The *ach-laut* is formed by first placing the tongue in the position for [a:] and then swiftly expelling residual air centralized at the back of the hard palate. As previously observed with the *ich-laut*, one need not inhale to make an effective *ach-laut*. The residual air already floating in the mouth is sufficient for an *ach-laut* that will project with clarity and confidence.

While the *ach-laut* is often described as a guttural sound, it should not sound like one is clearing the throat. Although it originates in the back of the mouth, the air moves swiftly and directly to the front of the mouth, travelling along the hard palate. It is crucial that the following vowel or consonant not be formed where the *ach-laut* originated.

Occurrence

1. *ch* preceded by the vowels *a*, *o*, or *u* (including diphthong [ao])
Note that the *ach-laut* may occur multiple times within one word.

die Nacht	[naχt]	night
der Buchenbaum	[buːχənbaom]	beech tree
das Loch	[lɔχ]	hole
auch	[aoχ]	also
die Nachtandacht	[ˈnaχt|andaχt]	evening church service
die Nachbarschaftssache	[ˈnaːχbaːrʃaftszaχə]	neighborhood thing

Special circumstances: initial *ch* and loan words

When *ch* begins a word, it is difficult to determine whether it is an *ich-laut* or an *ach-laut*. Most often, initial *ch* is pronounced [ç]. However, when *ch* occurs in a loan word (often Greek origin), it is pronounced [k]. When in doubt, please consult a dictionary.

das China	[çiːnaː]	China (country)
die Chemie	[çeˈmiː]	chemistry
das Orchester	[ɔrˈkɛstɐ]	orchestra
der Chor	[koːɐ]	choir

| [ʝ] Curly-tail J | | Voiced palatal fricative |
| Spelling: *j* | | |

| der Jammer | [ʝamɐ] | lamentation |

Production: This phoneme is not identical to its English counterpart [j].
In English, this sound is classified as a glide or semi-consonant. In German, [j̯] is a voiced counterpart to the *ich-laut* [ç], i.e., its cognate. The
production is identical to that of the *ich-laut*, the only difference being
that this phoneme is voiced. In other words, the vocal folds are engaged,
causing this fricative to be pitched. Practice executing [ç], then adding a
tone. It resembles an exaggerated [j] with aspiration. As with all other
voiced consonants, it will be rhythmically timed on the beat. This differs
from both the *ich-laut* and *ach-laut*, which are produced before the beat.

16.2 Use of R: [ɾ] vs. [ɐ]

The treatment of *r* has long been disputed and discussed. This is similar
to the controversy surrounding the various uses of *r* in English. In spoken German and French, one uses the uvular *r* [ʁ], a voiced uvular fricative. In fact, this phoneme is very close to [χ], except it is voiced. The
use of [ʁ] is *not* recommended in singing, primarily since it is centered
at the back of the mouth. This text promotes the use of flipped *r* [ɾ], and
also the vowel [ɐ] as a substitute for *r* in certain circumstances.

[ɾ] Fish-hook R   Voiced alveolar tap
Spelling: *r*

rauschen	[ɾaoʃən]	to rustle, to babble
die Türen	[ty:ɾən]	doors
die Freude	[fɾɔødə]	joy
starren	[ʃtaɾən]	to stare

Production: In order to produce a flipped *r*, the tip of the tongue taps the
alveolar ridge only *once*. This phoneme is also called the one-tap trill.

Exercise for singers with difficulty producing [ɾ]

Speak "tada" (as a magician would) very slowly at first, mindful of solely using the tip of the tongue to produce [t] and [d]. Gradually increase the speed, so that [d] becomes a flipped [ɾ]. The tongue must remain loose as the speed increases. Once [ɾ] is formed consistently, speak the following words: treat, dream, trance, drape. Then, speak the following, mindful of only using the tongue-tip: very, merry, berry, carry, tarry.

Occurrence of [ɾ]

1. Initial *r*

der Regen	[ɾeːgən]	rain
das Röslein	[ɾøːslaen]	little rose

2. Intervocalic *r*

während	[vɛːɾənt]	during, while
die Tiere	[tiːɾə]	animals

3. *r* plus a consonant

der Frühling	[fɾyːlɪŋ]	spring
die Erde	[eːɾdə]	earth

4. Doubled *r*

irre	[ɪɾə]	crazy
harren	[haɾən]	to race, to hurry

N.B.: If *r* is doubled, it may be rolled for the purpose of word-painting. Often a prolonged flip will suffice. This is left to the singer's discretion. Generally, it is not advisable to roll *r* [r] in art song repertoire. However, when singing operatic repertoire, it is often necessary to use [r] for the purpose of projection and clarity. For further information, please consult Chapter 24 (Lyric Diction in Opera).

[ɐ]   Turned A   Near-open central vowel
Spelling: r, -er (suffix), er-, ver-, der-, vor- (prefixes)

die Uhr	[uːɐ]	clock
länger	[lɛŋɐ]	longer
erweitern	[ɛɐ'vaetɐrn]	to expand, to extend
verstehen	[fɛɐ'ʃteːən]	to understand
derselbe	[deːɐ'zɛlbə]	the same
vorhin	[foːɐ'hɪn]	earlier, just now

Production: This vowel occurs in Received Pronunciation (RP) when the final vowel is a, e.g., idea [aɪ'dɪə], sofa [soʊfə], Amanda [ə'mændə]. In RP this is referred to as an intrusive r, as it does not belong to the original spelling (Jones 1962). However, in English IPA transcriptions, this vowel is expressed as a *schwa*. To North American ears, [ɐ] is an R-colored vowel. Due to the strong relationship between English and German, it is quite logical that this vowel is used to replace r in German.

If one flips the r when pronouncing a word ending in final -er, it no longer sounds idiomatic and draws attention to a sound rarely heard in speech. This is similar to emphasizing the unstressed *schwa* in French, which is scarcely pronounced when spoken. Singers should strive for an authentic inflection in each language in which they sing and the correct pronunciation of -er is a key element for German. Although both Siebs and Duden recommend actors to pronounce -er as [ər] on the stage, this does not extend to singing except in the circumstances listed below. As explained in Chapter 13 (Introduction to German Diction for Singers), *Bühnendeutsch* (Stage German) was created by Theodor Siebs to unify German pronunciation in public forums, including radio, television, and theatre. For lyric diction, this text promotes the modern use of *Hochdeutsch*.

Occurrence of [ɐ]

1. final -*er* (suffix) at end of word

| später | [ʃpɛːtɐ] | later |
| der Kummer | [kʊmɐ] | sorrow |

N.B.: When *er* occurs at the end of a word element, it is *not* considered to be a final -*er* and thus is pronounced [ər]. This decision is made according to optimal clarity and projection for singing.

| bedauerlich | [bə'daoərlıç] | regrettable |
| die Sauberkeit | [zaobərkaet] | cleanliness |

2. *er-*, *ver-*, *der-*, *vor-* (prefixes)

erkennen	[ɛɐ'kɛnən]	to recognize
verbergen	[fɛɐ'bɛrgən]	to hide
dereinst	[deːɐ|'aenst]	once
die Vorahnung	['foːɐ|aːnʊŋ]	premonition

N.B.: It is imperative to recognize the function of an initial *vor*. If it is not a prefix, *vor* is pronounced [fɔr].

| die Vorderhand | [fɔrdərhant] | upper hand |
| vordere | [fɔrdərə] | front, anterior |

3. Final *r* in a monosyllabic word, -*bar* (suffix)

dir	[diːɐ]	to you
die Spur	[ʃpuːɐ]	trace
vier	[fiːɐ]	four
der Nachbar	[naːχbaːɐ]	neighbor

Special circumstance: -ern

Words ending in -ern may be verbs, adjectives, or dative plurals. In this case, it is strongly advisable to use [ərn] instead of [ɐn]. The use of flipped r reinforces clarity, projection, and comprehension of these difficult words. Practice the following words, taking care to flip the r cleanly.

erleichtern	[ɛɐ'laeçtərn]	to ease, to facilitate
schimmernd	[ʃɪmərnt]	glimmering
schlummern	[ʃlʊmərn]	to slumber

16.3 The German *schwa*: vocalic chameleon

The term *schwa* comes from a Hebrew word, transliterated as *sheva* or *shewa*, meaning nothingness. The *e* in the transliteration is a short phonetic sound, referred to as a neutral, obscure, or indeterminate vowel. Indeed some phoneticians refuse to classify this sound as a vowel, citing that the sound is indeed too indefinite. Although the same IPA symbol is used, the *schwa* has a distinct sound in each of the languages in which it is represented. This presents the singer with a unique challenge.

The quality of the German *schwa* is unique to the German language. **The color is directly related to the quality of the vowel immediately preceding the *schwa*.** In order to best describe this phenomenon, I have coined the term *vocalic chameleon*. One must maintain the same tongue and lip position when pronouncing the ensuing *schwa*. The sound quality varies in openness according to its environment. However, compared to the English *schwa* it is more forward, has a greater degree of focus, and a higher tongue position. One must strive to avoid the common mistakes of either opening the German *schwa* all the way to [ɛ] or over-rounding the lips so that it becomes the French *schwa*, also known as [œ].

[ə]   Schwa   Central (tongue)
Spelling: *e* (unstressed)

die Ruhe	[ruːə]	peace, stillness
geboren	[gəˈboːrən]	born
du arbeitest	[duːǀarbaetəst]	you work

Occurrence: The German *schwa* is found in final and unstressed syllables, including prefixes, suffixes, and inflectional endings. However, this rule does not apply to all unaccented syllables. Prefixes such as *er-, ver-, zer-, emp-,* and *ent-* should always be pronounced [ɛ].

In actual practice, singers use the *schwa* primarily for final *e* and certain unaccented middle syllables. For all other unaccented syllables (specifically the prefixes *ge-* and *be-*, the adjective endings *-es, -en, -em,* and the verb endings *-et, -en, -est*), singers tend to make the error of forming the vowel further forward, thus achieving a quality akin to [ɛ]. However, all references use the *schwa* in transcribing these syllables. It is critical that one listen carefully to native speakers to recognize the constant changes in color due to its relationship to the surrounding vowels.

Oral practice for the German *schwa*
1. Practice speaking the following words, mindful of pronouncing the *schwa* in the position of the previous vowel. Take great care that the articulators (lips and tongue) and the jaw do *not* move to form the *schwa*.

die Liebe	[liːbə]	love
die Nichte	[nɪçtə]	niece
die Seele	[zeːlə]	soul
die Nägel	[nɛːgəl]	nails
die Rechte	[rɛçtə]	rights, privileges
die Ruhe	[ruːə]	peace, stillness, rest
der Kunde	[kʊndə]	customer

die Bote	[boːtə]	messenger
kochen	[kɔχən]	to cook
die Fahne	[faːnə]	flag, banner
die Verwandte	[fɛɐˈvantə]	relatives
die Söhne	[zøːnə]	sons
ergötzen	[ɛɐˈgœtsən]	to amuse, to delight
rühren	[ryːɾən]	to touch
die Sünde	[zʏndə]	sin, transgression

2. In the following words with double consonants, concentrate on pronouncing the *schwa* in the same position as the previous vowel. Do not let the articulation of the doubled consonants displace the position of the *schwa* or a different vowel will ensue.

bitte	[bɪtə]	please
die Sonne	[zɔnə]	sun
die Ebbe	[ɛbə]	ebb tide
die Puppe	[pʊpə]	doll
süße	[zyːsə]	sweet
alle	[alə]	all, everyone
küssen	[kʏsən]	to kiss
der Himmel	[hɪməl]	heaven, sky
die Waffe	[vafə]	weapon
klirren	[klɪɾən]	to clatter
die Kogge	[kɔgə]	sailboat (for trade), cog
entlocken	[ɛntˈlɔkən]	to entice
die Städte	[ʃtɛːtə]	cities

N.B.: Certain consonant spellings are treated as functioning double consonants, e.g., *ck*, *dt*. Please refer to Chapter 18 (Consonants) for further explanation.

Supplementary exercises

In the following exercises, speak and intone all words, then transcribe into IPA.

1. *ich-laut* vs. *ach-laut*

der Zecher, der Kuchen, das Büchlein, die Sucht, suchen, das Veilchen, das Bächlein, gebrauchen, mächtig, das Gedicht, hoch, möchte, der Lauch, durchsichtig, nächste, jedoch, die Schmach, der Flüchtling, nachsichtig, offensichtlich, das Nachtlicht, nachträglich, nachbarschaftlich, die Sachlichkeit, das Nachthemdchen

2. [ç] vs. [ɪk]

ewiglich, Ludwig, beleidigt, minniglich, freudigst, königlich, vierzigste, das Königreich, befriedigt, wonniglich, herzigste, hoffentlich, die Vergesslichkeit, inniglich, besänftigt, wichtigstem, die Gerechtigkeit

3. [r] [ər] [ɐ]

flüstern, bitter, davor, vorhergehen, die Mutter, den Müttern, das Rohr, mehr, offenbar, ihren, vorderste, wirren, sauer, schwirren, klar, schwerer, mir, schaudern, das Muster, wieder, berühren, treffen, rot, mehrere, der Unterricht, übergehen, das Wiedersehen, ersehen, verstimmen

4. [ç] [χ] [ɪk]

mächtig, die Macht, noch, lachen, lächerlich, wenigstens, die Handtücher, das Handtuch, lediglich, hoch, gesprochen, die Gespräche, höchste, durch, die Tochter, die Bücher, die Sache, ach, rechtsbündig, die Seligkeit

Chapter 17: Vowels

17.1 Vowel length

In German, all closed vowels are *long*. The colon [:] is used in IPA to illustrate vowel length. This principle does not exist in English and is difficult for non-natives to adopt. In essence, a closed vowel is held almost double the length of an open vowel. This lends a natural rhythm and lilt to the German language, not unlike stressed vowels in Italian.

Equally important as lengthening a closed vowel is allowing an open vowel to be short. Singers should sing each vowel as long as rhythmically possible, but not at the expense of the consonants. It is a common problem to not leave enough time for the clear production of the consonants by lingering on the vowel too long. This is especially critical in the crisp formation of voiceless clusters abounding in the German language.

Occurrence of closed vowels

1. before an *h*

sehr	[ze:ɐ]	very
die Bedienung	[bə'di:nʊŋ]	service

2. doubled vowel

das Haar	[ha:ɐ]	hair
der See	[ze:]	ocean, sea

3. before a single consonant (monosyllabic words, word element)

| der Tod | [toːt] | death |
| ebenso | [eːbənzoː] | likewise |

Occurrence of open vowels

1. before two or more consonants

| das Wetter | [vɛtɐ] | weather |
| naschen | [naʃən] | to snack, nibble |

N.B.: Vowels preceding *Eszett* (*ß*), *ich-laut* [ç], or *ach-laut* [χ] may be closed or open. One must consult a dictionary in these cases. Most words employ an open vowel, as all three phonemes represent multiple consonants orthographically, *ss* and *ch*, respectively. Please see section 17.5 for a full list of common exceptions using these phonemes.

17.2 Monophthongs

Monophthongs, also known as pure vowels, consist of a sole phoneme. Their purity is characterized by a clear tone that does not waver or oscillate from the very beginning of the pitch until the very end. The quality of a given vowel is determined by the position of the tongue, lower jaw, and lips, as these can alter the shape of the cavity through which the air passes. Moreover, different shapes create different resonances. Lips that are accidentally rounded will impede the production of a "tongue vowel". Often an involuntary movement of the articulators will result in the production of an unwanted diphthong. Great care must be taken to avoid this common error. This may also be regulated by the singer's keen aural sensitivity.

Vowels may be categorized according to relative length and tongue position (close, open), inherent sound quality (bright, dark), height in the mouth (high, mid, low), or the distance from the opening of the mouth (front, central, back). This text divides German monophthongs into four categories: bright, central, dark, and mixed.

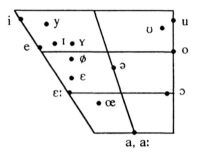

Figure 17.1. Monophthongs
Source: Klaus Kohler, *Handbook of the International Phonetic Association* (Cambridge: Cambridge University Press, 1999), 87.

Bright vowels [iː] [ɪ] [eː] [ɛ] [ɛː]

[iː]   Lowercase I   Bright (tongue), close
Spelling: *i, ih, ie, ieh*

der Jasmin	[jasˈmiːn]	jasmine
ihnen	[iːnən]	to them
wieder	[viːdɐ]	again
das Vieh	[fiː]	beast

Exceptions: die Nachtigall [naχtɪgal], die Lyrik [lyːrɪk], die Lilie [liːliə], fix [fɪks], bin [bɪn], hin [hɪn], in [ɪn], vierzehn [fɪrtseːn], vierzig [fɪrtsɪç]

Production: The tongue is arched forward with the back high, the sides lightly touching the upper molars, and the tip resting against the lower teeth. Upon properly positioning the tongue, the jaw will automatically lower slightly and rotate back. The lips are not directly involved in the formation of this vowel and therefore should be relaxed. As the tongue is arched as far as possible without becoming a consonant, one must be mindful of any unwanted tension. This phoneme has greater intensity than its English counterpart and is perceived as being considerably more closed. N.B.: Since [iː] is a closed vowel, it is always pronounced *long*.

[ɪ]	Small capital I	Bright (tongue), open

Spelling: *i*

die Sinne	[zɪnə]	senses, wits

Production: The tongue is arched forward with the back high, the sides slightly touching the upper molars, and the tip resting against the lower teeth. In comparison to [iː], the front of the tongue moves back slightly and depresses. The jaw will automatically rotate back, while the lips are relaxed and neutral. Compared to English, this phoneme is noticeably brighter and more forward. N.B.: For the spellings *ich* and *-ig*, the sound is indeed halfway between [iː] and [ɪ]. Some sources recognize this hybrid phoneme as [i], which is a closed vowel, slightly lower than [i].

[eː]	Lowercase E	Bright (tongue), close

Spelling: *e, ee, eh*

reden	[reːdən]	to speak/to talk
der Kaffee	[kafeː]	coffee
mehr	[meːɐ]	more

Exceptions: es [ɛs], des [dɛs], weg [vɛk], die Hexe [hɛksə]

Production: The tongue is arched forward with the back high (slightly lower than [iː]), the sides lightly touching the upper molars, and the tip resting against the lower teeth. The jaw lowers slightly and rotates back. The lips are relaxed and neutral. The vowel [eː] is closed, bright, frontal, and high. In order to correctly form [eː], the tongue must be arched high at the front and the articulators must remain stable until the end of the pure vowel. It is a common mistake to let a diphthong form at the very end by moving the lips or dropping the tongue. If it feels too comfortable, it is probably not the correct vowel! Great care must be taken not to move the articulators during the production of this strongly closed vowel. Since [eː] is a closed vowel, it is always pronounced *long*.

This is a difficult vowel to achieve for English native speakers, as it does not exist in English. The closest comparison would be the diphthong [eɪ], e.g., say [seɪ]. The German [eː] is very intense in quality and is identical to its French counterpart, e.g., *été* [ete]. There is only a minor difference between [eː] and [iː].

Practice speaking and then singing the following words, noticing the minimal change in the arch of the tongue between [eː] and [iː]:
der See/sieh, das Meer/mir, dehnen/dienen, flehen/fliehen, nehmen/die Nieren, stehlen/stiehlen, wer/wir, die Beere/die Biere, das Heer/hier, die Regel/der Riegel, er/ihr, gehen/gierig

---

[ɛ]   Epsilon   Bright (tongue), open
Spelling: *e, ä*

das Hemd	[hɛmt]	shirt
die Blätter	[blɛtɐ]	leaves

Exceptions: die Erde [eːɾdə], erst [eːɾst], das Erz [eːɾts], der Herd [heːɾt], werden [veːɾdən], der Wert [veːɾt]

Production: The tongue-tip is in contact with the lower teeth, while the back is mid-high (slightly lower than [ɪ]). The sides of the tongue gently touch the sides of the upper molars, while the rest of the tongue feels like it is moving backwards, flattening its curvature at the front. The jaw naturally rotates back, while the lips are relaxed. This vowel should feel bright and vertical in nature. In German, this phoneme is slightly more closed than its English counterpart. The tongue has a stronger arch, feeling noticeably brighter and more forward.

N.B.: An alternate spelling for *ä* is *ae*, e.g., *die Gäste* or *die Gaeste* [gɛstə].

[ɛː]   Epsilon   Bright (tongue), near-close
Spelling: *ä, äh*

| die Schwäne | [ʃvɛːnə] | swans |
| die Hähne | [hɛːnə] | roosters |

Production: This phoneme is halfway between [eː] and [ɛ]. In spoken German, this vowel is often interchanged with [eː], but in lyric diction a clear distinction must be made. The best method of achieving the correct sound of this phoneme is through exercises alternating between [eː], [ɛː], and [ɛ]. In jest, one may consider this vowel to be the "lazy closed [eː]." This is the vowel that many singers achieve, falsely believing it to be closed. It is easier to attain [ɛː] when starting from [ɛ] and progressively becoming more closed, ending with [eː]. Care must be taken not to arch the tongue to the extreme, or it will result in [iː]. It is highly recommended to listen to native speakers to get this phoneme in the ear.

Occurrence: Following the rules for closed vowels, one uses [ɛː] before a single consonant, or before *h*, e.g., *später* [ʃpɛːtɐ], *mähen* [mɛːən]. There are no instances of doubled *ä* in German.

Starting with the right-hand column, practice speaking, intoning, and then singing the following words, mindful of the slight changes in the tongue position. Then, repeat the steps in the opposite direction.

[eː]	[ɛː]	[ɛ]
die Rede [reːdə]	die Räder [rɛːdɐ]	die Retter [rɛtɐ]
(lecture)	(wheels)	(saviors)
der Meter [meːtɐ]	das Märchen [mɛːrçən]	messen [mɛsən]
(meter)	(fairy tale)	(to measure)
das Wesen [veːzən]	wäre [vɛːrə]	wessen [vɛsən]
(being)	(would)	(whose)
beten [beːtən]	bäten [bɛːtən]	betten [bɛtən]
(to pray)	(would offer)	(to bed)
die Beeren [beːrən]	die Bären [bɛːrən]	die Bässe [bɛsə]
(berries)	(bears)	(basses)
zehren [tseːrən]	zärtlich [tsɛːrtlıç]	zerren [tsɛrən]
(to weaken, to sap)	(tenderly)	(to pull)
das Meer [meːɐ]	das Mädchen [mɛːtçən]	melden [mɛldən]
(ocean, sea)	(maid, girl)	(to announce)
stehlen [ʃteːlən]	die Stähle [ʃtɛːlə]	die Stelle [ʃtɛlə]
(to steal)	(steels)	(place, position)
nehmen [neːmən]	nämlich [nɛːmlıç]	nennen [nɛnən]
(to take)	(namely)	(to name)
der Lehrer [leːrɐ]	lähmen [lɛːmən]	das Lächeln [lɛçəln]
(teacher)	(to lame)	(smile)
stets [ʃteːts]	die Städte [ʃtɛːtə]	die Stätte [ʃtɛtə]
(constantly)	(cities)	(site)
die Demut [deːmuːt]	dämlich [dɛːmlıç]	dämmern [dɛmɐrn]
(humility)	(stupid, dumb)	(to dawn)

Central vowels [aː][a][ə][ɐ]

[aː]   Lowercase A   Central (tongue), open

Spelling: *a, aa, ah*

tragen	[traːgən]	to carry
das Paar	[paːɐ]	pair
das Jahr	[jaːɐ]	year

Exceptions: an [an], am [am], ab [ap], das [das], was [vas], man [man]

Production: The tongue-tip is in contact with the lower teeth, while the back is mid-high (slightly lower than [ɛ]). The tongue feels like it is moving backwards and flattens its curvature at the front. The jaw naturally rotates back slightly, as for [ɛ]. This vowel should feel bright and vertical. Some phoneticians classify this phoneme as frontal and this is helpful to visualize in its production. This vowel does not exist in English, except for in two diphthongs [aɪ] and [aʊ]. It is identical to its Italian counterpart, pronounced both long and short, e.g., *cara* [kaːra].

[a]   Lowercase A   Central (tongue), open

Spelling: *a*

| der Spatz | [ʃpats] | sparrow |

Exceptions: zart [tsaːrt], nach [naːχ], die Schmach [ʃmaːχ], das Maß [maːs], die Bratsche [braːtʃə], die Sprache [ʃpraːχə]

The only difference between the production of [aː] and [a] is vowel length. The quality is exactly the same (open). Note that it follows the same rules regarding the occurrence of closed and open vowels, e.g., der Rabe [raːbə] vs. der Rabbi [rabiː].

[ə] [ɐ]

Please see Chapter 16 (Characteristic German Phonemes) for full descriptions of these central vowels: German *schwa* [ə], and Turned A [ɐ].

Dark vowels [oː][ɔ][uː][ʊ]

[oː]   Lowercase O   Dark (rounded lips), close
Spelling: *o, oh, oo*

loben	[loːbən]	to praise
gestohlen	[gəˈʃtoːlən]	stolen
doof	[doːf]	dumb, idiotic

Exceptions: sooft [zoːˈ|ɔft], die Koordination [koː|ɔrdinaˈtsioːn], das Akkordeon [aˈkɔrdeɔn], von [fɔn], vom [fɔm], op [ɔp]

Production: The tongue-tip is in contact with the lower teeth and the lips are protruded and rounded without any labial tension. The middle of the tongue is raised, while the back remains low, but slightly higher than [uː]. One must imagine a high vertical space at the back of the mouth, although the front forms a small, round aperture. This is identical to its French counterpart in intensity and quality, e.g., *beau* [bo]. It is much more closed than the English [o] that only occurs in an unstressed position that is not final. Great care must be taken not to move the lips or tongue during the production of this strongly closed vowel. Note that since [oː] is a closed vowel, it is always pronounced *long*.

[ɔ]   Open O   Dark (rounded lips), open
Spelling: *o*

| der Koffer | [kɔfɐ] | suitcase |

Exceptions: der Trost [troːst], das Obst [oːpst], groß [groːs], hoch [hoːχ], das Kloster [kloːstɐ], das Ostern [oːstɜrn], der Schoß [ʃoːs]

Production: The tongue-tip remains in contact with the lower teeth, though it feels slightly retracted. The back of the tongue is raised while the middle and front both lie quite flat. In fact, the tongue is as retracted as possible, without becoming a fricative consonant, e.g., [ʁ] or [χ]. The lips are rounded and protruded, forming a small, oval aperture, while maintaining a sense of vertical space inside the mouth. The jaw is relaxed and rotated slightly back. It is not advisable to drop the jaw very much. This phoneme is identical to its Italian and English (RP) counterparts, e.g., *sarò* [saˈrɔː], *bought* [bɔt]. It is imperative that this vowel not decay into [ɑ] by opening the lips or moving the jaw during production. It is difficult to maintain [ɔ] on a longer note value.

[uː]   Lowercase U   Dark (rounded lips), close
Spelling: *u, uh*

mutig	[muːtɪç]	courageous
der Ruhm	[ruːm]	fame, glory

Exceptions: die Betreuung [bəˈtrɔøʊŋ], die Anstauung [anʃtaoʊŋ], das Individuum [ɪndiˈviːduʊm], das Kontinuum [kɔnˈtiːnuʊm], zum [tsʊm], die Verdauung [fɛɐˈdaoʊŋ], die Zerstreuung [tsɛrˈʃtrɔøʊŋ], un- [ʊn]

Production: The lips are protruded and rounded, mindful that there is no labial tension. The middle of the tongue is high, while the tip touches the lower teeth and the back is low. One must imagine a high vertical space at the back of the mouth, although the front forms a small, round aperture. It is crucial that one not add a *schwa* [ə] or shadow vowel upon the release. In German, [uː] is longer and thus is perceived as being more closed than its English counterpart. Great care must be taken not to open the lips during production of this phoneme, similar to [oː]. As with all pure vowels, the integrity must remain for the entire duration of the vowel. Since [uː] is closed, it is always pronounced *long*.

[ʊ]   Upsilon   Dark (rounded lips), open
Spelling: *u*

das Unternehmen   [ʊntərˈneːmən]   company, enterprise

Exceptions: das Buch [buːχ], das Tuch [tuːχ], suchen [zuːχən], der Kuchen [kuːχən], der Fuß [fuːs], der Fluß [fluːs], der Gruß [gruːs]

Production: It is very important to note that this vowel is *not* identical to its English counterpart, although the same IPA symbol is used, e.g., book [bʊk]. In German, the closest comparison is in fact the closed [uː]. According to the *Handbook of the International Phonetic Association*, the German [ʊ] has a slightly lower tongue position than [uː], retracting at the front. It is halfway between [uː] and the English [ʊ]. The tip of the tongue remains in contact with the lower teeth, but moves slightly backward at the blade. The lips remain strongly rounded and protruded, as for [uː] and [oː]. Similar to [ɔ], it is difficult to maintain this open vowel for a longer duration. When a composer has set this phoneme on a longer note value, it is recommended to close the vowel slightly. It is wise to listen to native German speakers to perfect the quality of this enigmatic vowel.

Mixed vowels [yː] [ʏ] [øː] [œ]
Mixed vowels are formed by the action of two articulators simultaneously. Mixed vowels do not exist in English, but are directly related to their French counterparts, e.g., *une* [ynœ], *deux* [dø]. The four German

mixed vowels may be classified as closed or open and follow the same
rules regarding their occurrence as other monophthongs.

[y:]   Lowercase Y   Mixed (tongue + rounded lips), close
Spelling: *ü, üh, y*

müde	[my:də]	tired
die Kühnheit	[ky:nhaet]	audacity, boldness
typisch	[ty:pɪʃ]	typical

N.B.: Foreign loan words often have shortened closed vowels, e.g., das
Baryton [baɾy'to:n], die Psychologie [psyçolo'gi:], die Physik [fy'zi:k],
psychologisch [psyço'lo:gɪʃ], die Hypothek [hypo'te:k], der Zylinder
[tsy'lɪndɐ], Ganymed [gany'me:t], die Zypresse [tsy'prɛsə]

Production: While placing the tongue in the position for [i:], round and
protrude the lips to form [u:]. It is a common error to underestimate the
amount of rounding that is needed for this phoneme to be accurate. It is
identical to its French counterpart, e.g., *tu* [ty]. When practicing this
phoneme, it is helpful to first intone [i:] and then think of [u:], keeping
the breath engaged and the sound constant. Both articulators (tongue
and lips) must be in their respective, specific positions for the mixed
vowel to be definite. It is highly recommended to learn this sound
through aural training. Since [y:] is a closed vowel, it is always pronounced *long.*

[ʏ]   Small capital Y   Mixed (tongue + rounded lips), open
Spelling: *ü, y*

| stürzen | [ʃtʏrtsən] | to plunge, to plummet |
| hypnotisch | [hʏp'no:tɪʃ] | hypnotic |

Exceptions: der Zyklus [tsy:klʊs], düster [dy:stɐ], die Wüste [vy:stə], die
Bücher [by:çɐ], die Tücher [ty:çɐ], zyprisch [tsy:prɪʃ], süß [zy:s], die
Süßigkeit [zy:sɪçkaet]

Production: This phoneme is the open counterpart to [y:]. While placing
the tongue in the position for [ɪ], round the lips to form [ʊ]. Compared
to [y:], the lips are not as rounded, nor is the tongue quite as arched.
When practicing this phoneme, it is helpful to intone [ɪ] and then think
of [ʊ], keeping the breath engaged and the sound constant. It is a common error to open this vowel too much, forming [œ] by mistake. Both
tongue and lips must be in their respective, specific positions for the
mixed vowel to be definite. This is the only German mixed vowel that
does not have a French counterpart. It is highly recommended to listen
to native German speakers to perfect the quality of this enigmatic vowel.

[ø:]   O-slash   Mixed (tongue + rounded lips), close
Spelling: *ö, öh*

| der König | [kø:nɪç] | king |
| die Höhe | [hø:ə] | altitude, elevation |

Production: While placing the tongue in the position for [e:], round and
protrude the lips to form [o:]. It is a common error to underestimate the
amount of rounding needed for this phoneme to be accurate. It is identical to its French counterpart, e.g., *feu* [fø]. When practicing this phoneme, it is helpful to intone [e:] and then think of [o:], keeping the
breath engaged and the sound constant. Both tongue and lips must be in
their respective, specific positions for the mixed vowel to be definite. It
is highly recommended to learn this sound through aural training. Since
[ø:] is a closed vowel, it is always pronounced *long*.

[œ]   Lowercase O-E ligature   Mixed (tongue + rounded lips), open
Spelling: *ö*

schöpfen   [ʃœpfən]   to create

Exceptions: größer [grøːsɐ], höchst [høːçst], Goethe [gøːtə]

Production: This phoneme is the open counterpart to [øː]. The tongue is in the position for [ɛ], while the lips form [ɔ]. The tongue is not as arched and it feels much lower in the mouth compared to [øː]. It is identical to its French counterpart, *le* [lœ]. When practicing this phoneme, it is helpful to intone [ɛ] and then think of [ɔ], keeping the breath engaged and the sound constant. Both tongue and lips must be in their respective, specific positions for the mixed vowel to be definite. It is recommended to learn this sound through aural training and listening to native speakers.

Alternative spellings

As previously seen with the vowel *ä*, alternative spellings are possible for all four mixed vowels. In each case, an *e* is added after the vowel.

spuelen or spülen	[ʃpyːlən]	to rinse
beruehmt or berühmt	[bəˈryːmt]	famous
kuessen or küssen	[kʏsən]	to kiss
Mueller or Müller	[mʏlɐ]	(surname)
Schoenberg or Schönberg	[ʃøːnbɛrk]	(surname)
die Floehe or die Flöhe	[fløːə]	fleas
moechte or möchte	[mœçtə]	would like to
der Koerper or der Körper	[kœrpɐ]	body

Oral drills: Practice speaking, intoning and singing the following words.

[iː]	vs.	[ɪ]	[eː]	vs.	[ɛ]	[oː]	vs.	[ɔ]
wider		Widder	Heer		Herr	Hose		Hopfen
Lied		litt	wen		wenn	so		sollen
schief		Schiff	Kehle		Keller	Ton		Tonne
Stiel		still	Fehl		Fell	wohnen		Wonne
Miene		Minne	den		denn	oder		Otter
ihren		irren	beten		betten	ohne		Onkel
hier		Hirn	stehlen		stellen	Zofe		Zopf
Bier		Birne	eben		Ebbe	hohl		Holz
Wien		Wind	Beet		Bett	Bote		Post

[øː]	vs.	[œ]	[yː]	vs.	[ʏ]	[aː]	vs.	[a]
Höhle		Hölle	Wüste		wüsste	Kahn		kann
gewöhnen		gewönnen	düster		Dünste	Abend		Apfel
Söhnen		sönne	fühle		fülle	Wahl		Wald
Chöre		Körner	rügte		rückte	Vater		Wasser
krönen		können	Hüte		Hütte	aber		Abteil
Flöte		Völle	pflügte		pflückte	Ahnung		Anna
stören		Stöcke	kühnste		Künste	Plan		Platz
Röte		Röcke	übel		üppig	Staat		Stadt
Goethe		Götter	Führer		fünf	haben		hatten

[uː]	vs.	[ʊ]	[eː]	vs.	[ɛː]
Brut		Brust	sehen		sähen
Uhr		Urteil	gehen		gähnen
Pfuhl		Pfund	nehmen		nämlich
Mut		Mutter	Beeren		Bären
Buch		Bucht	geben		gäben
Schule		Schuld	legen		lägen
Buhle		Bulle	wehren		wären

17.3 Diphthongs [ae] [ao] [ɔø]

When one vowel glides into a successive vowel and produces a smooth, imperceptible blend within one syllable, it is referred to as a diphthong. It is advisable to spend 90% of the note value on the first vowel, moving seamlessly through the second vowel (a.k.a. vanish vowel) for the remaining 10% of the note value. There should be no movement of the lips, tongue, or jaw during this smooth transition between vowels.

There are only three diphthongs in the German language. Modern dictionaries agree on two different spellings, defined by the two leading references in the German language (Siebs and Duden). This text advocates those found in Siebs, represented by [ae], [ao], and [ɔø].

	Siebs	**Duden**	
heimlich	[haemlɪç]	[haimlɪç]	secretly
das Taubenpaar	[taobənpaːɐ]	[taubənpaːɐ]	pair of doves
die Freude	[frɔødə]	[frɔydə]	joy

Duden's first two diphthongs correspond exactly to those found in Italian, e.g., *mai* [mai], or *aura* [aura]. The relationship between the first and second vowels in an Italian diphthong is about 60–40. The second vowel receives much more weight. This ratio is not desirable in German, as this would negatively influence word stress. The closed [iː] is too substantial in color and intensity to be a suitable vanish vowel.

Siebs' diphthongs are unique to the German language and accurately represent a nuance in vowel shading. The vanish vowels are only slightly lower than their Duden counterparts. However, this makes a significant difference in terms of stress and perceived importance. Further, they are pronounced with the least possible closing of the jaw, which is favored by singers and actors alike.

[ae]
Spelling: *ei, ey, ai, ay*

das Eisen	[aezən]	iron
Heyse	[haezə]	Heyse (surname)
der Mai	[mae]	May
Bayreuth	[bae'rɔøt]	Bayreuth (city)

Production: After spending 90% of the note value on [a], arch the tongue quickly to form [e] distinctly for the remaining 10% of the note. There should be no movement of the lips or the jaw during this smooth transition between vowels, as everything happens internally.

[ao]
Spelling: *au*

der Schaukelstuhl	[ʃaokəlʃtuːl]	rocking chair

Production: After spending 90% of the note value on [a], round the lips to form [o] distinctly for the remaining 10% of the note. Although there is a slight rounding of the lips, take great care that the lower jaw does not close during this smooth transition between vowels. It is helpful if the jaw is not extended too low for [a], but rather simply rotated back. Then, it may stay in the same position throughout.

[ɔø]
Spelling: *eu, äu*

die Beleuchtung	[bə'lɔøçtʊŋ]	lighting
die Häuser	[hɔøzɐ]	houses

Production: After spending 90% of the note value on [ɔ], arch the tongue quickly to form [ø] distinctly for the remaining 10% of the note. The tongue is in the same position as for [eː]. There should be no movement of the lips or the jaw during this smooth transition between vowels, as everything happens internally.

Comparison of German and English diphthongs

German			English	
dein	[daen]	your	dine	[daɪn]
Maus	[maos]	mouse	mouse	[maʊs]
treu	[trɔø]	faithful	Troy	[trɔɪ]

The main difference between German diphthongs and their English counterparts is in the nature of the second vowel. In each case, the German vanish vowel is closed (vs. open in English). As a result, the tongue is in a higher position and the quality is much more focused.

Speak and intone the following diphthongs, noting the slight changes in both the tongue and the lips, while passing smoothly between vowels:

[ae] – [aː] – [eː] – [ae]
leiden, laden, lehnen, leiden
reiten, Rad, reden, reiten
dreist, Draht, dreht, dreist

[ao] – [aː] – [oː] – [ao]
drauf, Draht, droben, drauf
kaufen, Kater, kosen, kaufen
Graus, Gras, groß, Graus

[ɔø] – [ɔ] – [øː] – [ɔø]
träumen, trommeln, trödeln, träumen
Bäume, Bombe, Böhme, Bäume
Säume, Sonne, Söhne, Säume

17.4 Vowels in loan words

German borrows many words from both Greek and French. In loan
words there is a preponderance of closed vowels, which rarely indicate
word stress. It has been emphasized throughout this text that all closed
vowels are indicated by the use of the colon [:] and are pronounced *long*.
However, in German loan words, one encounters several closed vowels
within a single word. As a result, the colon is only used where the word
stress falls on a closed vowel. All other closed vowels are thus shortened.

die Apotheke	[apoˈteːkə]	pharmacy, apothecary
die Melodien	[meloˈdiːən]	melodies
psychologisch	[psyçoˈloːgɪʃ]	psychological
die Hypothek	[hypoˈteːk]	mortgage
die Kooperation	[ko|opeɾaˈtsioːn]	cooperation
das Telefon	[teleˈfoːn]	telephone
die Bibliothek	[biblioˈteːk]	library
die Klimatisierung	[klimatiˈziːɾʊŋ]	air-conditioning

17.5 Common exceptions

Please memorize the following list of common exceptions in German
with respect to vowel length and quality.

an, am, ab	[an][am][ap]	at/on, at/on the, off
bin	[bɪn]	(I) am
bis	[bɪs]	until
das	[das]	the
der Besuch	[bəˈzuːχ]	visitation, company
das Buch	[buːχ]	book

die Bücher	[byːçɐ]	books
des	[dɛs]	of
düster	[dyːstɐ]	gloomy
die Erde	[eːrdə]	earth
erst	[eːrst]	first
das Erz	[eːrts]	ore
es	[ɛs]	it
der Fluch	[fluːχ]	curse
der Fuß	[fuːs]	foot
das Gespräch	[ɡəˈʃprɛːç]	conversation
die Geburt	[ɡəˈbuːrt]	birth
groß	[ɡroːs]	large, big, tall
größer	[ɡrøːsɐ]	larger, bigger, taller
der Gruß	[ɡruːs]	greeting
der Herd	[heːrt]	stove, hearth
herab	[hɛˈrap]	down
die Hexe	[hɛksə]	witch
hin	[hɪn]	to (direction)
hoch	[hoːχ]	high
höchst	[høːçst]	highest
in, im	[ɪn] [ɪm]	in, in the
das Kloster	[kloːstɐ]	monastery
der Kuchen	[kuːχən]	cake
man	[man]	one
das Maß	[maːs]	measure, amount
mäßig	[mɛːsɪç]	moderately, measured
der Mond	[moːnt]	moon
mit	[mɪt]	with
nach	[naːχ]	after, to, following
das Obst	[oːpst]	fruit
op	[ɔp]	whether

das Ostern	[oːstərn]	Easter
das Pferd	[pfeːrt]	horse
die Schmach	[ʃmaːχ]	disgrace, ridicule
der Schoß	[ʃoːs]	lap, womb, bosom
stets	[ʃteːts]	constantly, invariably
suchen	[zuːχən]	to look for
süß	[zyːs]	sweet
der Trost	[troːst]	comfort
das Tuch	[tuːχ]	cloth
die Tücher	[tyːçɐ]	cloths
um, un-	[ʊm] [ʊn]	around, not/im-/un-/in-
von, vom	[fɔn] [fɔm]	from/of, from/of the
was	[vas]	what
weg	[vɛk]	away
werden	[veːrdən]	to become
der Wert	[veːrt]	value, worth
die Wüste	[vyːstə]	desert
zart	[tsaːrt]	tender, gentle
zum	[tsʊm]	to

Supplementary exercises

In the following exercises, transcribe all words into IPA:

1. [iː] vs. [ɪ]

die Kinder, die Ruine, die Stille, mir, paranoid, innerhalb, ihretwegen, dir, liefern, erschienen, der Blick, kapieren, schieben, das Geschwister, der Finger, bedienen, schminken, befiehlt, die Sinne, ist, vierzehn, vier

2. [eː] [ɛ] [ɛː]

ähnelt, aufheben, das Hemd, die Tränen, mähen, schenken, der Nebel, die Bläser, fester, der Edelstein, das Meer, das Mädchen, tätig, ehrlich,

der Bär, der Seefahrer, lächerlich, der Klempner, die Museen, die Trennung, später, der Mensch, der Verkehr, die Krähe, der Wächter, wäre

3. [aː] vs. [a]

die Gassen, die Tageszeitung, amtlich, der Wohnwagen, der Gast, ahnen,
der Aal, angeln, das Frageszeichen, der Draht, andere, strahlen, bange,
die Auswahl, die Astern, klammern, der Bundesstaat, die Sammlung, das
Ehepaar, der Tannenbaum

4. [oː] vs. [ɔ]

der Hocker, oben, stolpern, die Sonne, das Brot, das Telefon, die Wonne,
das Ohr, hohe, die Wolken, der Strohhalm, zerronnen, sich lohnen, das
Moor, locker, der Zoo, wollen, die Krone, die Post, fromm

5. [uː] vs. [ʊ]

unter, das Ruder, bunt, das Ufer, die Schulter, einlud, verunsichern, die
Juden, stumm, tun, die Truhe, der Mund, der Schuh, die Kunst, ruhig,
der Buhle, die Schuld, die Luft, die Uhren, der Schlummer, fluchen

6. Mixed vowels

köstlich, der Trödelmarkt, örtlich, das Bügeleisen, können, tödlich, das
Ägypten, möchte, überfallen, empören, rötlich, die Gebühr, die Töpfe,
pflücken, die Höhle, der Kühlschrank, anonym, die Röhre, das Glück, die
Ansprüche, das Wörtchen, die Vögel, die Hölle, der Amethyst, dürr

7. Diphthongs

schleichen, kauen, grausam, sich freuen, das Fräulein, vermeiden, heute,
launisch, vergleichen, aufstehen, die Hausfrau, staunen, das Mailand,
betreuen, der Bayer, die Malerei, das Zeugnis, die Zäune

Chapter 18: Consonants

"Consonants are nearly always movements at the beginning or end of a vowel. As we have noted, they are best thought of as gestures of the tongue and lips, like the gestures one makes with one's hand when writing, fluid movements that produce particular shapes" (Ladefoged 2005). Successful consonant production depends on identifying which articulators are involved, achieving the correct position of articulation, and avoiding other muscles from coming into play. If a false articulator is used, e.g., the jaw, the consonant will be hampered and compromised.

As most of the following consonants are similar or identical to their English counterparts, a full description of their production is not repeated in this chapter. Detailed information regarding the formation of consonants common to English and German may be found in Chapter 10 (Consonants). Further, please re-read section 10.1, addressing the importance of efficiency in production, which applies to all languages.

18.1 Voiced vs. voiceless

In lyric diction, consonants may be divided into two distinct groups: voiced and voiceless. Voiced consonants carry the pitch and ensure a seamless legato when sung to their full potential. The pitch essentially never stops when singing through a voiced consonant. By contrast, voiceless consonants must be articulated in between the notes. If their production is labored, the singer is inevitably rhythmically late.

As in English, the timing of voiced and voiceless consonants differs. In general, voiced consonants are to be sung *on the beat*, while voiceless consonants are to be sung *before the beat*. This ensures that the singer does not lag behind the musical pulse and the vowel is always securely on the beat. As voiced consonants carry the pitch, they do not delay the vowel. One must allow enough time to articulate unvoiced consonants, always "taking time" from the previous speech sound. In the following example, take note of the timing for voiced and voiceless consonants.

"Die Lotosblume, op.25, no.7" from *Myrthen,* R. Schumann/H. Heine

In German, the plosive consonants have a greater degree of aspiration compared to their English counterparts. It is a common but unfounded fear that producing aspirated consonants robs the singer of the breath needed for the completion of a successful phrase. In fact, aspirated consonants use residual air, in other words, air that is already present in the mouth. One need not inhale to produce a highly aspirated consonant. As a result, strong aspirates do not use the air required for singing. Strangely, their release allows the singer to have *more* air at the end of the phrase. This is due to the fact that the singer is not holding in the air in an effort to conserve, but rather releasing the air.

Another erroneous concern is that voiceless consonants break the legato singing line. Nothing could be further from the truth. A properly formed and released voiceless consonant bridges the gaps between words, forging a fluid legato line. When there is an absence of legato, this is due to a space or hole in the vocal line.

In German, most voiceless consonants have a corresponding voiced consonant. These pairs are called *cognates,* and are formed with the exact same articulation process.

Table 18.1. Cognates

Voiceless	Voiced
[p]	[b]
[t]	[d]
[k]	[g]
[f]	[v]
[s]	[z]
[ʃ]	[ʒ]
[ç]	[j]

N.B.: The only voiceless consonants without a voiced counterpart are [tʃ] and [χ]. By contrast, several voiced consonants do not have a voiceless partner, e.g., [l], [m], [n], [ŋ].

18.2 Double consonants

In everyday German speech, a double consonant results in a shortened vowel. In lyric diction, one builds upon this principle and actually elongates the double consonant as well. This is not carried out to the same extent as in Italian. Elongated double consonants may be used for dramatic effect, e.g., *der Kummer* [kʊmɐ], meaning grief. It is highly recommended to listen to native German singers to acquire a feeling for this use of word-painting. Note that double consonants are *not* expressed in IPA, although they are consistently extended and preceded by a short vowel. Further, there are two spellings that are considered to be functioning double consonants: *ck, dt*.

"Widmung, op.25, no.1" from *Myrthen*, R. Schumann/F. Rückert

In the above example, note that the double consonant is sounded halfway through the note value on the words *Himmel* and *bessres*. By rhythmically anticipating the double consonant, it is elongated without impeding the overall rhythmic flow of the phrase. One must take care to vibrate through the prolonged [m], as well as maintain an even airflow through the extended [s]. The listener's attention is drawn to both of these words through the expressive elongation of the double consonants.

18.3 Individual consonants

Plosives (Stops) [b][p][d][t][g][k]

[b]   Lowercase B   Voiced bilabial plosive
Spelling: *b, bb*

der Berg	[bɛrk]	mountain
krabbeln	[krabəln]	to crawl

[p]   Lowercase P   Voiceless bilabial plosive
Spelling: *p, pp, b* (latter only at end of word element)

der Parkplatz	[paɾkplats]	parking lot/space
doppelt	[dɔpəlt]	double
gelb	[gɛlp]	yellow

Production: The cognates [b] and [p] require the same action of the lips and forward release. They are identical to their English counterparts. Note that the lips should never purse or roll inwards in an effort to produce a stronger consonant.

[d]   Lowercase D   Voiced alveolar plosive
Spelling: *d, dd*

| der Donnerstag | [dɔnəɾstaːk] | Thursday |
| paddeln | [padəln] | to canoe, to paddle |

[t]   Lowercase T   Voiceless alveolar plosive
Spelling: *t, th, tt, dt, d* (latter only at end of word element)

die Treue	[trɔøə]	fidelity, loyalty
die Apotheke	[apoˈteːkə]	pharmacy, apothecary
der Rettich	[rɛtɪç]	radish
die Verwandte	[fɛɐ̯ˈvantə]	relatives
der Grund	[grʊnt]	reason, cause

N.B.: The spelling *dt* functions and is pronounced as a double consonant.

Production: The cognates [d] and [t] require the same action of the tongue. They are virtually identical to their English counterparts. Specifically, the German [t] is more aspirated, demanding slightly more time for its execution.

[g]   Lowercase G   Voiced velar plosive
Spelling: *g, gg*

| der Garten | [gartən] | garden |
| anbaggern | [anbagərn] | to flirt with, to hit on |

[k]   Lowercase K   Voiceless velar plosive
Spelling: *k, kk, ck, g* (latter only at end of word element)

die Erkältung	[ɛɐ̯ˈkɛltʊŋ]	common cold
das/der Sakko	[zakoː]	blazer, sportcoat
knicken	[knɪkən]	to bend
genug	[gəˈnuːk]	enough

N.B.: das Orchester [ɔrˈkɛstɐ], das Café [kaˈfeː], der Charakter [kaˈraktɐ]

N.B.: The spelling *ck* functions and is pronounced as a double consonant.

Production: The cognates [g] and [k] require the same action of the tongue. They are virtually identical to their English counterparts. Specifically, the German [k] is more aspirated, demanding slightly more time for its execution. It is recommended to imagine these consonants as being palatal to ensure that both consonants are not produced too far back in the mouth. In forming [k] and [g], variations in the exact point of articulation exist, depending on the nature of the following vowel (Jones 1962).

Practice speaking and intoning *kalt* [kalt] and *das Kino* [kiːnoː], noting how the different position of the tongue affects the exact point of articulation for [k].

"Süßer Freund, du blickest, op.42, no.6" from *Frauenliebe und -leben*, R. Schumann/A.v. Chamisso

In the above example, note how the *ck* in *blickest* functions as a double consonant. Namely, it is anticipated rhythmically and thus elongated, falling halfway between the repeated eighth notes. The double consonant in *Süßer* (sweet) adds to the exquisite color of the highest and longest note in the phrase. The fact that the husband is gazing at her with absolute wonder may be illustrated by a lean on the word *blickest*. Lyric diction provides a myriad of interpretive possibilities.

Fricatives [v][f][z][s][ʒ][ʃ][h][j][ç][χ]

All German fricatives are classified as continuants and therefore may last as long as there is breath supply.

[v]   Lowercase V   Voiced labiodental fricative
Spelling: *w, v*

der Löwe	[lø:və]	lion
die Universität	[univɛrzi'tɛ:t]	university

[f]   Lowercase F   Voiceless labiodental fricative
Spelling: *f, ff, v, ph* (latter only in borrowed foreign words)

das Fenster	[fɛnstɐ]	window
hoffentlich	[hɔfəntlıç]	hopefully
viele	[fi:lə]	many

physisch   [fy:zɪʃ]   physical, corporal

Production: The cognates [v] and [f] are produced with the exact same
articulation process and are identical to their English counterparts. It is
imperative that the lips be relaxed. Any tension in the labia will result in
a tight consonant that is difficult to sustain. Both [v] and [f] may be anticipated for expressive use. This is left to the singer's discretion.

[z]   Lowercase Z   Voiced alveolar fricative
Spelling: *s*

die Suppe   [zʊpə]   soup

[s]   Lowercase S   Voiceless alveolar fricative
Spelling: *s, ss, ß*

der Trost   [troːst]   solace, consolation
der Schlüssel   [ʃlʏsəl]   key
der Fleiß   [flaes]   diligence

Production: The cognates [z] and [s] are produced with the exact same
articulation process and are identical to their English counterparts. Take
care to sing through [z], keeping the air in constant motion.

[ʒ]   Ezh   Voiced postalveolar fricative
Spelling: *g, j*

die Etage   [eˈtaːʒə]   floor (e.g., 1st floor)
der Journalist   [ʒʊrnaˈlɪst]   journalist

N.B.: In German, words using [ʒ] are borrowed from French. In loan words, not all closed vowels are long (or expressed with the colon [ː]).

[ʃ]   Esh   Voiceless postalveolar fricative
Spelling: *sch, s* (before *p, t*)

fantastisch	[fanˈtastɪʃ]	fantastic
das Spiel	[ʃpiːl]	game, match
stumm	[ʃtʊm]	mute

Production: The cognates [ʒ] and [ʃ] are produced with the exact same articulation process and are identical to their English counterparts. Note that the consonant blends *sp* and *st* result in [ʃ] only at the beginning of a word or word element. Otherwise, they are pronounced [sp] and [st], e.g., der Geburtstag [ɡəˈbuːrtstaːk], gestern [ɡɛstərn].

[h]   Lowercase H   Voiceless glottal fricative
Spelling: *h*

heftig	[hɛftɪç]	acute, severe

Production: This phoneme is identical to its English counterpart. N.B.: If *h* occurs after a vowel, it is silent, e.g., sehr [zeːɐ], die Mühe [myːə].

[ʝ] [ç] [χ]
Please consult Chapter 16 (Characteristic German Phonemes) for complete descriptions of Curly-tail J [ʝ], *ich-laut* [ç], and *ach-laut* [χ].

Nasals [m][n][ŋ]
[m]   Lowercase M   Voiced bilabial nasal
Spelling: *m, mm*

| der Maler | [maːlɐ] | painter |
| schwimmen | [ʃvɪmən] | to swim |

[n]   Lowercase N   Voiced alveolar nasal
Spelling: *n, nn*

| die Nacht | [naχt] | night |
| die Sonne | [zɔnə] | sun |

[ŋ]   Eng   Voiced velar nasal
Spelling: *ng, n* (before *k*)

| lange | [laŋə] | long |
| trinken | [trɪŋkən] | to drink |

Production: All three nasal consonants are identical to their English counterparts. All are classified as continuants and therefore may last as long as there is breath supply. Unless produced properly, nasal consonants can hinder legato. Further, one should be sure to keep a sense of vertical height at the back of the mouth to combat the fact that the soft palate is lowered.

Rhythmic timing: As in English, both [m] and [n] may be executed before or on the beat, depending on the melodic context.

Laterals [l]
[l]   Lowercase L   Voiced alveolar lateral
Spelling: *l, ll*

| der Leiter | [laetɐ] | leader, manager |
| wollen | [vɔlən] | to intend/want to |

Production: This phoneme is identical to its English counterpart (the clear *l*). There are no other allophones of *l* in German. It releases in a quick downward movement that immediately prepares the next consonant or vowel. Note that the jaw is not connected to the production of [l]. It is crucial that singers have jaw/tongue independence for the proper, efficient production of this phoneme.

N.B.: When found in combination with another voiced consonant, it is imperative that [l] be considered the primary consonant and be pitched on the beat. If the first voiced consonant is emphasized, a shadow vowel inevitably occurs. This principle exists in English, as well. Examples include *bleiben* [blaebən], *blind* [blɪnt], *glauben* [glaobən], *das Glas* [glaːs].

Trills [r]

This text advocates the sole use of a one-tapped trill (a.k.a. flipped *r*) in lyric diction. One may choose to roll *r* (expressed as [r]) when singing certain German operatic or oratorio repertoire.

[r]   Fish-hook R   Voiced alveolar tap
Spelling: *r, rr*

| die Reise | [raezə] | trip, journey |
| die Herren | [hɛrən] | gentlemen |

Production: The tongue-tip begins lightly touching the lower teeth, moving vertically to quickly tap the alveolar ridge once. It returns immediately to the lower teeth in a swift motion. For efficient production, the tongue must be relaxed. Note that only the tip of the tongue is involved. The flipped *r* [r] is identical to its French and Italian counterparts, e.g., *train* [trɛ̃], *paura* [pauːra], respectively.

Affricates [ts][tʃ]

[ts]   T-S ligature   Voiceless dental or alveolar affricate

Spelling: *ts, tz, z, c, ti* (latter two in borrowed foreign words)

rechts	[rɛçts]	right
der Satz	[zats]	sentence, phrase
zwei	[tsvae]	two
Cäcilie	[tsɛˈtsiːliə]	Cecilia
die Nation	[naˈtsioːn]	nation, country

N.B.: die Skizze [skɪtsə], die Pizza [pɪtsə], abends [aːbənts], die Aktien [aktsiən]

[tʃ]   T-Esh ligature   Voiceless postalveolar affricate

Spelling: *tsch*

der Klatsch	[klatʃ]	gossip

Production: Both [ts] and [tʃ] are identical to their English counterparts.

Additional consonants borrowed from foreign words: *q, x*

[kv]

Spelling: *qu*

das Quartier	[kvarˈtiːɐ]	quarter (neighborhood)

[ks]

Spelling: *x, chs*

die Boxen	[bɔksən]	music speakers
sechs	[zɛks]	six

N.B.: Contrary to English, [gz] does not exist in German. The prefix *ex-* is solely pronounced [ks], e.g., *die Examen* [ɛˈksaːmən].

18.4 Consonant blends, contractions

In general, consonants are pronounced individually, unless they combine to form one speech sound, e.g., *sch* [ʃ]. German has a preponderance of consonant blends, which are produced in one gesture of articulation. Often, there are many succeeding consonants forming a cluster. This demands that one move rapidly through each consonant, clearly speaking each, and omitting none. One must also take care not to insert vowels in between consonants or after final consonants (a.k.a. shadow vowels). As in English, if both consonants in the blend are voiced, it is important that the second consonant be treated as the primary consonant, voicing it on the beat, e.g., *bl, gl, br, dr*. Note that all consonant blends occur within the space of one syllable. Indeed, there may be as many as eight consonants in succession, depending on the given context.

sprechen	[ˈʃprɛçən]	to speak, talk
du schi**mpfst**	[duː ˈʃɪmpfst]	you complain
die Kam**pfsz**ene	[ˈkampfstseːnə]	fight scene
du beka**mpfst Str**eit	[duː bəˈkɛmpfst ˈʃtraet]	you fight controversy

Common consonant blends

bl bleiben, die Blamierung, blind, das Blech, blamieren, blöd, die Blüte

br bringen, brechen, der Brand, brennen, das Brötchen, der Bruch

chs wachsen, der Lachs, drechseln, sechs, wechseln, die Achsel, der Ochs

dr drinnen, der Draht, dringen, droben, dröhnen, die Drogerie, drollig

fl das Fleisch, die Flöhe, fliehen, geflimmert, fliessen, die Flamme

fr froh, der Frühling, der Frieden, die Freundin, fromm, frisch, frei

gl glühen, die Gläser, der Glanz, gleich, die Glatze, gleiten, die Glut

gn gnädig, das Signal, Wagner, leugnen, die Gnade, der Gnom, segnen

gr größer, grün, der Gram, das Grab, die Grüße, grimmig, die Grenze

kl klingeln, die Klarheit, klassisch, der Klee, das Kloster, das Klavier

kn der Knecht, der Knabe, knapp, knistern, der Knödel, der Knoblauch

kr der Krach, kriechen, der Krieg, die Krönung, die Krawatte, der Kreis

kt der Punkt, die Aspekte, bedankt, verschenkt, die Akte, respektieren

ld das Feld, das Geld, hold, der Held, der Wald, bald, die Schuld, mild

nd der Abend, das Kind, die Hand, der Verstand, das Band, die Gegend

ng der Sänger, der Finger, singen, der Gesang, der Lehrgang, hängen

nk trinken, bedanken, sinken, denken, die Bank, das Getränk, links

pf pfiffig, der Pfeffer, der Pfennig, kämpfen, das Pferd, der Dampf

pl das Plakat, die Pläne, plaudern, plötzlich, plosiv, plündern, plappern

pr die Probe, prost, die Pracht, der Prinz, primär, das Problem, privat

ps der Psalter, psychisch, die Psyche, die Kapseln, der Psychiater

qu die Qual, die Quelle, quadratisch, der Quatsch, quälen, das Quartett

sk die Muskatnuß, die Maske, die Sklaverei, skeptisch, der Skandal

sp die Knospe, lispeln, haspeln, die Wespe, raspeln, die Espe

st gestern, lästern, das Ostern, das Muster, das Poster, der Knast

sz die Szene, das Szenarium, szenisch, das Szepter, der Auszug

tr die Trennung, der Traum, trösten, die Tränen, treffen, die Treue

ts nichts, ist's, gibt's, rückwärts, der Abfahrtstag, abseits, angesichts

tz der Besitz, die Sätze, der Platz, der Spatz, die Hitze, klotzig, setzen

Additional consonant combinations

dsch der Dschungel, die Dschunke

ph der Physiker, die Philosophie, physisch, die Philharmonie, die Phase

sch der Schlummer, schenken, der Schrank, schwimmen, die Schublade

th roth, das Thema, das Theater, der Thunfisch, Thule, ätherisch

tsch tschechisch, das Tschechien, klatschen, quatschen, knutschen

Some consonant blends occur as a result of a contraction, when a vowel preceding the consonants [l], [n], and [r] is omitted. In these cases, the initial consonant is *devoiced*. In other words, the consonant is no longer fully voiced. In order to achieve a devoiced consonant, one should strive to produce a voiced consonant but stop the production midway. This is a principle similar to implosion. In IPA, a devoiced consonant is expressed with a subscript, e.g., [d̥]. This text does not employ this symbol, as it is understood that devoicing occurs in all such contractions. N.B.: the consonants subject to devoicing are limited to [b], [d], and [g].

edel	[eːdəl]	elegant
ein edler Mann	[eːdlɐ]	an elegant man
mager	[maːgɐ]	meager, gaunt
die magre Frau	[maːgrə]	the skinny woman

Practice speaking the following words with a fully voiced consonant, noting the appearance of an intrusive shadow vowel. Then, devoice the initial consonant of the blend, as if it were imploded/exploded:

edle, die Wandlung, magre, der Wandrer, die Handlung, Wagner, regnerisch, ebnen, irdne, die Ordnung, leugnen, der Redner, obrer, der Adler

Supplementary exercises

In the following exercises, transcribe all words into IPA.

1. Plosives (Stops) [b][p][d][t][g][k]

Rembrandt, täglich, gern, ausbilden, die Tastatur, die Nachtigall, das Buch, sabbern, aggressiv, das Tier, kribbeln, beflaggen, das Publikum, damals, die Bibliothek, die Kirche, das Gepäck, die Kupplung, klein, das Thema, schleppen, die Kehle, das Laub, spöttisch, der Zug, drücken, der Papierkorb, der Ausdruck, der Ritter, der Dezember, die Städte, wickeln

2. **Fricatives** [v][f][z][s][ʒ][ʃ][h]

die Jury, die Wolken, der Ausweis, die Schere, wohnen, das Ventil, der
Schüler, festhalten, die Kurve, spucken, der Feind, küssen, der Spion, die
Forelle, das Treffen, der Stoff, das Messer, vorüber, abservieren, lesen,
der Hase, der Spaß, verboten, aktiv, stehlen, das Phantom, die Hälfte,
die Süßigkeiten, die Phase, heilen, gelieren, streben

3. **Nasals** [m][n][ŋ]

die Wangen, nimmer, vernichtet, klingeln, innig, winken, der Mensch,
der Rang, die Milch, die Badewanne, die Spange, annähern, das Lamm,
rennen, der Markt, nein, bummeln, die Tonne, die Nummer, der Mangel,
die Tankstelle, die Füllung, die Überschwemmung

4. [ç] vs. [χ]

eckig, der Bach, zugig, tauchen, zackig, suchen, der Kranich, auch, die
Sprüche, der Bauch, tüchtig, leicht, durch, räuchern, (du) sprachst, euch,
der Nachbar, die Chemie, (du) brauchst, der Chirurg, machen, der Chi-
nese, die Flucht, manchmal, die Achtung, das Mäuschen, das Herzchen,
das Buch, richten, die Rache

5. [ɾ] vs. [ʁ]

derart, die Freiheit, rasch, heiter, arbeiten, erkennen, die Karre, schrei-
ben, irre, vorbereiten, vergleichen, röntgen, die Erscheinung, der Bruder,
eher, derselbe, weiterhin, der Kerl, berühren, der Zwirn, die Rettung,
erzählen, werden

6. **Contractions** (devoicing)

ebnen, übler, goldne, handle, der Wandrer, andrer, unsrer, regnerisch,
der Bildner, der Redner, die Ordnung, wandle, obrer, leugnen, Friedrich,
Leibnitz, ew'gen, freud'ge, eurer, eigne, Wagner

Chapter 19: Advanced Concepts in Diction

The following chapter addresses advanced concepts in lyric diction that promote the idiomatic treatment of German, without compromising clarity. This includes the lyric and phrasal doubling of consonants, the execution of phrasal consonant clusters, as well as the use of implosion/explosion in incidental words. The varied treatment of consonants is extremely important, especially in terms of legato singing. As in English, consonants should always be merged without the occurrence of a shadow vowel, resulting from a drop or movement of the articulators.

19.1 Lyric and phrasal doubling of consonants

When a double consonant is elongated for the purpose of emphasis or word-painting, this is referred to as *lyric doubling*. The consonant becomes a greater part of the melodic line, as it is anticipated rhythmically and thus elongated. Note that a doubled voice consonant is voiced on the previous pitch, since it is actually produced early. In the following example, the word *unnennbare* consists of two pairs of *nn* and translates to mean "unspeakable, unutterable". Such a word at the end of such a profound song deserves special treatment, provided by Wolf in the form of a hemiola and a strong tempo change. If a singer augments this by doubling both *n's*, it highlights the meaning of this word and serves to naturally broaden the final phrase. It is quite unusual to sing for this amount of time on an [n], especially within one word.

"Im Frühling," H. Wolf/E. Mörike

When a final consonant merges with an identical initial consonant of an adjacent word, it is possible to form a double consonant. This is referred to as *phrasal doubling* and is based solely on context. Its use is highly recommended when the words involved are worthy of emphasis in the overall phrase. Moreover, expressive doubling presents the singer with greater interpretive possibilities. However, if the two words joined in this manner have little meaning or importance grammatically, elision may be used instead. Ultimately, this is left to the singer's discretion.

"Meine Liebe ist grün, op.63, no.5," J. Brahms/F. Schumann

In the above example, note the phrasal doubling that occurs in *viel liebestrunkene*. In each word of this phrase, [l] is featured prominently, ending with *Lieder*. The anticipated [l] is voiced on the first pitch and then released on the B-flat (taking care to spin through this pitch), the tongue moving swiftly and directly to form [i:]. All words "move" toward the end of the phrase, whereby the singer hands over the melody to the piano for a climactic postlude. N.B.: As *liebestrunkene* is a compound word, it is critical to stress this word solely on the first syllable.

19.2 Phrasal consonant clusters

The term *phrasal consonant cluster* refers to the joining of consonants for the purpose of sustained legato. A cluster is formed when two adjacent words end and begin with a consonant. This happens very frequently in German and often is a cause for unneeded panic on the part of the singer. For example, practice speaking the phrase *In dem Schatten meiner Locken* [ɪn deːm ʃatən maenɐ lɔkən], noting that all words are joined. The resulting phrasal consonant clusters are *nd* [nd], *msch* [mʃ], and *nm* [nm]. In this example, it is important to maintain the spin while singing through the nasal consonants ([m][n]). When these continuants are truly voiced, the pitch continues at the same intensity as the vowels. The line never ceases, whether moving through vowels or consonants (voiced or voiceless). There is *always* time to pronounce all consonants within a cluster, even if it seems that the composer has left little space.

"Erstes Liebeslied eines Mädchens," H. Wolf/E. Mörike

In the above example, note the phrasal consonant clusters that are formed. The execution of voiceless clusters, such as *tschm* [tʃm] in *mit Schmiegen,* is facilitated by taking time from the previous word/note. As a result, the rhythm will not be compromised. One must find the correct balance between clear, efficient articulation of the consonant clusters and a strong lean on the vowel or consonant directly following the cluster. For example, the emphasis of [m] in *Schmiegen* and [l] in *schlüpft's* anchors the words and propels the phrase in a forward direction. Note that both of these voiced consonants fall *on the beat.*

"Auf dem Wasser zu singen, op.72," F. Schubert/F.L. Graf zu Stolberg

In the above example, the elongation and anticipation of double consonants maintain the direction and intensity of the melodic line. The actual vowel on *sanft* will be quite short to allow for the subsequent phrasal consonant cluster *nftsch* [nftʃ] formed by *sanft schimmernden.* This translates as "soft shimmering," providing great opportunity for word-painting. It is crucial to remain calm while allowing the tip of the tongue and the lips to do the work. The even breath stream provides the wave or *Welle* upon which all vowels and consonants effortlessly ride.

19.3 Treatment of monosyllabic, incidental words

An incidental word refers to a small word of weak grammatical importance, e.g., conjunction, preposition, article, or auxiliary verb. They are frequently monosyllabic and are very prevalent in the German language. Modifiers describe other words and thus are always "moving" to the stronger words in the sentence, e.g., adjectives and adverbs. This creates a natural, idiomatic inflection, which is indispensable for the conveyance and communication of a poem.

Implosion/explosion

Implosion/explosion promotes a stronger legato line by allowing for greater continuity of sound. It also serves to effectively highlight the hierarchical importance of words. As in English, a consonant is imploded when its production is stopped prior to becoming aspirated (for a

voiceless consonant) or fully voiced (for a voiced consonant). A consonant is exploded as the air pressure is suddenly released. In everyday
German speech, implosion/explosion occurs quite frequently. For example, in the phrase *mit dem* (with the), [t] is imploded, while [d] is exploded. There is a brief moment of suspension as the tongue lingers in
the position of [t] without allowing it to become aspirated. The tongue-
tip is firmly attached to the alveolar ridge, while a light pressure builds
up. Then, [d] quickly releases into the subsequent vowel.

If one does not follow the implosion/explosion pattern in lyric diction, it results in a German that sounds over-mannered and pedantic.
The only exceptions occur if a particular word is emphasized for artistic,
interpretive purposes, or if clarity or comprehension would otherwise be
compromised. Note that implosion/explosion is *not* expressed in IPA.

"Lied der Mignon, op.62, no.2," F. Schubert/J.W. v. Goethe

In the above example, implosion/explosion occurs with the text
missgönnt der and *nicht die*. Take care that the exploded [d] does not
poke out of the melodic line upon release. This is avoided by matching
the degree of pressure building up in the implosion to the explosion. The
legato line is easy to realize and the sense of forward direction is clear.

Occurrence of implosion/explosion of consonants

1. Within a word

mitteilen [mɪtaelən], weggelassen [vɛkgəlasən], süddeutsch [zyːtdɔøtʃ],
abbiegen [apbiːgən], abblenden [apblɛndən], forttreiben [fɔrtraebən],
mitdenken [mɪtdɛŋkən], weggeben[vɛkgeːbən], entdecken [ɛntˈdɛkən]

2. Adjacent words, same consonant

und zu [ʊnt tsuː], mit tausend [mɪt taozənt]

3. Adjacent words, cognates

mit dem [mɪt deːm], mit der [mɪt deːɐ], hat den [hat deːn], hat die [hat diː], und die [ʊnt diː], nicht dein [nɪçt daen], bist du [bɪst duː]

[p] / [b]

abbrechen	[apbrɛçən]	to discontinue
halbbewußt	[halpbəvʊst]	half-aware

[t] / [d] and [t] / [t]

norddeutsch	[nɔrtdɔøtʃ]	northern German
das Handtuch	[hantuːχ]	towel

[k] / [g] and [k] / [k]

der Fluggast	[fluːkgast]	flight passenger
die Wegkreuzung	[veːkrɔøtsʊŋ]	crossroads

In the following example, note the use of implosion/explosion on the words *mit tausend Thränen*. It is particularly effective if the exploded [t] is notably aspirated upon release. This draws one's attention to both *tausend* and *Thränen*. One can vary the degree of aspiration to further personalize the performance. Implosion/explosion aids in revealing a magical suspension and the ultimate arrival of a lengthy melodic ascent.

"Peregrina II," H. Wolf/E. Mörike

If clarity or comprehension is in danger of being compromised, it is best not to use implosion/explosion. In the following example, *tritt die* is pronounced without imploding the [t], allowing the aspirate to flow cleanly into the subsequent [d]. Were it imploded, it would be impossible to discern the word *tritt* (treads), an important word in this phrase.

"Die Nacht, op.10, no.3," R. Strauss/H.v. Gilm

| Aus | dem | Wal | - | de | tritt | die | Nacht, |
| ao | sdeːm | va | | ldə | trɪ | t diː | na | χt |

Vowel changes: strong and weak forms

Monosyllabic, incidental words may be "strong" or "weak" depending on grammatical and musical context. This principle, known as *gradation*, occurs in German but to a much lesser extent than in English. In German, solely the length of the vowel is affected, e.g., *der Mann* [deɐ man] vs. *mit der* [mɪt deːɐ]. A weak form is merely a shortened version of the same vowel, i.e., the colon is not used. Often, the decision regarding which form to use has already been determined by the composer.

Table 19.1. Strong and weak forms

	Strong	**Weak**	
dem	[deːm]	[dem]	to the
der	[deːɐ]	[deɐ]	the (masculine)
die	[diː]	[di]	the (feminine)
für	[fyːɐ]	[fyɐ]	for
hat	[haːt]	[hat]	(he/she) has
vor	[foːɐ]	[foɐ]	in front of, before

Supplementary exercises

In the following exercises, speak and intone all of the words, taking care to execute implosion/explosion. Further, transcribe into IPA.

1. abbauen, abbinden, abbrechen, anfärbbar, antreibbar, aufhebbar, taubblind, der Erbbesitz, der Farbbildschirm, der Schriebbedarf, halbbedeckt, die Gelbbeeren, der Laubbach, das Scheibband, vererbbar

2. die Bilddarstellung, die Enddaten, der Erddruck, der Felddienst, der Golddraht, die Morddrohung, das Norddeutschland, das Sanddorf, der Endteil, die Schilddrüse, süddeutsch, der Blinddarm, der Endtermin, der Grundtarif, die Geldtasche, das Grundthema, der Landtag, der Liedtext, die Abenddämmerung

3. der Berggipfel, der Burggraben, die Fluggesellschaft, weggebracht, der Zuggurt, das Weggeben, weglassen, weggenommen

Chapter 20: Common Pitfalls

When singing in German, there are many common errors that befall singers. Many mistakes are related to inefficient consonant production, improper movement of the articulators, use of unwanted diphthongs, or the adoption of colloquialisms from the German vernacular or *Umgangssprache*. This chapter addresses various common pitfalls that one encounters in German lyric diction and may be used as a reference guide.

1. Improper use of R

It is not recommended to use the uvular R [ʁ] in German lyric diction. While this phoneme is common in everyday speech, it is not used in singing. This text recommends the sole use of [ɾ] or [ɐ] for all art song repertoire. Occasionally, rolled [r] may be chosen for word-painting. This is an interpretive device that is left to the singer's discretion. Moreover, in oratorio and operatic repertoire, [r] may be used to aid in projection when singing against a thick orchestral texture.

2. Shadow vowels

Consonants should be merged without allowing any space in between phonemes, or any movement of the articulators. Shadow vowels may be avoided by certifying that a given consonant is completely finished production before the articulators move to form the next sound. Consonant blends must be pronounced in a single gesture, while keeping the integrity of the individual consonant. One must take care to sing through voiced blends and keep releasing the air during voiceless blends. If the initial consonant is treated as the primary (as opposed to the second consonant), often a shadow vowel will result. This common error results in an instant Italianate accent.

bleiben	[blaebən] not [bəlaebən]	to stay, to remain
träumen	[trɔømən] not [tərɔømən]	to dream

In monosyllabic words ending in [ɐ] or [l], it is easy for a shadow vowel to be falsely inserted. This occurs when the articulators move out of the position for the previous phoneme. In the case of [ɐ], this phoneme cannot exist as its own syllable, or it results in a vowel akin to [ɑ]. One should never draw attention to the weak syllable.

viel	[fiːl] not [fiːəl]	much, lots
wir	[viːɐ] not [viːɑ]	we

3. Use of diphthongs instead of monophthongs

During the production of any monophthong, it is imperative that the articulators involved in forming a given phoneme remain in the same position. Indeed, any movement of the tongue or the lips interferes with and influences the existing phoneme. This results in a different vowel than originally intended, or a sound that is not free, since the tongue is part of the vowel.

As English has ten diphthongs, English native speakers often feel the need to "wind off" a German vowel, adding a glide or a vanish vowel to the pure vowel at the very last moment. Sometimes singers anticipate the next word or syllable, unconsciously moving the tongue or the lips. This commences the formation of the next sound before it is time to do so. German is characterized by many pure monophthongs that are highly focused in nature. In order to achieve authenticity in [iː], [eː], or [oː], it is imperative that the intensity and integrity of the vowel remain, from the initial onset until the beginning of the subsequent phoneme.

4. Mispronunciation of the *schwa*

As previously discussed in Chapter 16 (Characteristic German Phonemes), the German *schwa* is known as the *vocalic chameleon*. It changes color depending on its environment. In order for this to occur, it is crucial that the *schwa* be pronounced in the exact position of the previous vowel. For this to happen, the articulators must also remain in the same position. If the tongue moves before or during production of the *schwa*, the result will be [ɛ]. Similarly, [œ] is formed if the lips round before or during production of the *schwa*. Compared to other languages this treatment of the *schwa* is unique. As a result, this prevalent unstressed phoneme is hardly noticeable, as it constantly matches its surroundings. Further, the natural ebb and flow of the German language is fully palpable.

5. False use of glottal onsets

While a fresh, clean glottal onset is an important component of German lyric diction, it may be used too frequently and improperly. All glottal onsets should be *soft* in nature, initiated in the position of the impending vowel. Often a preceding consonant that is released in a forward motion will negate the necessity for a strong glottal attack. Plosives are especially useful in this respect and aid in keeping the legato line, as the aspirate fills the gap between words without bleeding into the next word. Singers tend to start every word commencing in a vowel with a strong glottal attack. However, the use of a glottal onset is dependent on context and word setting. For example, if a phrase begins with a vowel, there is never a need to start with a glottal onset. A hard glottal attack should be avoided at all costs. This is a bad habit borrowed from both English and German colloquial speech.

6. Mispronunciation of contractions

Contractions abound in German, often a result of a missing *schwa*. The newly formed consonant cluster may be quite awkward to pronounce and is often mispronounced in one of two ways: 1) insertion of shadow vowel, 2) aspiration of initial consonant in blend, instead of devoicing. It is easy for a shadow vowel to occur when fully voicing the initial consonant. Moreover, if the initial consonant is aspirated, it suggests that one is at the end of a word or word element, which is not the case. Instead, it must be devoiced, a process very similar to implosion.

| andrer | [andɾɐ] not [andəɾə] | other, another |
| eignen | [aegnən] not [aeknən] | one's own |

7. Omitting sounds in consonant clusters

When presented with consonant clusters within one word or in the context of a sentence, it is easy to rush and omit the occasional consonant. It cannot be stressed often enough that one *always* has time to execute all of the consonants, no matter what the tempo. If all consonants are produced efficiently with an economy of movement, they will flow smoothly and imperceptibly into the next phoneme.

| es spricht | [ɛs ʃpɾɪçt] not [ɛʃpɾɪçt] | (it) speaks |
| das Sehnen | [das zeːnən] not [daseːnən] | longing, yearning |

8. Using jaw as an active articulator

The lips, teeth, tongue, hard and soft palates are considered to be articulators. Active articulators, e.g., lips, tongue, soft palate, move in precise movements to form consonants and vowels. Conversely, passive articulators are approached or contacted, e.g., teeth, hard palate. Although the jaw falls open naturally to allow for enough space to form certain phonemes, it is *not* directly involved in the production or maintenance of any vowels or consonants. Similarly, the jaw is never involved in supporting the breath while singing.

9. Tongue tension

The base of the tongue attaches just above the larynx. If the tongue is curled back and held, it results in a swallowed, tense sound. If the tongue is lifted too high at the back, it becomes too close to the soft palate, resulting in a fuzzy tone. Similarly, the tongue is never involved in supporting the breath while singing.

PART IV: ENGLISH AND GERMAN—COMMON GROUND

Chapter 21: Commonalities Between English and German

This section presents a summary of the main commonalities between English and German. It is intended to be a quick reference guide.

21.1 Common vowels and consonants

Vowels

English: [i] [ɪ] [ɛ] [ɔ] [o] [ʊ] [u]
German: [iː] [ɪ] [ɛ] [ɔ] [oː][ʊ] [uː]

The monophthong [o] exists in English, but only in certain unstressed positions, e.g., omit [oˈmɪt]. In German, this shortened phoneme is present in loan words of non-Germanic origin, e.g., *orientalisch* [oɾiɛnˈtaːlɪʃ].

N.B.: A phoneme halfway between [i]/[iː] and [ɪ] is represented as [ɪ]. This occurs in both English and German and is indicated by certain spellings. Some sources transcribe this sound as [i], also known as "Barred I". This text prefers to use [ɪ] exclusively. This hybrid sound is classified as a closed vowel, but it is slightly lower and less intense than [i].

English: final *y* or *–ies*

fancy   [fænsɪ]   cities   [sɪtɪs]

German: *ich, -ig*

sicherlich   [zɪçərlɪç]   ruhig   [ruːɪç]

Consonants

English: [b] [d] [f] [g] [h] [k] [m] [n] [ŋ] [p] [r] [s] [t] [v] [ts]
German: [b] [d] [f] [g] [h] [k] [m] [n] [ŋ] [p] [r] [s] [t] [v] [ts]

Table 21.1. Common cognates in English and German

Voiceless	Voiced
[p]	[b]
[t]	[d]
[k]	[g]
[f]	[v]
[s]	[z]
[ʃ]	[ʒ]

21.2 Treatment of monosyllabic, incidental words

Table 21.2. Strong and weak forms in English and German

		Strong	**Weak**
English	am	[æm]	[əm]
	and	[ænd]	[ənd]
	as	[æz]	[əz]
	can	[kæn]	[kən]
	for	[fɔə]	[fə]
	from	[fɹʌm]	[fɹəm]
	has	[hæz]	[həz]

Continued on next page

Table 21.2—Continued

		Strong	Weak
	have	[hæv]	[həv]
	of	[ʌv]	[əv]
German	dem	[deːm]	[dem]
	der	[deːɐ]	[deɐ]
	die	[diː]	[di]
	für	[fyːɐ]	[fyɐ]
	hat	[haːt]	[hat]
	vor	[foːɐ]	[foɐ]

21.3 Concise comparison of the *schwa*

English: Idiomatic inflection in English is characterized by the principle of stress and "unstress". The substitution of pure vowels for the *schwa*, e.g., [ɪ], [ɛ], [ɑ], results in a stilted, pedantic treatment of the language. The *schwa* is spelled with all vowels and is identical to [ʌ]. It only exists in unstressed syllables.

German: In German, the *schwa* changes its color according to its environment and hence is known as the *vocalic chameleon*. It is always formed and pronounced in the position of the previous vowel. The *schwa* is only spelled with *e* and is not identical to any other phoneme. It only exists in unstressed syllables.

21.4 Voiced and voiceless consonants: rhythmic timing

In both English and German, voiced consonants are to be sung *on the beat*, as they do not delay the vowel. An anticipated voiced consonant results in an unwanted scoop or slow onset. Conversely, voiceless consonants are timed *before the beat*, in between the notes in the melodic line. All consonant clusters are to be articulated cleanly and efficiently. There is always time to pronounce every consonant in a given cluster.

Practice speaking and intoning the following consonant combinations, taking care to avoid any space between consonants. In both languages, the resulting phrasal cluster should feel as if it were one word.

[s] /[ts]

In order to pronounce this cluster cleanly, divide it into two parts ([s] and [ts]), rather than three separate consonants ([s][t][s]).

English: beasts [bists], tastes [teɪsts], texts [tɛksts], rests [ɹɛsts], wastes [weɪsts], guests [gɛsts], feasts [fists], ghosts [goʊsts], boasts [boʊsts], casts [kæsts], hastes [heɪsts], twists [twɪsts], firsts [fɜsts], lasts [læsts]

German: die Szene [stseːnə], das Ausflugsziel [aosfluːkstsiːl], die Auszahlung [aostsaːluŋ], die Betriebszeit [bə'triːpstsaet], das Einkaufszentrum [aenkaofstsɛntrʊm], die Tageszeitung [taːgəstsaetuŋ], das Todeszeichen [toːdəstsaeçən], losziehen [loːstsiːən], ist's [ɪsts]

"Abendempfindung," W.A. Mozart/J.H. Campe

Bald	ent-flieht	des __	Le -	bens __	bun - te __	Szene, __
ba	lt∫ɛ ntfliː	tdɛ	sleː	bə	nsbʊ ntə	stseː nə

[ts]

English: cats [kæts], dates [deɪts], tzatziki [tsæt'siki], tsetse fly [tsitsi flaɪ], crates [kɹeɪts], bats [bæts], hits [hɪts], fights [faɪts], puts [pʊts], quartz [kwɔəts], waltz [wɔlts], slots [slɑts], abates [ə'beɪts]

German: der Zahn [tsaːn], der Fetzen [fɛtsən], zurück [tsuˈrʏk], das Zimmer [tsɪmɐ], die Ärztin [ɛrtstɪn], das Netz [nɛts], der Abfahrtstermin [ˈapfaːrtstɐˌmiːn], das Gesundheitsamt [gəˈzʊnthaets|amt]

[s] / [ʃ]

English: this shop [ðɪsʃɑp], this shoe [ðɪsʃu], pass Sheila [pæsʃilə], grass shed [gɹæsʃɛd], canvas shade [kænvəsʃeɪd], this shutter [ðɪsʃʌtə], this shoulder [ðɪsʃoʊldə], this shower [ðɪsʃaʊə], this shrimp [ðɪsʃɹɪmp]

German: es springen [ɛsʃprɪŋən], das schlafende Kind [dasʃlaːfəndəkɪnt], es sprach [ɛsʃpraːχ], das Schlimmste [dasʃlɪmstə], es schien [ɛsʃiːn], daß später [dasʃpɛːtɐ], das schöne Haus [dasʃøːnəhaos]

"Epheu, op.22, no.3," R. Strauss/F. Dahn

an der er - sten   Lieb' - um-ran-kung   hängt ihr gan-zes   Le - bens-schick-sal,
a nde:ɐ|e: rstə   nli: p|ʊ mra ŋkʊ   ŋ   hɛ ŋt|i: ɐgantsə   sle: bə nsʃɪ   k zaː l

"Morgen!, op.27, no.4," R. Strauss/J. Mackay

und auf   uns   sinkt des   Glük - kes stum-mes   Schwei   -   gen...
ʊ nt|a   of|ʊn   s zɪŋktdɛ   sglʏ   k ə sʃtʊ m ə   s ʃ va   egən

[s] / [z]

English: life's zest [laɪfszɛst], he lacks zeal [hilækszil], trees sway [tɹizsweɪ], his soulmate [hɪzsoʊlmeɪt], kiss Zelda [kɪszɛldə]

German: das sind [daszɪnt], dieses Singen [diːzəszɪŋən], es seufzet [ɛszɔøftsət], was sind [vaszɪnt], daß sie [daszi:], uns sehr [ʊnsze:ɐ]

"Weep you no more, sad fountains," J. Dowland

That	now	lies	sleep	-	ing,	that	now	lies	sleep	-	ing,
ðæ	tna	ʊla	ɪzsli		pɪ	ŋ	ðæ	tna	ʊla	ɪzsli	pɪ	ŋ

[t] /[ʃ]

English: that ship [ðætʃɪp], light shop [laɪtʃɑp], hot shower [hɑtʃaʊə], caught shoplifter [kɔtʃɑplɪftə], white shoes [ʍaɪtʃuz], bought shade [bɔtʃeɪd], won't share [woʊntʃɛə], not short [nɑtʃɔət]

German: die Windschutzscheibe [vɪntʃʊtsʃaebə], die Freundschaft [frɔøntʃaft], der Bildschirm [bɪltʃɪrm], der Goldschmied [gɔltʃmiːt], die Handschrift [hantʃrɪft], der Radschlüssel [raːtʃlʏsəl]

[ts] /[ʃ]

English: that's shameful [ðætsʃeɪmfʊl], it's shiny [ɪtsʃaɪnɪ], forgets charade [fɔəˈgɛtsʃəˈɹeɪd], hits Shawn [hɪtsʃɔn], hates shed [heɪtsʃɛd], gets shy [gɛtsʃaɪ], let's show [lɛtsʃoʊ], dates Cher [deɪtsʃɛə]

German: die Weihnachtsstimmung [vaenaχtsʃtɪmʊŋ], die Wirtsstube [vɪrtsʃtuːbə], die Arbeitsstelle [arbaetsʃtɛlə], das Universitätsstudium [univɛrziˈtɛːtsʃtuːdiʊm], die Geburtsstadt [gəˈbuːrtsʃtat], die Rückwärtssteuerung [rʏkvɛrtsʃtɔøərʊŋ], der Weihnachtsstollen [vaenaχtsʃtɔlən]

[k] /[ts]

English: restricts [ɹɪˈstɹɪkts], acts [ækts], objects (v.) [əbˈdʒɛkts], afflicts [əˈflɪkts], conflicts (n.) [kɑnflɪkts], architects [ˈɑəkəˌtɛkts], convicts (v.) [kənˈvɪkts], rejects (v.) [ɹɪˈdʒɛkts], directs [dɪˈɹɛkts], collects [kəˈlɛkts], predicts [pɹɪˈdɪkts], neglects [nəˈglɛkts], addicts [ædɪkts]

German: die Aktionen [akˈtsioːnən], die Lektion [lɛkˈtsioːn], die Direktion [dirɛkˈtsioːn], die Kollektion [kɔlɛkˈtsioːn], der Freundschaftskreis, [frɔøntʃaftskraes], die Wirtschaftskrise [vɪrtʃaftskriːzə]

21.5 Common consonant blends

Table 21.3. Common consonant blends in English and German

	English			German		
[bl]	blister	[blɪstə]		der Blick	[blɪk]	glance
[bɹ]	bright	[bɹaɪt]	**[br]**	brechen	[brɛçən]	to break
[dɹ]	dread	[dɹɛd]	**[dr]**	der Draht	[draːt]	wire
[fl]	flower	[flaʊə]		die Flasche	[flaʃə]	bottle
[fɹ]	frantic	[fɹæntɪk]	**[fr]**	fromm	[frɔm]	pious
[gl]	gloom	[glum]		glühen	[glyːən]	to glow
[gn]	ignore	[ɪgˈnɔə]		regnen	[reːgnən]	to rain
[gɹ]	grand	[gɹænd]	**[gr]**	grausam	[graozaːm]	horrible
[kl]	classic	[klæsɪk]		klein	[klaen]	small
[kɹ]	crown	[kɹaʊn]	**[kr]**	die Krähe	[krɛːə]	crows
[ks]	thanks	[θæŋks]		wachsen	[vaksən]	to grow
[kt]	perfect	[pɜfəkt]		der Sekt	[zɛkt]	champagne
[mb]	tremble	[tɹɛmbəl]		der Imbiß	[ɪmbɪs]	snack
[ŋ]	young	[jʌŋ]		der Gesang	[gəˈzaŋ]	voice
[ŋk]	think	[θɪŋk]		die Bank	[baŋk]	bank
[pl]	please	[pliz]		die Pläne	[plɛːnə]	plans
[pɹ]	prince	[pɹɪns]	**[pr]**	der Preis	[praes]	price
[ps]	shops	[ʃɑps]		die Psyche	[psyːçə]	mind
[sk]	scream	[skɹim]		die Maske	[maskə]	mask
[ʃ]	shame	[ʃeɪm]		schlafen	[ʃlaːfən]	to sleep

Continued on next page

Table 21.3—Continued

	English		German		
[sl]	slender	[slɛndə]	slawisch	[sla:vɪʃ]	Slavic
[sp]	spacious	[speɪʃəs]	die Knospe	[knɔspə]	bud
[st]	storm	[stɔəm]	gestern	[gɛstərn]	yesterday
[tɹ]	tradition	[tɹə'dɪʃən] **[tr]**	treu	[trɔø]	true
[ts]	awaits	[ə'weɪts]	nichts	[nɪçts]	nothing
[ts]	waltz	[wɔlts]	der Satz	[zats]	sentence

Table 21.4. Similar blends in English and German

	English		German		
[ld]	child	[tʃaɪld]	**[lt]** mild	[mɪlt]	soft
[nd]	behind	[bɪ'haɪnd]	**[nt]** das Kind	[kɪnt]	child
[kw]	quality	[kwɔlɪtɪ]	**[kv]** die Quelle	[kvɛlə]	source

Chapter 22: Legato Singing

If asked to name a legato language, most people would not immediately think of either English or German. Perhaps this is due to the sheer number of consonants or the presence of aspirates. Contrary to popular belief, legato is not merely connective singing between vowels. Legato is achieved through the merging of all phonemes on a column of released air. Vowels and consonants work together to form a seamless melodic line supported by the body, and executed by the imagination.

In any language there are obstacles to legato. If singers unconsciously place a rest between an adjacent vowel and consonant, a break in the line will ensue. Another common error results from permitting the vowel to die before sounding the following consonant. All vowels must maintain the same degree of intensity until the next phoneme takes over. It is possible for both English and German to sound and feel like they have inherent legato. Often, the proper use and release of consonants is integral to achieving a fluid legato line.

22.1 Glottal attacks: friend or foe?

The term *attack* sounds fiercer in meaning than it truly is. In actuality, an attack is the commencement of an action. This text prefers the term *onset*, referring to how exactly a vowel or consonant is started.

Singers should strive to commence each speech sound with the conscious release of the breath, especially words beginning with a vowel. This process begins with a silent inhalation that calms the body and ensures that there is no build-up of unnecessary friction in the vocal tract. Every utterance must begin on the impulse of the breath. After all, healthy singing is directly connected to healthy diction.

Both English and German use glottal onsets regularly. Legato and glottal onsets need not be a contradiction in terms. A "healthy" glottal increases clarity, as well as the expressive potential for a given word. The omission of glottal onsets results in the unintentional formation of other words or complete misunderstandings. Moreover, neither English nor German is intended to be sung like French. If singers attempt to achieve legato solely by singing vowel-to-vowel, this inevitably fails. Instead, it is recommended to practice the use of the healthy, soft glottal onset, commencing with speaking, then intoning, and finally singing.

In the following example, note the frequency of soft glottal onsets. In each case, the new onset occurs wherever the vowel is articulated, in other words, *not* where the previous consonant has finished. Upon production of the word "sing", the tongue quickly flattens to form [ɑ]. As each vowel begins on the breath, it is helpful to visualize that this phoneme is produced in a more forward position than that of [ŋ].

"If music be the food of love (1st setting)," H. Purcell/Colonel Heveningham

Sing   on, sing on, sing   on, sing on till   I____ am___fill'd,__ am__   fill'd____with__joy;
sɪ   ŋ |ɑ nsɪ ŋ |ɑ nsɪ ŋ |ɑ nsɪ ŋ |ɑ ntɪ l |ɑ   ɪ æ   mfɪ   ld |æ   mfɪ   ldwɪ   ðdʒɔ ɪ

Adjacent vowels, vowel sequences

Often one encounters adjacent vowels in the context of a sentence. It is advisable to have a soft, glottal onset to illustrate the beginning of each word starting with a vowel. However, it is also important to sustain each vowel as long as possible before passing seamlessly to the next. In both

English and German, leaning on the next word sometimes obliterates the need for a glottal onset between adjacent vowels, e.g., following an R-colored vowel or diphthong, e.g., *ein armer Arzt* [aen|aɾmɐ|aɾtst], their age [ðɛə|eɪdʒ]. As long as clarity or comprehension is not an issue, the use of a glottal onset is left to the singer's discretion.

eine andere Übung	[aenə|andərə|y:bʊŋ]	a different exercise
euer uralter Onkel	[ɔørɐ|ʊɐ|altɐ|ɔŋkəl]	your ancient uncle
alle Achtung	[alə|aχtʊŋ]	well done
aber ohne eine Idee	[a:bɐ|o:nə|aenə|iˈde:]	but without an idea

all at once an ape appeared	[ɔl|ət|wʌns|ən|eɪp|əˈpɪəd]
as always I am alert	[æz|ɔlweɪz|aɪ|əm|əˈlɜt]
I ate an apple and an orange	[aɪ|eɪt|æn|æpəl|ənd|ən|ɔɹəndʒ]
eventually Eve enjoys every area	[ɪˈvɛntʃuəlɪ|iv|ɛnˈdʒɔɪz|ɛvəɹɪ|ɛɹɪə]

22.2 Rhythmic release and timing of consonants

It is a common but unfounded fear that the aspirated release of a final consonant results in a disturbance of the legato line. This could not be further from the truth. In reality, an aspirated consonant fills the gap between the words, resulting in greater legato and removing the need for strong glottal onsets before subsequent words. The vocal line would be broken only if there were an inserted space or rest. Further, one must remember that not only the vowel carries the tone. The sound of a consonant still continues the line, be it voiced or voiceless.

In the following two musical examples, note how the actual release of certain consonants removes the need for a strong glottal onset. In the Brahms excerpt, the aspirated [t] of *zieht* releases forward into the tongue position for [ɛ], directly commencing the word *es*. It is crucial that this incidental word *not* be highlighted. This is accomplished by the rhythmic timing of the release of [t] for the last eighth note within the half note value. In fact, the air released by [t] bridges the gap without effectively joining the words together. A common error occurs if [i:] is held too long, not leaving the singer enough time to finish *zieht*, resulting in [tɛs]. Similarly, in the Dowland excerpt, the release of [t] in "sit" relates to the release of [p] in "weep", as well as that of [t] in "faint". These crisp, aspirate consonants may also be timed rhythmically by executing the releases to occur on the tied notes. This fills in any potential gaps in the melodic line and results in ultimate clarity.

"Wie Melodien zieht es mir, op.105, no.1," J. Brahms/K. Groth

"Come again, sweet love," J. Dowland

In the next example, the release of [kt] in *sinkt es* is directly related to the above Brahms excerpt. There is always time to finish a word completely before moving on to the next. The air released by a rhythmically timed [kt] on the dot of the dotted rhythm bridges any potential gap in the melodic line, while also not highlighting the incidental word *es*.

"Der Nußbaum, op.25, no.3" from *Myrthen*, R. Schumann/J. Mosen

As previously discussed in Chapters 11 and 19 (Advanced Concepts in Diction), implosion/explosion is a valuable tool used to further legato singing, while de-emphasizing monosyllabic incidental words, e.g., sit down [sɪt daʊn], *mit dem* [mɪt deːm]. However, if a given word is emphasized for artistic purposes, or if clarity or comprehension would otherwise be compromised, it is not advisable to use implosion/explosion.

In the following example, *blind zu* is treated with a normal aspirate release of [t] into a subsequent, rearticulated aspirated [t]. The decision not to employ implosion/explosion is based on the importance of the word *blind* in the context of the poem, as well as the tempo of the piece. If *blind* and *zu* were merged together, the meaning would be unclear and it would be impossible to hear the two words as separate entities.

"Seit ich ihn gesehen, op.42, no.1" from *Frauenliebe und -leben*, R. Schumann/A.v. Chamisso

The key to attaining true legato in any language is to sing each and every phoneme without stopping the air for a nanosecond. It is rather difficult to sing through the nasal consonants [m], [n], as well as the lateral [l]. Singers tend to shy away from fully voicing these consonants, often acquiring a smaller space in which to resonate. A dead, straight tone without vibration is never desired in classical vocal repertoire, unless it provides an expressive color for the purpose of word-painting.

Practice singing the following words, continuously spinning the air:			
calm morning	sun, moon, and stars	come near to me	one night
home no more	some never moan	omnipotent	calm night

22.3 Phrasal elision

When identical consonants are adjacent to each other in the context of a sentence, it is possible to assimilate these sounds, resulting in elision, e.g., with thoughts [wɪθɔts], at times [ətaɪmz]. This occurs in both English and German and depends solely on context and clarity. In general, it is not necessary to pronounce both consonants, unless one intends to create a phrasal double consonant. This would only be done if one means to emphasize a particular word. Please consult Chapter 19 (Advanced Concepts in Diction) for further information on phrasal doubling.

In the example below, the decision to omit the final [m] in *deinem*, and *meinem* is based on natural inflection. If the [m] were pronounced twice, it would create a phrasal double consonant, which would greatly accentuate *Mund*. Given that this word appears twice in one sentence, it does not warrant stress. Further, it is arguably more important to convey the opposites of *deinem* vs. *meinem* in reference to the exchange of the kiss. The entire phrase peaks on the word *meinem*. By omitting the [m], one has increased time on the *schwa*, creating greater vertical space.

"Die Liebende schreibt, op.86, no.3," F. Mendelssohn-Bartholdy/J.W. v. Goethe

| ein | Kuß | von dei - nem | Mund | auf | mei - | nem | Mun - de, |
| a | en ku | s fɔ nda | enə | mu | nt |a | ofma | enə | mu ndə |

22.4 Final thoughts on R

As previously outlined, it is necessary to have clean glottal onsets in English for the sake of clarity and precision of meaning. However, when an R-colored diphthong precedes a vowel, it is possible to substitute [ɹ] for the *schwa* [ə]. In these cases, [ɹ] is pronounced at the beginning of the next word, creating a seamless legato. Ultimately, this depends on personal taste and context. The following examples may be pronounced with the use of a soft glottal onset, or with a joining [ɹ]:

Where am I?	[ʍɛə|æm|aɪ]	or	[ʍɛ ɹæm|aɪ]
you are all	[ju|aə|ɔl]	or	[ju |a ɹɔl]
before us	[bɪˈfɔə|ʌs]	or	[bɪˈfɔ ɹʌs]
for honor	[fɔə|ɑnə]	or	[fɔ ɹɑnə]
forever and a day	[fɔəˈ|ɛvə|ænd|ə deɪ]	or	[fɔ ˈɹɛvə|ænd|ə deɪ]

Supplementary exercises

1. Speak and then sing the following words, consciously engaging the breath to employ a soft glottal onset:

artig, üblich, immer, der Oberarzt, ihm, die Uhren, ihn, die Oper, innen, ungarisch, euer, die Änderung, das Elend, interessant, eventuell, unter, das Obst, ohne, die Ahnung, örtlich, ähnelt, offenbar, andere, das Urteil, der Anfang, die Erinnerung, umarmen, einzeln, die Inschrift, überhaupt, die Ökonomie, intelligent

2. Speak and then sing the following sentences, being careful not to use any hard glottal attacks. The breath must remain in motion the entire duration of the sentence.

Eine alte Oma aß einen Apfel.	An old grandmother ate an apple.
Anna opferte einfach alles.	Anna sacrificed simply everything.
Er ist immer arg ängstlich.	He is always highly fearful.
Ohne ihn ist alles einsam.	Without him, everything is desolate.

Chapter 23: Close but No Cigar

This section deals with phonemes in English and German that are very similar, but not identical. It is important to distinguish between these phonemes, as they are not interchangeable. This section is intended to be a quick reference guide.

1. [j] vs. [ʝ]
English: The glide [j] is most commonly used before [u]. It has several different spellings and is classified as a voiced palatal approximant, e.g., tune [tjun], allure [əˈljʊə].

German: The voiced palatal fricative [ʝ] is spelled only with the letter *j*, e.g., *jagen* [ʝaːgən], *der Jammer* [ʝamɐ]. It is considered to be the voiced counterpart to the *ich-laut* [ç].

2. Diphthongs: [aɪ] vs. [ae], [aʊ] vs. [ao], [ɔɪ] vs. [ɔø]
In both languages, all three diphthongs occur within the space of one syllable. However, the amount of time one remains on the primary, initial vowel varies slightly.

English: One sings the initial vowel for 75% of the note value, passing through the second, vanish vowel for the last 25% of the note.

German: One sings the initial vowel for 90% of the note value, passing through the second, vanish vowel for the last 10% of the note.

Table 23.1. Comparison of English and German diphthongs

English			German			
[aɪ]	fine	[faɪn]	[ae]	fein	[faen]	fine
[aʊ]	brown	[bɹaʊn]	[ao]	braun	[braon]	brown
[ɔɪ]	Roy	[ɹɔɪ]	[ɔø]	die Reu	[rɔø]	regret

N.B.: The main difference between German diphthongs and their English counterparts is in the nature of the second vowel. In each case, the German vanish vowel is closed (vs. open in English). As a result, the tongue is in a higher position and the quality is much more focused.

3. [ɛ] and [ɪ] in English and German
Compared to their English counterparts, German [ɛ] and [ɪ] are brighter and more forward, resulting in a higher arch to the tongue. They do not feel low and relaxed. Correspondingly, both vowels have a higher vertical space in the mouth and are decidedly energized.

4. [ʊ] in English and German
It is a common error to pronounce this phoneme identically in both English and German. Although they use the same IPA symbol, they are not interchangeable.

English: The English [ʊ] is much more open, e.g., book [bʊk], awful [ɔfʊl]. In fact, it is closer to [œ] in terms of tongue position and quality. It is difficult to sustain and quite challenging to attain for ESL singers.

German: The German [ʊ] is closely related to [uː], but formed with slightly less lip-rounding and focus, e.g., *die Mutter* [mʊtɐ], *unmöglich* [ʊnmøːklɪç]. Compared to its English counterpart, this enigmatic vowel has greater intensity and involves the protrusion of the lips.

5. [ŋg] vs. [ŋ]

English: Both [ŋg] and [ŋ] exist in English and are spelled with *ng*. If a word is monosyllabic, or is formed from an existing verb, [ŋ] is used, e.g., thing [θɪŋ], longing [lɑŋɪŋ]. Moreover, [ŋg] is used if 1) the first syllable of the word does *not* form a word, e.g., finger [fɪŋgə]; 2) the first syllable of the word means something completely different from the full word, e.g., single [sɪŋgəl]; 3) an adjective is in the comparative or superlative form, e.g., younger [jʌŋgə].

German: Only [ŋ] is used, without exception. It is spelled with *ng*.

Table 23.2. Comparison of [ŋ] and [ŋg] in English and German

	English			German		
[ŋ]	sing	[sɪŋ]	[ŋ]	singen	[zɪŋən]	to sing
	singer	[sɪŋə]		der Sänger	[zɛŋɐ]	singer
[ŋg]	finger	[fɪŋgə]	[ŋ]	der Finger	[fɪŋɐ]	finger

6. [əɹ] vs. [ər]

In English and German, the spelling *er* is very common. In English, unstressed *er* is pronounced as a *schwa* [ə], e.g., player [pleɪə], permit (v.) [pə'mɪt]. In German, unstressed *er* is pronounced [ɐ] if it is at the end of the word, or [ɛɐ] if it is a prefix, e.g., *bitter* [bɪtɐ], *erhalten* [ɛɐ'haltən].

English: The combination [əɹ] occurs when unstressed *er* is followed by a vowel or *y*, e.g., exaggerate [ɪg'zædʒəɹeɪt], mastery [mæstəɹɪ].

German: The combination [ər] occurs when unstressed *er* is at the end of a word element, or in the form of *-ern*, e.g., *bedauerlich* [bə'daoərlɪç], *gestern* [gɛstərn]. This decision is made according to optimal clarity and projection for singing.

7. Final -s

English: Final -*s* is always pronounced [z], preceded by a vowel or a consonant, e.g., Brahms [bɹɑmz], sews [souz], dishes [dɪʃəz].

German: Final -*s* is always pronounced [s], preceded by a vowel or a consonant, e.g., *Brahms* [braːms], *deswegen* [dɛsveːgən], *dies* [diːs]. Note that this may occur at the end of a word or word element.

8. Treatment of the *schwa* [ə]

As previously discussed, the English *schwa* is the unstressed counterpart to [ʌ], having the same sound, no matter what the context. By contrast, the German *schwa* is also known as the *vocalic chameleon*, as it constantly changes its color depending on its environment. Although the quality of the *schwa* is not identical in English and German, the treatment of this neutral, obscure vowel is similar in one respect.

In both English and German lyric diction, it is important to economize the movement of the articulators. The German *schwa* is pronounced in the exact same position as the previous vowel. This enables the phoneme to blend into the surrounding tones and shapes, thus appearing highly unstressed. Similarly, since the English *schwa* is so prevalent, often occurring multiple times within one word, one often remains in the same vocal position as a result. For example, in words such as deliberate [dɪˈlɪbəɹət] and experiment [ɪkˈspɛɹəmənt], note that the sound akin to [ʌ] is not actually repeated. In fact, the second part of both words maintains the same shape, using a neutral, unquantifiable vowel sound. Less movement means greater economy of breath, and leads to increased legato capability and stamina in the musical phrase.

Chapter 24: Lyric Diction in Opera

Singing operatic repertoire presents different challenges with regards to lyric diction. Consonants clearly projected in a concert or recital setting may appear lost in the presence of a full orchestra. In general, consonants need to be faster and stronger when performing operatic repertoire. It is crucial to practice these adjustments even when rehearsing or performing operatic repertoire with the piano. In an audition, the panel needs to hear how the voice will project once the orchestra has been added. The intimacy of the text in a singer-plus-piano situation is transformed into large-scale theatre in a singer-plus-orchestra scenario. The voice becomes an instrument that must carry over copious other musicians. This chapter presents several strategies for effective lyric diction in opera.

German:
1. Use of rolled [r] and flipped [ɾ]
In Chapter 7 (Characteristic English Phonemes), the allophones of *r* were described with reference to singing English oratorio and operatic repertoire. Please refer to this chapter for review. While it is not recommended to use [r] in German lied (unless it is used for word-painting), it may be used quite freely in operatic repertoire. However, one must be mindful that the tempo does not slow to allow for an extended [r]. This trilled phoneme penetrates a thick, orchestral texture with ease, reaching the back seats in a large hall. Further, in using [r] regularly, it helps to keep the diction in a frontal position, which is always advantageous.

In song repertoire, [ɐ] is used as an *r* substitute in monosyllabic words, e.g., *mir*, prefixes, e.g., *er-, ver-, der-, vor-*, and the *-er* suffix. In opera it is advisable to enhance projection by using flipped *r* [ɾ] instead. The subtle differences between [ɐ] and [ə], though apparent in an intimate recital hall, do not read on an operatic stage. It is not advisable to use [r], as it is deemed too strong for these contexts.

Table 24.1. Use of R in song and operatic repertoire

	Art Song	**Opera**	
erfahren	[ɛɐˈfaːɾən]	[ɛrˈfaːɾən]	to learn
die Mutter	[mʊtɐ]	[mʊtəɾ]	mother
die Uhr	[uːɐ]	[uːɾ]	clock
rastlos	[ɾastloːs]	[ɾastloːs]	restless
der Ritter	[ɾɪtɐ]	[ɾɪtəɾ]	knight, cavalier

In the following musical example, note the increased use of [ɾ]. The decision to use [ɐ] on *mir ist* removes the need for a new glottal onset. Any uses of [ɾ] (except in *Jungfer*) may be increased to [r], if greater projection is desired. This is left to the singer's discretion. Note that no glottal onset is indicated for *die Ehre*. A strong lean on [eː] will suffice, ensuring that the singer's full tone does not cease.

"The Presentation of the Rose" from *Der Rosenkavalier*, R. Strauss

English and German:

2. Shadow vowels

Although not encouraged in art song repertoire, it is perfectly acceptable to employ shadow vowels in opera. These intrusive vowels aid in overall projection and are especially useful after final [b], [d], and [g]. A strong release of these plosives naturally results in either [ə] or [ɪ]. As the voice penetrates an orchestral texture, the effect greatly enhances comprehension and clarity throughout. It may be used to illustrate particularly strong words, e.g., stab [stæbə], grand [gɹændɪ], or when greater projection is needed. This applies to both English and German. Note that it is not advisable to insert shadow vowels between consonant blends, e.g., *bl, br, dr, pl, pr*, as this results in an unwanted scoop in the melodic line.

3. Alternative to [h]

It is very difficult for [h] to project over an orchestra or small chamber ensemble. In opera, it is strongly suggested to substitute the *ich-laut* for [h] whenever possible. This is an easy endeavor before front vowels such as [i], [ɪ], and [ɛ]. When faced with back vowels or diphthongs, e.g., how [haʊ], it is helpful to imagine a more frontal production of [h]. One will not produce a true *ich-laut*, but this image results in a more forward position, aiding both projection and penetrative power.

"The Presentation of the Rose" from *Der Rosenkavalier*, R. Strauss

In the above example, note the substitution of [ç] for [h] on the word *himmlische*. As the preceding word employs [iː], the tongue is already strongly arched. Thus, the singer may remain in the same position to pronounce a quick [ç], releasing into a bright, forward, spinning [ɪ]. For *nicht*, the [n] may be anticipated (voiced on the F-sharp) or sung directly on the beat (voiced on the A-sharp). This is left up to the singer, based on the ease of negotiating the leap. Sometimes it is desirable to have just a vowel on top, given the tessitura of this section.

4. Cognate substitutions or omission

Certain consonants are highly difficult to project in operatic repertoire. When faced with a final [p] that must be strong and clearly audible, one may employ [b] instead. The cognate substitution occurs directly before the final cut off. The same may be done for a final [f], by using [v]. These changes are not noticeable when singing with orchestra.

Certain settings of initial [g] may be sung with greater ease by using an unaspirated, Italianate [k] instead. This is especially useful for higher pitches whereby a strong initial [g] is required. By substituting the cognate, the ear is tricked into hearing the original phoneme.

Another common substitute in opera is using [tʃ] in place of [dʒ]. This aids projection considerably, as [tʃ] is highly aspirated. It is impossible to hear the difference over an orchestra and once again, it serves to keep the diction forward. Since [tʃ] is voiceless, it is also produced before the beat, thus much earlier than its original counterpart [dʒ]. This aids in the clarity of the English text.

Table 24.2. Cognate substitution in opera

	Art Song	**Opera**	
der Stab	[ʃtaːp]	[ʃtaːb]	rod, staff
der Wurf	[vʊrf]	[vʊrv]	throw, pitch
grimmig	[grɪmɪç]	[krɪmɪç]	grim, fierce
generous	[dʒɛnəɹəs]	[tʃɛnəɹəs]	

In high tessituras, over a full orchestra, it is often desirable to omit adjacent, related consonants. This is especially useful in establishing a stronger legato line. If correctly executed, the listener is not conscious of an omission. This is only possible if the given consonants are identical, cognates, or strongly related, e.g., both nasal. Lyric consonant omission is undetectable in high tessituras, especially in operatic repertoire. Ultimately, its use is left to the singer's discretion.

"Sein wir wieder gut" from *Ariadne auf Naxos*, R. Strauss

	zu	ver-sam	-	meln	al	-	le	Ar	-		ten	von	Mut	
	tsu:	fɛ	ɐza	m ə	ln ǀa	l ə	a:			ɾtə	nfɔ	m u:	(t)

In the above example, note that [n] is omitted in *von Mut,* giving the singer greater vertical space and vowel length. It is recommended to anticipate the voicing of [m] on the G, allowing the vowel to be the ultimate arrival of this magnificent ascent. The decision to use [ɐ] instead of [ɾ] in *versammeln* is based on the resulting emphasis of [z].

Similarly, [n] is omitted in *von mir* in the example below. In this case, it is advisable to pitch the [m] directly on the high B-flat. A strong, voiced [m] on *mir* will result in a dramatic arrival, finishing with a pitched [ɾ] or [r]. The decision to voice [n] directly on the beat for *nimm* is based on the rhythmic precision this provides.

"Es gibt ein Reich" from *Ariadne auf Naxos*, R. Strauss

du	nimm_____	es	von	mir.	
du:	nɪ	m ǀɛ	sfɔ	mi:	ɾ

Chapter 25: Concise History of the English Language

English is classified as a Germanic language, though it has deviated in its development over the centuries, as a result of countless influences from other countries. Notably, the development of English has been influenced by the Roman Catholic Church (ca. 597–1964), the Vikings (ca. 787–1042), England's colonization of large parts of the world, including the Americas (1600–1850), and advances in science and technology, borrowing words from Greek and Latin (1850 to present) (Woods 1987). English has also been immensely influenced by military, political, and social factors. Had English remained a strictly Germanic language, it would strongly resemble Dutch, Danish, Icelandic, or German. The resulting wide vocabulary in English provides a wealth of choice in expressive possibilities to the singer. One can formulate the same thought or idea in countless ways, e.g., to help (Anglo-Saxon), to aid (Old French), Peter's book (Anglo-Saxon), roof of the house (Old French), harder (Anglo-Saxon), more difficult (Old French).

According to historian Charles Barber, all living languages change and evolve primarily due to socio-economical, political, geographical, and cultural influences (Barber 1993). This rate of change varies greatly and is fascinating when comparing languages. For example, Iceland was colonized by the Norwegians thousands of years ago. Since the rate of change has been quite slow, a modern Icelander would have little trouble reading a medieval Icelandic saga. By contrast, without formal training it would be impossible to comprehend an English document from 1100. In fact, one can easily jump to the false conclusion that this seemingly foreign language bears no connection to Modern English.

When determining familial relationships it is imperative that one consult the earliest forms of the respective languages. Upon comparing English, German, Swedish, Dutch, Danish, Norwegian, and Frisian, there are strong similarities with regard to phonemes, structure, and syntax. Many English words resemble those of French, e.g., people/peuple, battle/bataille, palace/palais, to change/changer. However, these are primarily loan words taken from French or Latin. When one compares the earliest forms of English with French, there is no relationship. The following chart depicts the similarities of three related languages:

Table 25.1. Similarities in Swedish, German, and English

Swedish	German	English
sten	Stein	stone
ben	Bein	bone
ek	Eiche	oak
hem	Heim	home
rep	Reif	rope
get	Geiss	goat
en	ein	one

Source: Charles Barber, *The English Language: A Historical Introduction* (Cambridge: Cambridge University Press, 1993), 58. Reversed version of the original.

N.B.: Over centuries, words have not necessarily retained the same meaning. For example, at one time *Reif* did indeed mean *rope* in German, but this meaning has since been lost.

All Germanic languages descend from one parent language, Proto-Germanic (PG), which is a dialect of Indo-European. There are three branches of PG: West Germanic (High German, Low German, Dutch, Frisian, English), North Germanic, a.k.a. Old Norse (modern Scandinavian languages), and East Germanic (Gothic). PG was a highly inflected language, structurally based on grammatical additives, e.g., prefixes, suffixes, and other endings. Modern German and classical Latin still retain a high level of inflection, including the use of cases. Conversely, modern English is dependent on word order to show the meaning of a sentence and the function of words.

Following the dissolution of the Roman Empire, Germanic tribes spread throughout Europe via military expeditions—the Goths through Spain/Italy and the Anglo-Saxons through Britain. The rise of the nation-state furthered the consolidation of Germanic languages. A centralized political force resulted in the triumph of a single dialect or standard literary language. The history of the English language is generally divided into three periods: Old English, Middle English, and Modern English.

1. Old English (1st Anglo-Saxon settlements in England to ca. 1100)
The Anglo-Saxon conquest resulted in a settlement of a whole people whose language remained dominant. As a result, there are few traces of Celtic influence on Old English (OE). Their Germanic dialects provided the basis for modern English. Old English did borrow some words for Christian concepts, e.g., church (old Greek), apostle, monk, bishop (all from Latin). However, due to its Germanic inflectional nature, vocabulary development resulted from compounding and the use of prefixes and suffixes. During the latter part of the OE period, two large groups invaded Britain, having tremendous influence on the English language: Norsemen (Old Norse) and Normans (Old French). Words loaned from Scandinavia were mainly everyday words belonging to a central vocabulary, e.g., *sweostor* (sister). The cultures were very similar, and the Vikings mingled with the English on equal terms.

2. Middle English (ca. 1100–1500)

The main dialects of Middle English (ME) were Scots, Northern English, West Midland, East Midland, Southern, and South Eastern. A standard literary language did not exist. Latin and French became quite prestigious, but eventually, the balance tipped in favor of English. Although French had enjoyed a lengthy high status, it never became the mother tongue to the majority of population. This might be due to the fact that the Normans did not outnumber the English like the Anglo-Saxons had outnumbered the Britons (Barber 1993). One of the major changes in English during this period was the virtual disappearance of SOV (subject/object/verb) and VSO (verb/subject/object) types of word order.

During the thirteenth and fourteenth centuries, an enormous amount of French loan words entered the language. These words reflected the imposed culture and political dominance of the Normans. They included terms related to rank (baron, count, prince) and the law (accuse, prison, crime, justice) (Barber 1993). Chaucer was a major figure in the upsurge of English literature in the fourteenth century. It was not until the end of the fifteenth century that the literary language was largely standardized.

3. Modern English (New English) (ca. 1500 to present day)

During the fifteenth and sixteenth centuries many religious disputes affected the establishment of English as the sole literary language in England. Reformers wrote books and pamphlets that were distributed to wide audiences. The Bible was translated into English and church services gradually came to be conducted in English (from Latin). Part of a gentleman's education at the time was to travel the Continent, thus bringing foreign words, which were then adapted into English, e.g., Italian (fuse, fresco, opera), Spanish (armada, cargo). In Renaissance English, there were also a large number of Latin loan words, e.g., genius, species, cerebellum, militia, radius, specimen, focus, tedium, lens. However, often the original meaning was not adopted. For example, focus meant "hearth, fireplace", and lens was short for "lentil", as the double-convex lens of an optical glass resembled a lentil seed (Barber 1993).

In Modern English there is still evidence of the French aristocratic stamp made by the inclusion of many medieval French words. Words connected to ordinary people tend to retain English names, while upper-class objects have preserved French names, e.g., house, daughter, son, man, woman (English), manor, palace, heir, butler, servant (French). Germanic words tend to be more popular and emotionally charged vs. French words, which are inevitably more refined or formal, e.g., doom, folk, hearty, stench (Germanic), judgment, nation, cordial, odor (French) (Barber 1993). Over centuries, subjunctive forms have largely been lost, e.g., "If he was" vs. "If he were". Instead, it is now more common to use modal auxiliaries (might, should, could, would).

Table 25.2. Changes in pronunciation since late Middle English

Chaucer	Shakespeare	Present Day	Modern spelling
[tiːd]	[təid]	[taɪd]	tide
[greːn]	[grin]	[gɹin]	green
[mɛːt]	[meːt]	[mit]	meat
[mak(ə)]	[mɛːk]	[meɪk]	make
[gɔːt]	[goːt]	[goʊt]	goat
[foːd]	[fuːd]	[fud]	meat
[huːs]	[həus]	[haʊs]	house
[kʊt]	[kʊt]	[kʌt]	cut
[rɪŋg]	[rɪŋg]	[ɹɪŋ]	ring
[niçt], [niːt]	[niçt], [nəit]	[naɪt]	night
[kneː]	[kniː]	[ni]	knee

Source: Charles Barber, *The English Language: A Historical Introduction* (Cambridge: Cambridge University Press, 1993), 197. Altered version of the original: addition of brackets, Present Day IPA modified to correspond to this textbook.

4. Developments in Modern English (17th century to present day)

In 1699, the great classical scholar Richard Bentley observed that every language "is in perpetual motion and alteration" (Barber 1993). When one attempts to regulate a language, one freezes it in a desired state by refining, correcting, and defining its correct usage. In fact, no living language can be prevented from changing. In 2006, this was clearly evident with the final implementation of the *Neue Rechtscheibung*, a modernization of the standard German language, amid rampant adversity.

In the eighteenth century, language was increasingly used as a social marker. Suddenly, there were many prescriptive books written on what expressions and idioms one should avoid, and the language of the people was duly condemned. This is not unlike the wave of "political correctness" that dominated the latter decades of the twentieth century.

Over the past three hundred years, the expansion of English vocabulary has occurred mainly via the assimilation of scientific words (from Greek, Latin, French), and the inclusion of new words from the fields of finance, politics, arts, and fashion.

Many oddities and inconsistencies in modern English spelling are due to the fact that letters are still preserved that represent sounds which long ago ceased to be pronounced, e.g., knight, castle, wrong. Homophones are very common, which are words that make a distinction in spelling but not in pronunciation, e.g., meet/meat, sea/see. Some new distinctions that arose were never recognized in spelling, leading to the confusing fact that diphthongs are often represented by a single letter, as the phoneme was originally a pure vowel in the Middle English period, e.g., go [gou], date [deɪt]. Correspondingly, modern monophthongs are often spelled with digraphs, e.g., author [ɔθə], each [itʃ]. Clearly, the considerable inconsistencies in modern English spelling make it very challenging to learn as a foreign language.

Appendix A: Glossary of Phonetic and Anatomical Terms

Affricate: the resulting phoneme when a plosive (stop) consonant is immediately followed by a fricative or aspirant. Both consonants are formed in a single gesture at the same place of articulation.

Allophone: one of many variant sounds forming the same phoneme, e.g., aspirated [t] of English and German vs. unaspirated [t] of Italian and French

Alveolar: an articulation by the tongue-tip on the ridge directly behind the upper front teeth, e.g., [t], [d], [s], [z], [ɾ], clear [l], [n]

Approximant: a speech sound whereby the articulators approach each other, slightly narrowing the vocal tract; results in a phoneme in between a vowel and a consonant, e.g., [ɹ]

Articulation: a gesture of the vocal organs so as to shape the sounds of speech

Aspirate: a consonant pronounced with an initial release of breath, e.g., [h], or a puff of air upon its release, e.g., [t], [k], [p]

Assimilation: a historical or contextual process by which a phoneme becomes similar to an adjacent sound, e.g., his shoe [hɪʒʃu]

Bilabial: articulated with both lips coming together, e.g., [b], [p], [m]

Blade: the part of the tongue immediately behind the tip

Cardinal vowels: eight pure vowels whose tongue positions are as remote as possible from a neutral position; systematized by phonetician Daniel Jones

Closed vowel: a vowel whereby the tongue is positioned as close as possible to the roof of the mouth, without creating a constriction that would result in a consonant; sometimes called high vowel, referring to the arch of the tongue

Cognate: a pair of consonants formed with the exact same articulation process, voiced and voiceless, e.g., [b]/[p], [d]/[t], [g]/[k]

Consonant: a speech sound in which the breath is partly obstructed. When combined with a vowel, it forms a syllable.

Continuant: a consonant whose duration of production is limited only by the capacity of breath, e.g., [f], [s], rolled [r], [v], [z], [h], [ʃ], [ʒ], [θ], [ð], [m], [n]

Dental: an articulation by the tongue-tip against the upper front teeth, e.g., [θ], [ð]

Diphthong: the union of two vowels pronounced in one syllable, formed by a seamless change from one vowel quality to another

Elision: the omission of a vowel, consonant, or syllable in a word creating greater ease in pronunciation, e.g., vegetable [vɛdʒtəbəl]

Explosion: the sudden release of air pressure in the pronunciation of stop consonants (same as plosion)

Formant: one of the ways in which the air in the vocal tract vibrates that characterizes a sound, forming an overtone, or group of overtones; a peak in an acoustic frequency spectrum typically independent of fundamental frequency

Fricative: a consonant made by the friction of breath travelling through a narrow opening or constricted passage, e.g., [v], [f], [θ], [ð], [χ], [ç], [z], [s], [ʒ], [ʃ], [h], [ʍ]; also known as spirant

Glide: a phoneme that begins as a vowel but is ultimately heard as a consonant; also known as semi-vowel or semi-consonant, e.g., [w], [j]

Glottal attack/onset: general term for how glottal vibrations begin; may be soft (vocal folds are adducted simultaneously with air flow through the glottis), hard (vocal folds are firmly closed, creating subglottal pressure before tone begins), or breathy (air flows through vocal folds before the glottis has closed)

Glottal stop: sound produced by a sudden opening or closing of the glottis; the momentary, complete closure of the vocal folds

Glottis: the opening from the pharynx into the larynx and in between the vocal folds; affects modulation of the voice by contracting or dilating

Gradation: a change in the quality or length of a vowel within a word, indicating certain inflectional differentiations, e.g., am [æm] vs. [əm]

Guttural: consonant whose point of articulation is near the back of the oral cavity, e.g., velar [k], [g], uvular [χ], [ʁ]

Hard palate: the thin bony structure that forms part of the roof of the mouth; creates a partition between the nasal passages and the mouth

Homophones: words that sound the same but have different meanings

Implosion: an inward burst of air pressure whereby the vocal folds move downward, expanding the vocal tract and decreasing the air pressure therein; results in an unaspirated or devoiced consonant

Labial: sound requiring partial or complete closure of lips, e.g., [b], [p], [f], [v], [m], [w]

Labiodental: an articulation formed by the cooperation of the lower lip and the teeth, e.g., [f], [v]

Labiovelar: an articulation formed by the cooperation of both lips and the soft palate, e.g., [w]

Larynx: an organ found in the neck that is involved in sound production and that houses the vocal folds; situated just below where the tract of the pharynx splits into the trachea and the esophagus

Lateral: an articulation produced by the passage of breath around the sides of the tongue, e.g., [l]

Monophthong: a pure vowel sound, whose single articulation at both beginning and end is fixed

Nasal: a vowel or consonant whereby the air in the vocal tract is prevented from going out of the mouth, but allowed to escape through the nose, e.g., [m], [n], [ŋ]; characterized by a lowered soft palate

Obstruent: a consonant produced by blocking the passage of air through the mouth; e.g., plosive (stop), fricative, affricate

Open vowel: a vowel whereby the tongue is positioned as far as possible from the roof of the mouth; sometimes called low vowel, referring to the position of the tongue

Overtone: harmonic, secondary tone higher than the fundamental tone; regular variation of air pressure at a higher rate than the fundamental rate of repetition of the sound wave

Palatal: an articulation whereby the body of the tongue is raised against the hard palate, e.g., [j]

Palate: upper roof of the mouth that separates the oral and nasal cavities; hard and soft palate refers to front and back parts

Postalveolar: an articulation produced by the blade of the tongue touching or approaching the spot directly behind the alveolar ridge, before the hard palate, e.g., [ʃ], [ʒ]

Pharynx: cavity at the back of the mouth near the root of the tongue; upper part of the throat connecting the oral and nasal cavities with the esophagus

Phoneme: a unit of significant, distinct sound in a specified language; the smallest unit of speech that distinguishes meaning

Phonetics: the study of the physical sounds of human speech using a system of symbols representing individual phonemes; study of properties, production, and perception of speech sounds

Phonology: sub-field of linguistics dealing with the context in which sounds function in a given language or across languages

Plosive: a consonant whereby the air in the vocal tract is completely blocked, then released audibly, e.g., [g], [k], [t], [d], [b], [p]

Resonance: the way in which air in the vocal tract will vibrate when set in motion; prolongation of sound through reverberation

Retroflex: a consonant whereby the tongue-tip curls back against the hard palate, e.g., [ɻ]

Root: the lowest part of the back of the tongue immediately above the epiglottis; the part by which an organ is attached to the body

Schwa: an indeterminate, neutral, central, obscure vowel occurring in unstressed syllables

Sibilant: a consonant produced with a hissing sound; air stream is directed toward the sharp edge of the teeth, e.g., [s], [ʃ]

Soft palate (velum): the soft, fleshy part of the roof of the mouth located in the rear; raising the soft palate blocks air from exiting the nose

Stop: see plosive

Tongue: flexible, muscular organ located in the bottom of the mouth and divided into four parts: back (below soft palate), front (below hard palate), blade (below the alveolar ridge), tip (most forward part)

Triphthong: union of three vowels pronounced within one syllable, e.g., fire [faɪə]

Uvula: the small, fleshy lobe hanging down from the soft palate

Velar: an articulation produced by the back of the tongue against the soft palate, e.g., [k], [g], [χ], [ŋ]

Velum: see soft palate

Vocal folds: two small muscular infoldings of mucous membrane stretched horizontally across the larynx that vibrate during phonation; also known as vocal cords

Vocal tract: the air passage between the vocal folds and the lips; includes laryngeal cavity, pharynx, oral and nasal cavities

Voiced: a consonant made with the vibration of the vocal folds

Voiceless: a consonant made without the vibration of the vocal folds

Vowel: a sound produced at the centre of a syllable without an obstruction of the vocal tract; vocal folds vibrate but without audible friction

Appendix B: Supplements

English tongue twisters

Practice speaking and intoning the following English tongue twisters:

1. Bilabial [p][b][m][w][ʍ]

The flexibility of the lips is integral to clear, projected text. Lack of lip mobility impedes both consonant and vowel production.

A poor pauper paused on purpose to pawn a porpoise
Pretty Polly Perkin polished pastel plates and plaster plaques
Betty beat a bit of butter to make a better batter
The bottom of the butter bucket is the buttered bucket bottom
The musician made music and moved multitudes
The mighty master murdered the maddened magistrate
One wan weary white woman wildly weeping
The woman wound the wool well while the wild wind whistled
Wishy-washy Wilfred wished to win a wager

2. Tongue-tip and alveolar ridge [t][d][l][n]

A tidy tiger tied a tie tighter to tidy her tiny tail
Ten tiny toddling tots trying to train their tongues to trill
Twelve twinkling stars twinkled twelve times
Twenty twisted tangled threads, twining taut the treetops
Two toads totally tired trying to trot to Tidsbury

Dancing dangerously down the dale dainty Dinah dashed dizzily past Dorothy

Dashing Daniel defied David to deliver Dora from the dawning danger

The dustman daily does his duty to dislodge the dirty dust deposited in disgusting dusty dustbins

A library littered with literary literature

Lotty loves lollies when lolling in the lobby

Lilith listlessly lisps lengthy lessons

A nightingale knew no night was nicer than a nice night to sing his nocturnes

Nine nimble noblemen nibbling nasty knobbly nuts

Tongue-tip and upper teeth [s][z]

A shifty snake selling snakeskin slippers

A single solid silver sifter sifts sifted sugar

A sick sparrow sang six sad spring songs sitting under a squat shrub

Down the slippery slide they slid sitting slightly sideways

Seventeen slimy slugs in satin sunbonnets sat singing short sad songs

Students study stenciling steadily

Sister Susie sneezes slightly, slicing succulent shallots

3. Back of tongue and soft palate [k][g][ŋ]

These are particularly good for singers who mispronounce [ŋ], or who have nasality due to a lazy soft palate.

Can consuming cold cod cutlets cause corns?

The crime completed, the coward crawled cautiously coastward

A carter carried crates of cabbages across a crooked court

A cricket critic cricked his neck at a critical cricket match

Quick quiet quills quote Quinney's quarrel

This crisp crust crackles crunchily

Grace's grey gloves glided to the ground
Gertrude Gray gazed at the grey goose gaily
The glow-worm's gleam glitters in glade and glen

4. Tongue-tip and upper teeth [θ] [ð]
On two thousand acres too tangled for tilling,
Where thousands of thorn trees grew thrifty and thrilling,
Theophilus Twistle, less thrifty than some,
Thrust three thousand thistles through the thick of his thumb
They thanked them thoroughly
Thelma saw thistles in the thick thatch
Sir Cecil Thistlethwaite, the celebrated theological statistician

5. Lower lip and upper teeth [f] [v]
Five frantic fat frogs fled from fifty fierce fishes
Forty fat farmers found a field of fine fresh fodder
Flora's fan fluttered feebly and her fine fingers fidgeted
Three fluffy feathers fell from feeble Phoebe's fan
Vera valued the valley violets
Violet vainly viewed the vast vacant vista

6. Tongue blade and hard palate [tʃ] [dʒ] [ʃ] [ʒ]
Cheryl's cheap chip shop sells cheap chips
Cheerful children chant charming tunes
Does this shop stock silk shirts?
Jean, John, Georges, and Gerald judged generally
Joan joyously joined jaunty Jean in jingling jigs
The chased treasure chest's thrice chipped
Shall Sarah Silling share her silver shilling?
Should such a shapeless sash such shabby stitches show?
When does the wrist-watch strap shop shut?

7. Aspirant [h]

Bees hoard heaps of honey in hives

How high His Highness holds his haughty head

He ate hot apples and halibut hastily

How has Harry hasted so hurriedly to the hunt?

Has Helen heard how Hilda hurried home?

Last year I could not hear with either ear

The hare's ears heard ere the hares heeded

8. Healthy glottal onsets

One old owl occupies an old oak

One old ox opening oysters

9. Glides and approximants [j][ɹ]

A yellow yo-yo young Hubert used

A purely rural duel truly plural is better than a purely plural duel truly rural

As around the rising rocket, the rushing rotors roared, the rattled roosters rollicked

Around the rugged rock the rural rascal ran to win the rural race

---

I wish to thank Samuel French Ltd. for their kind permission to reprint the above excerpts of their copyrighted work.

Parkin ANTHOLOGY OF BRITISH TONGUE-TWISTERS

© 1969 Samuel French Ltd. London

All rights reserved

Used by permission of Samuel French Ltd. on behalf of the Estate of Ken Parkin

German tongue twisters

Practice speaking and intoning the following German tongue twisters:

Vowels

1. [aː] vs. [a]

Nah dem Hage Tannen
schwanken,
Alles strahlet Abendprangen;
Klagend sang der alte Barde,
Daß der Waldesrand es hallte!
Knaben kamen da gegangen,
Sangen Psalmen, Banner
tragend—
Manchen prangt der Kranz am
Arme.
Alle waren arme Waller,
Rasten lange nah dem Walde.

2. [eː] vs. [ɛ]

Wenn der Rebe rechter Segen
Jede Seele mehr erreget,
Werde edel, selbstvergessen,
Schneller jedes Herz beweget!
Denn der hehren Lebensquelle,
Welche Edle stets belebt,
Werden Reben Segen geben—
Selbst der Menschen Weh
entschwebt.

3. [iː] vs. [ɪ]

Wie sie friedlich, sinnig blickt,
Innig mild sich still vertieft—
Sinnenlieb', die nie ersprießlich,
Wird sie sittig immer fliehn!
Kniend liegt sie—lieblich
sinnend,
Sie, die still die Himmel minnt;
Ihr Beginnen ist verdienstlich,
Bringt ihr Himmelslicht, gibt
Frieden!

4. [oː] vs. [ɔ]

Oben thront der Nonnen
Kloster.
Voll von Trost, voll hoher
Wonne
Wohnen dorten fromme
Nonnen,
Loben Gott vor Morgenrot.
O Sonne, thronst so wolkenlos!
Schon flog der Vogel hoch
empor.

Wohl knospen Rosen schon, wo
Moos—

So kommt der holde
Sommerflor.

5. [uː] vs. [ʊ]

Und durch zukunftsdunklen
Mund
Wurde Brutus' Schuld nun
kund:
«Gut und Blut trugst du zum
Bunde—
Dulden mußt du nun zur Stund',
Und der Fluch schuf Blut und

Wunde!»
«Mußtest du nun ruhn, um
stumpf
Uns'res Unmuts Sturm zu rufen?
Du—des Ungunst Mut uns
schuf,
Und uns trug zu Ruhmes
Stufen!»

6. [øː] vs. [œ]

Wer höhnt roh, wer stört so
Des Mönchs Wort?
Den schnöd Gold betört hold,
Der stört dort des Mönchs Wort!
Klöster krönen öde Höhen;

Hör' der Mönche Chöre tönen:
«Göttlich schön erlöst
Versöhnen,
Böse mögen's schnöd
verhöhnen...»

7. [yː] vs. [ʏ]

Über der Wüste düstere Gründe
Führet die zürnenden Brüder
vorüber;
Schüsse grüßen herüber,
hinüber,
Künden die Führer der
dürstenden Züge.

Sündigen Wüten, mit Flüchen
verbündet,
Kürzen—wie trüg'risch—die
Mühen der Wüste;
Drüben erst grüßen sie
Frühlingslüfte,
Küssen trüb flüsternd die Düfte
der Blüten!

8. Diphthong [ae]

Mein Meister freit ein reizend

Weib,
Er meint, es sei ein Zeitvertreib!

Allein, was treibt die kleine
Maid,
Den Greis zu freien in Eiligkeit?
Meint sie, beim Greis sei's

Dasein leicht,
Wenngleich sich keine
Gleichheit zeigt?

9. Diphthong [ao]
Auch das Laub rauscht auf der
Au—
Blauer Rauch schmaucht aus
dem Hause,
Trauben lauschen aus dem

Laube;
Kraut und Trauben zu
verkaufen,
Laufen aufwärts schlaue
Bauern.

10. Diphthong [ɔø]
Häuser, Bäume, Scheunen,
Zäune,
Kräuselt, heulend leuchtend
Feuer!

Scheu dort läuft schon eure
Meute,
Bäumt sich, träumt von neuer
Beute!

11. Mixture of diphthongs
[ae][ao][ɔø]
Ein leuchtender Tau
Weilt heut auf der Au.

Der Eichbaum beut Rast,
Sein Laub beugt den Ast.
Ein säuselnder Hauch
Streift leise euch auch.

Consonants
1. Plosives [b][p][d][t][g][k]
[b] vs. [p]
Bald bebt im Purpur die blonde
Braut,
Bunt blühen Blaublümelein am
Boden;
Breitblättriger Palmbaum

prangt beim Portal,
Breitbauschige Banner beleben
den Plan!
Ob Preis man, Prunk, und
bebänderte Pracht
Blöd beibringt als Brautgebinde
dem Paar...?

[d] vs. [t]

Betet, danket, darbet, duldet!

Nicht entrückt durch töricht
Denken,

Nicht enttäuscht, verderbt
durch Welttand,

Trifft der Tod dich nicht dort
drüben.

Fort mit der Demut dürft'ger
Tracht!

Nicht deucht dich's dumm und
töricht doch,

Daß dort der düst're Tod dir
droht,

Der tobend dröhnt und leicht
dich trifft!

[k] vs. [g]

Kummerkrank kauernd—kaum
karge Kost,

Krummgeknebelt—kalte Kette
des Kerkers;

Kommt kecker Kerl und kündet
Kühnem Krieger künft'gen

Kampf!

Gar gnädig gibt Gott
Gaben an Geld und Gut;

Ganz gern gab Gregor der
Große

Güter und Gold gegen Gottes
Gnadengut hin.

2. Fricatives

[v][f][z][s][ʃ][h][ç][χ]

[v] vs. [f]

Wie wär's wohl, wenn wir
weilten,

Wo wogende Wellen weich
winken,

Wo wonniges Wehen im Walde,

Wenn Westwinde wiegen und

weben?

Fischfrevler Franz fing frech

Vorm Flußfall fette
Fünffingerfische.

Vier fichtne, feste Fischfässer

Faßten vollauf den Fang—

Viele freilich flitzten flott
davon!

[z] vs. [s]

Es senkt sich sacht die Sonne,

Sanft säuselt's längs dem Flusse;

Leis singt selbst ems'ge Drossel,

Rings Sehnsucht süß
entfesselnd.

Selbstsucht ist solch böses
Laster,

Daß sogar es solche hassen,   sünd'gen.
Die sonst selbst nicht selten

[ʃ]
Spät aus spitz'gen Speichers   Schnell zum schmalen
Spalte   Schlossesschornstein,
Speis' und Speck im Spinde   Schrillen Schreis den
spähend.   Schloßschenk schreckend!

[h]   Hetzt herzhaft Hennen und
Hinterm Haus heult Hassan,   Hahn
Harrachs Hofhund, heißhungrig   Halb haushoch zum Heuhaufen
hervor—   hin!

[j]   jauchzend,
Jubelnd, johlend und   Jetzt im Jänner des Jahrs.

[ç] vs. [χ]   Lacht nicht Rache noch Sieg!
Nicht schlechte Wächter   Durch schlechte Streich'
scheuchen   Macht Knecht sich reich,
Wichte, welche frech lächelnd,   Schleicht nachts sacht, lächelt
Ziemlich bezecht—möchten   noch!
flüchtig entweichen.   Deucht's euch auch Nacht—
Nach solch nichtigem Krieg   Reichsacht doch wacht!

3. Laterals: [l]
Lang lauscht Lilli—endlich   «Lisple, lieblich, Liebeslallen;
lieblos lächelnd   Lächeln ließ mich längst solch
Lallt sie leise: Liebleids Langweil!»

4. Nasals [n][ŋ]

Nun nahen neue Wonnen
Nun glänzt und grünt manch
Land;
Von Hoffnungen trunken,

In Ahnung versunken
Wanken und schwanken,
Dem Undank zanken,
Kein Heim erwerben;

[n] vs. [m]

Wenn Männer den Mädchen
mal Ständchen bringen,
Im Nachen mit neckischem
Brummen, mit Singen,

Dann murmeln die Muhmen mit
Nasenrümpfen
Empfindsam und meinen, man
müsse nun schimpfen!

5. Trills [ɾ]

[ɾ] vs. [ʀ]

Schwer heran braust
Sturmeswetter,
Dräuend rasselt Donners
Grollen!
Sturm und Brandung rauschen
rasend,
Erde selber schwer

erschütternd,
Donner furchtbar
überdröhnend!
Wer war dort der
Mauerbrecher,
Der verheert mir Burg und
Ritter?
Zerrt hierher mir den Barbar!

Suffixes: *-ern* and *-ernd*

Erzitternd gewittern
Schmetternd erschütternde
Schauern!

Kletternd und kauernd,
Wandernd und lauernd,
Wimmernd zähnklappernde
Bauern!

6. Consonant blends

[ɾt][pf][kv]

[ɾt]

Zerstört der Herd,

Geschürt der Mord,
Schwirrt rauh der Nord,
Der's Mark verzehrt.
Geschart, gepaart

Nach Räuber Art;

Rückfahrt erschwert,

Trostwort verwehrt,

Betört irrt, der hier Recht

begehrt!

[f] [pf]

Für fünffachen Frevel fluchvoll

verpfändet,

Verfallen dem Pfeile finstrer

Verfolgung—

Verhalfen feinfühlige Frauen

zur Flucht.

Grashupfer schlüpft,

Der Tropf—und hüpft,

Mit Zopf und Zipfel—

Aus Sumpf zum Wipfel!

[kv]

Erquickende Quelle quillt

quirlend empor.

Quiekende Quinten quälen

quengelnde Quäker.

7. Affricates [ts]

Es zogen zwei Sänger zum

säuselnden See,

Zart sangen zur Zither sie

Tänze;

Daß Zeisig ganz sacht zur

selben Zeit

Sich zurückzog zu des

Waldsaumes Grenze.

Jetzt wetzt der Letzt',

Gehetzt entsetzt

Des Messers flitz'ge Spitz'!

I wish to thank European American Music Distributors, LLC for their kind permission to reprint the above excerpts of their copyrighted work.

Hey DER KLEINE HEY: DIE KUNST DES SPRECHENS
© 1997 Schott Music GmbH & Co. KG, Mainz
© 1956 and 1971 (revised edition) by Schott Music GmbH and Co. KG, Mainz
All Rights Reserved.
Used by permission of European American Music Distributors LLC, sole U.S. and Canadian agent for Schott Music GmbH & Co. KG, Mainz

Appendix C: Suggested Repertoire for Lyric Diction Study

While singers are developing their vocal technique it is useful for diction classes to keep the repertoire at a level that will not interfere with any technical study in the voice studio. It is highly recommended that students focus on the study of folk songs and strophic songs early in their vocal development and initial study of lyric diction. This enables students to concentrate on the production of individual phonemes. The following lists are guidelines for planning repertoire specifically for the study of lyric diction at both the undergraduate and graduate level:

Undergraduate Level

1. Freshman/Sophomore Level
English:

Arne, Thomas	Blow, Blow, Thou Winter Wind
	The Timely Admonition
	The Plague of Love
	When Daisies Pied
Barber, Samuel	The Daisies, op.2, no.1
Britten, Benjamin	Folk Song Arrangements (Complete)
Copland, Aaron	Old American Songs (Complete)
Dowland, John	By a Fountain Where I Lay
	Come Again!
	Five Knacks for Ladies

	Flow, My Tears
	Weep You No More, Sad Fountains
	What If I Never Speed?
Haydn, Joseph	A Pastoral Song
	The Mermaid's Song
	She Never Told Her Love
	Piercing Eyes
Head, Michael	Sweet Chance, That Led My Steps Abroad
	When I Think Upon the Maidens
Ireland, John	If There Were Dreams to Sell
	Sea Fever
	Spring Sorrow
Lawes, Henry	Beauty and Love
	Come, Lovely Phillis
	How Happy Art Thou
	I Prethee, Send Me Back My Heart
MacNutt, Walter	O Love, Be Deep
	Take Me to a Green Isle
Purcell, Henry	I Attempt from Love's Sickness to Fly
	Nymphs and Shepherds
	Strike the Viol
Quilter, Roger	Now Sleeps the Crimson Petal
	Weep You No More, Sad Fountains
Vaughan Williams, R.	Linden Lea
	The Sky Above the Roof

German:

Brahms, Johannes	49 Deutsche Volkslieder, WoO33
	Komm bald, op.97, no.5
	Sonntag, op.47, no.3
Mendelssohn, Felix	An die Entfernte, op.71, no.8
	Das Waldschloss

Der Blumenstrauß, op.47, no.5

Gruß, op.19, no.5

Morgengruß, op.47, no.2

Volkslied, op.47, no.4

Mozart, W.A.	Das Veilchen
	Komm, liebe Zither
	Warnung
Schubert, Franz	Heidenröslein, op.3, no.3

An die Musik, op.88, no.4

Litanei

An die Nachtigall, op.98, no.1

An mein Klavier

Geheimes, op.14, no.2

Lachen und Weinen, op.59, no.4

Meeres Stille, op.3, no.2

Der König in Thule, op.5, no.5

Seligkeit

Schumann, Robert	from *Myrthen, op.25*
	Die Lotosblume
	Du bist wie eine Blume
	Der Nußbaum
	Widmung

2. Junior/Senior Level

English:

Barber, Samuel	Sure on This Shining Night
Butterworth, George	Loveliest of Trees
Head, Michael	A Blackbird Singing
	Beloved
	The Ships of Arcady
Hoiby, Lee	The Shepherd

	Where the Music Comes From
Hundley, Richard	Come Ready and See Me
	Will There Really Be a Morning?
Purcell, Henry	Come all ye Songsters (*The Fairy Queen*)
	Fairest Isle (*The Tempest*)
	If Music be the Food of Love, 1st setting
	I'll Sail upon the Dog-star
	Music for a While (*Oedipus*)
	Sweeter Than Roses (*Pausanias*)
	What Can We Poor Females Do?
Quilter, Roger	Come away, Death, op.6, no.1
	Dream Valley, op.20, no.1
	Fair House of Joy, op.12, no.7
	Go, Lovely Rose, op.24, no.3
	June
	Love's Philosophy, op.3, no.1
	Music, When Soft Voices Die, op.25, no.5
	My Life's Delight, op.12, no.2
	O Mistress Mine, op.6, no.2
	The Faithless Shepherdess, op.12, no.4
Rorem, Ned	Early in the Morning
	Love
	The Nightingale
	Stopping by Woods on a Snowy Evening
Vaughan Williams, R.	Songs of Travel (nine songs)

German:

Brahms, Johannes	Dein blaues Auge, op.59, no.4
	O kühler Wald, op.72, no.3
	Ständchen, op.106, no.1
	Über die Heide, op.86, no.4

	Vergebliches Ständchen, op.84, no.4
	Wie bist du, meine Königin, op.32, no.9
	Wie Melodien zieht es mir, op.105, no.1
	Wir wandelten, op.96, no.2
Mendelssohn, Felix	Auf Flügeln des Gesanges, op.34, no.2
	Das erste Veilchen, op.19, no.2
	Die Liebende schreibt, op.86, no.3
	Neue Liebe, op.19, no.4
	Suleika, op.34, no.4
Mozart, W.A.	Abendempfindung
	Als Luise die Briefe ihres ungetreuen Liebhabers verbrannte
	An Chloë
Schubert, Franz	An den Mond, op.57, no.2
	Auf dem Wasser zu singen, op.72
	Bei dir! op.95, no.2
	Der Jüngling an der Quelle
	Der Musensohn, op.92, no.1
	Der Wanderer an den Mond, op.80, no.1
	Der Wanderer, op.4, no.1
	Die Blumensprache, op.173, no.5
	Die Forelle, op.32
	Erlafsee, op.8, no.3
	Frühlingsglaube, op.20, no.2
	Ganymed, op.19, no.3
	Im Frühling
	Nacht und Träume, op.43, no.2
	Nachtviolen
	Rastlose Liebe, op.5, no.1
	from *Schwanengesang*
	Das Fischermädchen

Ihr Bild

Ständchen

Schumann, Robert   from *Frauenliebe und -leben, op.42*

Er, der Herrlichste von Allen

Du Ring an meinem Finger

Seit ich ihn gesehen

Dein Angesicht, op.127, no.2

Marienwürmchen, op.79, no.14

Mein schöner Stern! op.101, no.4

Strauss, Richard   Ach Lieb, ich muss nun scheiden, op.21, no.3

All mein Gedanken, op.21, no.1

Allerseelen, op.10, no.8

Freundliche Vision, op.48, no.1

Graduate Level

English:

Argento, Dominick   Six Elizabethan Songs

Bridge, Frank   Love Went A-Riding

Britten, Benjamin   Cabaret Songs (four songs)

On this Island, op.11 (five songs)

Selections from *Albert Herring, A Midsummer*
Night's Dream, Billy Budd, The Turn of the Screw)

Copland, Aaron   Twelve Poems of Emily Dickenson

Elgar, Edward   Sea Pictures, op.37 (five songs)

Finzi, Gerald   A Young Man's Exhortation (ten songs)

Let Us Garlands Bring (5 songs)

Händel, G.F.   Selections from *Acis and Galatea, Messiah,*
Semele

Heggie, Jake   Paper Wings (four songs)

Songs to the Moon (eight songs)

Hoiby, Lee   The Message

	The Serpent
	What If?
Larsen, Libby	Cowboy Songs (three songs)
	Love After 1950 (five songs)
Mendelssohn, Felix	Selections from *Elijah*
Moore, Douglas	Selections from *The Ballad of Baby Doe*
Purcell, Henry	The Blessed Virgin's Expostulation
	Mad Bess (*The Indian Queen*)

German:

Brahms, Johannes	Zigeunerlieder (8 songs)
Mahler, Gustav	Rückert-Lieder (5 songs)
	Ich ging mit Lust durch einen grünen Wald
	Lob des hohen Verstands
	Rheinlegendchen
	Starke Einbildungskraft
	Wer hat dies Liedlein erdacht?
Marx, Joseph	Der bescheidene Schäfer
	Frage und Antwort
	Hat dich die Liebe berührt
	Nachtgebet
	Selige Nacht
	Waldseligkeit
Schubert, Franz	Heimliches Lieben, op.106, no.1
	Nachtstück, op.36, no.2
	from *Schwanengesang*
	Der Doppelgänger
	Frühlingssehnsucht
	Liebesbotschaft
	Selections from *Die schöne Müllerin, op.25*
Schumann, Robert	Selections from *Dichterliebe, op.48*
	Selections from *Liederkreis, op.39*

Strauss, Richard	Cäcilie, op.27, no.2
	Drei Lieder der Ophelia, op.67
	Du meines Herzens Krönelein, op.21, no.2
	Heimliche Aufforderung, op.27, no.3
	Ich schwebe, op.48, no.2
	Ich trage meine Minne, op.32, no.1
	Mein Herz ist stumm, op.19, no.6
	Nichts, op.10, no.2
	Schlagende Herzen, op.29, no.2
	Ständchen, op.17, no.2
	Traum durch die Dämmerung, op.29, no.1
	Zueignung, op.10, no.1
Wolf, Hugo	Anakreons Grab
	An eine Aeolsharfe
	Das verlassene Mägdlein
	Der Gärtner
	Der Tambour
	Die Bekehrte
	Die Spröde
	Elfenlied
	Frühling übers Jahr
	Im Frühling
	Lebe Wohl
	Peregrina I and II
	Verborgenheit
	Verschwiegene Liebe

Appendix D: Answers to Supplementary Exercises

Chapter 2: Proficiency in English IPA

1. [i], [i], [ɪ], [ɪ], [i], [i], [ɪ], [ɪ], [ɪ], [i], [i], [i], [ɪ], [ɪ], [ɪ], [i], [i], [ɪ]

2. [i], [ɛ], [ɛ], [i], [ɛ], [ɛ], [i], [i], [ɛ], [i], [i], [ɛ], [ɛ], [i], [i], [ɛ]

3. [æ], [ɛ], [æ], [æ], [æ], [æ] and [ɛ], [æ], [æ], [æ], [æ], [æ], [æ], [ɛ] and [ɛ], [ɛ], [æ], [æ], [æ], [æ], [æ]

4. [ə], [ə], [ə], [ə], [ʌ], [ʌ], [ə], [ə], [ə], [ʌ], [ʌ], [ʌ], [ə], [ʌ] and [ə], [ʌ], [ʌ] and [ə], [ə], [ʌ] and [ə], [ʌ] and [ə], [ʌ]

5. [ɔ], [ɔ], [ɑ], [ɑ], [ɑ], [ɑ], [ɔ], [ɔ], [ɔ], [ɑ], [ɑ], [ɔ], [ɔ], [ɔ], [ɑ], [ɔ], [ɔ], [ɔ], [ɑ]

6. [ʊ], [ʊ], [u], [u], [u], [ʊ], [ʊ], [u], [ʊ], [u], [u], [u], [ʊ], [u], [ʊ], [ʊ], [u], [u], [ʊ], [u], [ʊ], [u]

7. [aɪ], [oʊ], [eɪ], [aʊ], [ɔɪ], [aɪ], [eɪ], [ɔɪ], [aʊ], [oʊ], [ɔɪ], [aɪ], [aɪ], [ɔɪ], [oʊ], [eɪ], [aɪ], [aʊ], [eɪ], [ɔɪ]

8. [ɑə], [ʊə], [ɪə], [ɛə], [ɛə], [ɪə], [ʊə], [ɔə], [ɑə], [ɔə], [ʊə], [ɛə], [ɔə], [ɪə], [ɑə], [ɔə], [ɪə], [ɑə], [ɛə] or [ɪə], [ʊə]

9. [əˈgæst], [bɪˈhaɪnd], [ʃəˈlæk], [bɪəd], [nɑb], [lɑbɪ], [gæləp], [ɑkjupaɪ] or [ɑkjəpaɪ], [ɛksəpt], [nʌgət], [foʊld], [æbəs], [daɪəlɑg], [m̊aʊntən], [ænˈtik], [tʃɛdə], [ʃʌtə], [spid], [koʊd], [hæpən], [pʌdəl], [sʌpə], [ɹætəl]

10. [θɛft], [bəˈɹɑʒ], [səˈnɛɹoʊ] or [səˈnɑɹoʊ], [m̊ɪspə], [pɛɹəʃut] or [pæɹəʃut], [soʊʃəl], [dɪˈzaɪnə], [m̊aɪ], [pɑvətɪ], [saɪkɪk], [spɹɪŋ], [pəˈmɪʃən], [dɪvɪ], [sʌðən], [ʃʊgə], [kənˈfjuʒən], [zɛst], [hoʊl],

[fɹaɪtənɪŋ], [mɛsədʒ], [gæðə], [mɛʒə], [neɪʃən], [fə'nɑmənəl], [pʌzəl], [dʒə'ɹæf], [ʃʊd], [tiθ], [kɔf], [sidə], [hoʊm], [vɜbəl]

11. [θɪŋk], [mə'laɪn], [mɛɹɪ], [noʊm], [bɹɑŋks], [ɔtəm], [sʌmət], [nid], [ɹɪŋə], [kwɔm], [pɪntʃ], ['njuz,wɜðɪ], [ə'plɑm], [sɪnə], [juɲən], [njubaɪl]

12. [pjunətɪ], [kɹoʊm], [kwɔət], [bɪ'weɪl], [fɹeɪz], [tjuzdeɪ], [kænjən], [ə'wɛə], [bɜ], [ɹaɪ'nɑsəɹəs], [kjʊə], [weɪk], [ljut], [wʌndə], [mɪljən], [ɹaɪ], [mju'zɪʃən], [kwaɪt], [hju], [junə'vɜsətɪ], [ɹæpsədɪ], [ɪ'kweɪʒən], [djuk], [ɹɪgəl], [kwɔətəlɪ], [ə'sjum]

13. [tʃeɪnd], [dʒɛnəɹeɪt], [pɪdʒən], [sɜtʃ], [dʒæzmən], [fɑə'fɛtʃt], [lɛktʃə], [vɛdʒɪ], [dʒɪm'neɪzɪəm], [nætʃəɹəl], [stɹætədʒɪ], [dʒʌstəs], [mædʒəstɪ], [dɑdʒ], [fidʒɪ], [dʒoʊk], [dʒaɪənt], [tʃɔɪs], [lɑədʒ], [dʒɔ]

Chapter 3: Proficiency in German IPA

1. [iː], [iː], [ɪ], [iː], [ɪ], [iː], [ɪ], [iː], [iː], [ɪ], [iː], [ɪ], [ɪ], [i] and [iː], [ɪ], [ɪ], [iː], [ɪ], [ɪ], [ɪ], [iː], [ɪ], [iː], [iː]

2. [ɛ] and [eː], [ɛ], [eː], [ɛ] and [ɛ], [ɛ], [eː], [ɛ], [ɛ], [eː], [eː], [ɛ], [eː], [ɛ], [eː], [eː], [eː], [ɛ], [eː], [eː], [ɛ], [ɛ]

3. [ɛ], [ɛː], [ɛː], [ɛ], [ɛː], [ɛ], [ɛː], [ɛː], [ɛː], [ɛ], [ɛː], [ɛ], [ɛː], [ɛ], [ɛ], [ɛː], [ɛː], [ɛ], [ɛ], [ɛː], [ɛ]

4. [aː], [a], [aː], [a], [aː] and [a], [aː], [a], [a], [aː], [a], [aː], [a], [aː], [aː], [a], [aː], [a], [aː], [a] and [a], [a]

5. [oː], [ɔ], [oː], [oː], [ɔ], [ɔ], [oː], [oː], [ɔ], [ɔ], [oː], [ɔ], [ɔ], [oː], [ɔ], [oː], [oː], [ɔ], [oː], [ɔ]

6. [uː], [uː], [ʊ], [uː], [ʊ], [uː], [ʊ], [uː], [ʊ], [ʊ], [uː], [ʊ], [ʊ], [ʊ], [uː], [uː], [ʊ], [ʊ], [uː], [uː]

7. [ʏ], [yː], [ʏ], [yː], [yː], [ʏ], [yː], [yː], [ʏ], [ʏ], [yː], [yː], [ʏ], [yː], [ʏ], [yː], [yː], [ʏ], [yː], [ʏ]

8. [øː], [œ], [øː], [œ], [øː], [œ], [øː], [œ], [øː], [øː], [œ], [œ], [œ], [øː], [øː], [øː], [œ], [œ], [œ], [øː]

9. [ae], [ao], [ɔø], [ae], [ao], [ɔø], [ae], [ae], [ae], [ɔø], [ɔø], [ao], [ae], [ɔø], [ae], [ao], [ao], [ae], [ɔø], [ao], [ao], [ɔø], [ao], [ɔø]

10. [mʊtɐ], [halp], [blaeʃtɪft], [daŋkbaːɐ], [fraːgə], [babəln], [ʃtat], [praes], [knʊdəln], [valt], [grɛntsə], [pʊpə], [bəˈtriːp], [tantsən], [bagərzeː], [kœnən], [aˈkɔrt], [blɪkən], [teaːtɐ], [ʃlaːk], [briːf], [diːnst], [rʏkeːɐ], [ʃmɛkən]

11. [grøːsə], [nɛfə], [vaːˈrʊm], [ʃpraχə], [viːzʊm], [aofyːrən], [ʒeˈniː], [apzɔlviːrən], [ʃtuˈdɛnt], [fɪndən], [fɛɐˈ|anʃtaltən], [foˈneːtɪk], [graːs], [bəˈvaezən], [ʃɛŋkən], [ʒʊrnaˈlɪsmʊs], [klaːrhaet], [vɪçtɪç], [mʏsən], [dʊftən], [haot], [zɔmɐ], [ʃpraχkʊrs], [gəˈhøːrən]

12. [gəˈdaŋkə], [kɪn], [mançmaːl], [nɛçstə], [zɪŋkən], [mʊrməln], [anfaŋən], [kʊmɐ], [ʃpɪnə], [noːtfal], [drɪŋən], [kaom], [ɪnərhalp], [ʃlaŋk], [trɔməl], [gəˈvɪməl], [voːnʊŋ], [anmɛrkən], [ʃvaŋkən], [neːmən]

13. [meːɐ], [ʊntərɪçt], [ɛɐˈtsɛːlən], [faːtɐ], [raeə], [oːɐ], [vaetɐ], [ʃpɛrʊŋ], [deːɐˈzɛlbə], [faːraːt] or [faːɐraːt], [vɪrt], [rastloːs], [traoɐ], [briːfmarkə], [drae], [diːɐ], [ɛɐˈzeːən], [fɛɐˈʃteːən], [uːɐ], [kɔrigiːrən], [foːɐwɛrts], [rʊkzak], [fɛɐˈgɛsən], [tsɛrən]

14. [naχt], [mɛːtçən], [aχtʊŋ], [nɪçt], [mɪlç], [dʊrç], [dɔχ], [zeːnzʊχt], [brɛçən], [bɛçlaen], [ʃprʏçə], [buːχ], [aoχ], [ɪnɪç], [praχt], [høːɐ], [eːvɪç], [mança], [gəˈbrɔχən]

15. [tsaːn|artst], [kʊrts], [tsɛlziʊs], [vɪtsɪç], [kʊtʃə], [aofvɛrts], [raetsən], [tsɛːzaːr], [lʊtʃən], [katsə], [geːts], [paetʃə], [pflantsə], [rɛːtsəl], [nɪçts], [rʊtʃən], [tsyˈrɪlɪʃ], [zɪtsən], [hɛrtslɪç], [giːpts]

16. [taksiː], [kvɛlə], [ɛɐˈvaksənə], [kviːtʃən], [fɪks], [kvatʃ], [fɪˈksiːrʊŋ], [zɛks], [kvɛtʃən], [nɪksən], [kvaˈdraːt], [vaksən], [ɛˈksaːmən], [kvasəln], [kvaːl], [dakshʊnt], [kvarən], [flɛksibiliˈtɛːt], [kvɛːlən], [fʊks], [kvartaːl]

Chapter 6: The Structure of English

1. [fəˈtig], [lɪsənɪŋ], [ɹɛtʃəd], [kɹəˈtik], [saɪˈkoʊsəs], [bɔk], [eɪt], [ni], [klɔ], [ɹɪtən], [huz], [kɔk], [koʊm], [sæmən], [sinɪk], [hum], [naɪ], [ɹɛtəɹɪk]

2. [pipəl], [æpəl], [stipəl], [ɹɪpəl], [sɪmpəl], [tɹæmpəl], [eɪbəl], [bʌbəl], [bɔbəl], [tɹʌbəl], [ɹɪdəl], [aɪdəl], [litə], [kʌdəl], [oʊgəl], [kɑdəl]

3. dictionary, begin, comedy, department, probable, continue, photo-graphic, opportunity, economy, admission, envelop, delusion

4. leased/least, missed/mist, rye/wry, flu/flew

5. go-vernm-en-tal, spi-ri-tu-al, a-cce-ssi-ble, be-a-ti-tude, con-cert, in-tim-ate, a-bi-li-ty, o-ptim-i-stic, a-nxi-e-ty, a-lter-nate, re-co-gni-za-ble, ne-ce-ssa-ri-ly, in-fe-ctious

6. e'lectric, elec'tronic, e'lectrify, elec'trolysis, elec'trician, e'lectrical, electrifi'cation, 'photograph, pho'tographer, pho'tography, photo'gra-phic, 'analyze, a'nalysis, ana'lytical, a'nalogy, tech'nique, tech'nology, techno'logical, tech'nician, 'technical, 'medic, 'medical, 'medicine, me'di-cinal, e'conomy, eco'nomic, eco'nomical, ho'mogenize, homo'geneous, homoge'neity, 'real, 'really, 'realize, re'ality, 'realism, 'realist, rea'listic, reali'zation, di'vide, di'vision, di'visible, divisi'bility, di'visional, di'visive, di'visor, 'voluntary, vo'lition, volun'teer, volun'tarily, 'produce, 'product, pro'duction, pro'ductive, pro'ducible, pro'ductiveness, produc'tivity, pro'duce, pro'ducer, re'late, re'lation, re'lational, re'lationship, 'relative, 'relatively, rela'tivity, re'latedness

Chapter 7: Characteristic English Phonemes

1. [jɔə], [dɪ'naɪ], [sɪmbəl], [fɪzɪks], [madəfaɪ], [saɪkɪ], [ju], [jɜnɪŋ], [tɪɪst], [fɔətəfaɪ], [bjutəfaɪ], [joʊk], [θɛɹəpɪ], [vɪləfaɪ], [jultaɪd], [jild], [vɛɹɪ], [sʌmbədɪ], [jɪə], [lɪɹɪk], [hæpəlɪ], [juθ], [mɛməɹɪ], [lʌvlɪ], [kwɑntəfaɪ], [sɪləndə], [saɪ'kɑlədʒɪ]

Chapter 8: Vowels

1. [ə'bʌv], [hʌmbəl], [dʌbəl], [mʌðə], [ʌn'fɔətʃənət], [tʌsəl], [hʌzbənd], [ʃʌvəl], [bʌbəl], [dʒʌdʒmənt], [lʌvlɪəst], [kʌvət], [ʌðə], [kɪʌmbəl], [ə'mʌŋ], [ɹʌbəl], [jʌŋgə], [ʌn'hæpɪnəs], [ɹʌsəl], [tɹʌbəl], [sʌdən], [bɹʌðə], [ʌɲən], [ə'sʌndə]

2. [fɑðə], [lɑst], [kɔt], [fɔt], [kɹɑs], [ɔltəˈgɛðə], [gɑn], [swɑtʃəz], [flɔ], [ɪnˈstɔl], [glɑsɪ], [təˈmɔɹoʊ], [hɑpɪŋ], [hɔnt], [lɔjə], [bɑnd], [plɑdɪŋ], [tɔɹəd], [wɑndə], [ɔlˈðoʊ]

3. [ɹɪˈhɜs], [sɜdʒ], [dʒɜnɪ], [vɜs], [mɪsəɹɪ], [mæstə], [pəˈhæps], [æktə], [aɪən], [gɜl], [hɜbət], [sɜvə], [lɜnə], [kɜteɪl], [bɜnə], [nɛvə], [bɜd], [ɛvə], [sɛvə], [tɛðə], [əˈnʌðə], [bɜdən], [fɜvə], [wɜkə], [mɜmə], [mɜdə], [pəˈvɜtəd], [ʃɛpəd], [neɪbə], [kɜtsɪ], [pəˈfɔəm], [mɛʒə], [hɜt]

4. [tuθ], [wʊdəd], [bɹʊk], [spun], [suð], [tʊk], [gun], [ʃʊk], [mun], [gʊd], [kul], [pul], [fɔəˈsʊk], [sun], [lʊkt], [lus], [kɹʊkəd], [ful], [wud], [bʊk], [sʊt], [lun], [fud], [swund], [bəˈlun]

5. [ʌnˈtɪl], [mɪdɪənt], [ˈdaɪəˌlɛkt], [ʌndəˈniθ], [lɪtə], [ʌnˈlɛs], [soʊfə], [ʌnˈɹɪl], [sɛntə], [ˈʌndəˌwɜld], [ɹoʊzəz], [dʌv], [pɹɛzəns], [kʌm], [tʌf], [hoʊpləs], [kɪŋdəm], [əˈtɛmpt], [dʌn], [glʌv], [ɹaɪət], [nʌn], [tɹɛbəl], [ˈsʌmˌwʌn], [sʌn], [pɜpəs], [tʌtʃ], [pɛbəl], [dʌl], [ɹaɪfəl], [kwaɪət], [ʌnˈtaɪ]

6. [mɛʒə], [sɛnʃə], [vɜdʒə] or [vɜdjə], [kjʊə], [əbˈskjʊə], [lɛʒə] or [liʒə], [neɪtʃə], [ʃʊəlɪ], [pjʊə], [ɹæptʃə], [stætʃə], [sɪˈkjʊɹɪtɪ], [kæptʃə], [tɹɛʒə], [tɛɲə], [ljʊə], [əˈʃʊə], [ʃʊə], [ɛnˈkloʊʒə], [kəmˈpoʊʒə], [ɛnˈdjʊə], [fɜnətʃə], [vɛntʃə], [fjutʃə], [lɛktʃə], [kɹɪtʃə], [fɪtʃə], [ɪnˈʃʊɹəns]

7. [dɛsələt], [pɹoʊˈtɛkt], [poʊp], [pɹoʊˈlɪfɪk], [əˈgoʊ], [ɹoʊmd], [pɹoʊˈfaʊnd], [oʊˈmɪt], [smoʊldə], [pɹoʊˈtɛst], [fɑloʊ], [doʊ], [toʊd], [noʊˈvɛmbə], [gloʊb], [hoʊ], [fɹɪvələs], [məˈlɛst], [pɹoʊˈvaɪd], [mɪdɪˈoʊkə], [moʊld], [ɪˈɹoʊd], [pɹoʊˈnaʊns], [mɛlədɪ], [bɜɹoʊ], [wɪndoʊ], [θɜɹoʊ], [oʊˈbeɪ], [æɹoʊ], [pɹoʊˈhɪbət], [boʊst], [pɹoʊˈkleɪm], [pəˈlɪs]

8. [vɛɹɪ], [daɪə], [pjʊə], [dɛə], [dɛɹɪ], [hɪə], [mɪə], [daɪəɹɪ], [sɪnˈsɪəlɪ], [fɛə], [vɪə], [ɪə], [fɛɹɪ], [fɛəlɪ], [sɪˈkjʊə], [dɪˈvaʊə], [dɪˈvaʊɹɪŋ], [taɪɹɪŋ], [pjʊɹətɪ], [ɹɹɪ], [kwɪə], [tɹɹɪ], [kwɪɹɪ], [jɪəlɪ], [wɪɹɪ], [pʊɹə], [kjʊɹəs], [ɛɹɪ], [vɛɹɪ], [ɹɛɹəst], [tʃɪɹɪ], [tʃɪəfʊl], [kɛə], [dɪəlɪ], [hɪəbaɪ], [nɪəlɪ], [ɹɪˈvɪə], [sɪnˈsɪə], [taɪəd], [sɪˈkjʊɹətɪ], [vɛɹəlɪ], [kæɹɪ]

9. [lɜn], [mɜsɪ], [hɜd], [kɑlə], [jɜnɪŋ], [ɹɪˈmɛmbə], [bɜtʃ], [pɹɑktə], [feɪvəɹət], [tɹɛʒə], [vɜtju], [dʒɜnɪ], [pəˈsju], [wɜɹɪ], [mɜmə], [leɪbə],

[mɜtəl], [vɜdʒ], [bɹʌðə], [ɛnˈkʌɹədʒ], [fluɹəʃ], [lɛʒə] or [liʒə], [sɜdʒ],
[nɛktə], [pəˈplɛks], [dɪˈfɜ], [dɪfə], [wɜd], [gɜθ], [kæstə], [kʌmfət],
[hjumə], [kʌləfʊl], [pəˈpɔət], [kəˈɹeɪdʒəs], [kɜt]

10. [woʊfʊl], [neɪbəlɪ], [əˈlaʊ], [vɔɪs], [smoʊk], [sleɪ], [bɹɔɪl], [ɹoʊd],
[səˈblaɪm], [gɹeɪ], [fɜloʊ], [əˈnɔɪ], [θaʊzənd], [koʊmə], [ɹɔɪəl], [saɪləns],
[fɹaʊn], [feɪbəl], [bɛloʊ], [ɹɪˈzaɪn], [dɛkeɪd], [ðaʊ], [pɪloʊ], [peɪnfʊl],
[kɹaɪd], [haɪt], [ɹeɪnɪ], [foʊmɪ], [bɹeɪk], [dɪˈnaɪ]

11. [kɛəfʊlɪ], [sfɪə], [bɪˈfɔə], [ʃʊə], [bɪə], [hɔəs], [wɔə], [əˈljʊə], [staə],
[ɛnˈdɹɪɪŋ], [jɔə], [əbˈskjʊə], [kaəd], [ʍɛə], [bɪəd], [kɔət], [hɛə], [pjʊə],
[əˈlaəm], [flɔə], [lɪə], [ðɛə], [aʊtdɔə], [kaəv], [ɹeɪndɪə], [əˈdɔən],
[pɛəd], [bɪˈwɛə], [stɔəm], [ɛlsʍɛə], [ɪkˈsplɔə], [sɔəd]

12. [fɜmlɪ], [lʌv], [ɪnˈfɜ], [hoʊmwəd], [ɹʌf], [wʊdlənd], [nɛvə], [θɜst],
[ʌnˈdʌn], [mɛnəs], [səˈpæs], [hʌm], [wɜk], [pəˈɹuz], [ʌnˈhæpɪ], [nʌɹəʃ],
[dɹɪəst], [tɹeɪtə], [pɜpəs], [ʃʌv], [tɹʌbəl], [mɜ], [tjumə], [fæntəm], [ɜθlɪ],
[klʌŋ], [noʊbəl], [səˈpɹaɪz], [dɪˈtɜmən], [ʌndə], [pɜl], [mʌtʃ], [ɪnfəɹəns]

13. [pap], [ɔnt] or [ænt], [ˈpatˌhoʊldə], [əˈplɔd], [wɔk], [kamə], [fɔn],
[dɹæft], [bandɪŋ], [θɔt], [ɔltənət], [klɔ], [gan], [bəˈɹɑʒ], [bɔɹoʊ], [nat],
[kɔʃən], [gəˈɹɑʒ], [wand], [smɔl], [məˈɹɑʒ], [sɔɹoʊ], [sæbətɑʒ], [ɛnˈθɹɔl]

14. desire, conspire, admire, tower, sour, devour, our, inspire, wires,
dire, lyre, fire, liar, cower

Chapter 9: Glides and Approximants

1. [ʍɛt], [wɛt], [ʍɛðə], [wɛðə], [wɪtʃ], [ʍɪtʃ], [wɛə], [ʍɛə], [ʍɪf],
[ʍaɪn], [ʍaɪ], [ʍaɪl], [weɪl], [ʍeɪl], [weɪk], [wʌndə], [woʊ], [ʍətˈɛvə],
[watʃ], [ʍɪspə], [wɹɪ], [wɪəd], [waɪn], [wasp]

2. [djupləkeɪt], [tu], [kjubə], [ɪnˈdjus], [djuk], [djulɪ], [djutɪ], [ɪˈljud],
[pɹeɪljud], [ɪntəljud], [pəˈsjut], [əˈsjum], [plum], [kənˈsjum], [slu],
[ɹɪˈzjum], [ku], [tjuməlt], [stjudənt], [əˈljud], [stjupəd], [mʌltətjud],
[əˈstjut], [stup], [hu], [flut], [tʃuz], [flu], [dʒun], [fɹut], [luz], [ɹɪˈkɹut],
[blu], [tjuzdeɪ], [ɪnˈkluʒən], [ɪˈljuʒən], [kluz], [pjutə]

3. [jɔ ɹoʊn], [ði ʌðə|ɛnd], [fɑ ɹə'weɪ], [slʌbə|ɑn], [stɛ ɹət mi], [stɑ ɹənd mun], [ə pɛ ɹəv ʃuz], [mɔ ɹənd mɔə], [faɪə|ɛndʒən], [nɹɪə|ænd nɹɪə]

4. [blu], [fju], [tɹɪljən], [gɹu], [vju], [klu], [bɪ'jɑnd], [pju], [ɪn'klude], [dju], [ɪks'klud], [ə'skju], [juz], [glu], [fjud], [ju], [bjutəfʊl], [dɪ'ljude], [sjutə], [bjutɪ], [fjutʃə], [ɪm'bjud], [bjugəl], [bjuteɪn], [mjuzɪk], [ɑəgju], [kju], [pɹɪ'zjum], [hjumə], [ljud]

Chapter 10: Consonants

1. [lɑŋ], [ɹɑŋ], [jʌŋ], [ɪ'lɑŋgeɪt], [ɪlɑŋ'geɪʃən], [pɹo'lɑŋ], [tɪŋgəl], [mɑŋgə], [dʒɪŋgəl], [stɹɑŋgəst], [kɑŋgɹəs], [kɪŋ], [wɪŋd], [tʌŋ], [lɑŋɪŋ], [bæŋ], [swɪŋ], [sɪŋgəl], [hʌŋgə], [æŋgəl], [læŋgwədʒ], [lɪŋgə], [læŋgwəd], [ɹɪŋə], [pɹolɑŋ'geɪʃən]

2. [θwɔət], [tið], [tɹuθ], [nɔəθ], [w3ðɪ], [saʊθ], [bɹɪð], [tuθ], [kloʊð], [boʊθ], [maʊðz], [mʌðə], [ðoʊ], [w3θ], [mɛθəd], [ðʌs], [ðɛə], [θɪn], [ðæt], [pæθs] or [pæðz], [ðaɪ], [θim], [dɛθ], [smuð], [b3θ], [θ3st], [faðə], [θɹoʊ], [loʊð], [ɔθə]

3. [voʊg], [dʒ3m], [dʒab], [gɹoʊ], [t3dʒəd], [igə], [dʒaɪ'ɹeɪʃən], [gaʊn], [fɹɪdʒ], [dʒɛt], [dʒə'lapɪ], [dʒɛstə], [bɛgə], [dʒɪg], [bændʒoʊ], [g3kən], [kætəlag], [dʒunəpə], [bɪndʒ], [gɪl], [ɹɪgəl], [spə'gɛtɪ], [ɛpəlag], [taɪgə], [ɹɛdʒəmən], [gɛtoʊ], [ɛdʒ], [gɪgəl], [dʒʌmp], [tə'bagən]

4. [laks], [ɪg'zæm], [ɪk'stɹæpəleɪt], [ɛgzət], [sək'sɪŋkt], [ɪg'zɔst], [æksənt], [ɪk'spɛɹəmənt], [aksən], [baksəz], [ɪgzɔl'teɪʃən], [ɪk'stɪŋgwəʃ], [æksədənt], [ɪk'stɹim], [ə'fɪks], [ɪg'zæmpəlz], [ɪg'zɛmpt], [ɪg'zæktətjud], [ɪg'zɛmpləɹɪ], [sək'sid], [æksəs], [ɪk'spɹɪɹəns], ['hɛksə,gan], [ɪg'zjum], [ɪg'zædʒəɹeɪt], [ək'sɛntjueɪt], [ɪg'zanəɹeɪt], [æks]

Chapter 11: Advanced Concepts in Diction

1. [wɪ ði], [fɔ ɹɛvə |ɹənd ə deɪ], [wɪθaʊt |ə kɛə] or [wɪðaʊt], [wɪθ tʃaəlz], [aɪ həv tɹaɪd tu goʊ], [ʃʊə aɪ hæv], [ət |ə las], [ʃi ɛn'dʒɔɪz bɪɪŋ lʊkt |æt],

[ɔl fə ðɛm], [ði əˈkeɪʒən], [ɔl ðə ʍaɪl], [ʍʌt|ɑə ju weɪtɪŋ fɔə], [hɑəd |əv hɪɹɪŋ], [ðə bɜnɪŋ hɑət], [wɪð bjutɪ], [wɪ θɔənz], [wɪ θæŋks], [wɪ ðaɪn]

2. [lɑkt], [dɹimd], [tʌtʃt], [wɔkt], [gɹaʊndəd], [læft], [faʊndəd], [laɪkt], [wɜkt], [gɹæspt], [lʌvd], [sægd], [mɪst], [ɹʌʃt], [pækt], [kəmˈpoʊzd], [vænəʃt], [æskt], [feɪnd], [əˈtætʃt], [plɛdʒd], [stɑpt], [ɹʌbd], [kɹækt], [dɹægd], [tɔkt], [hoʊpt], [blɛst], [wɑtʃt], [dɹɑpt], [hipt], [ɪˈvoʊkt], [ɹɛkt], [fɪbd], [fʊlˈfɪld], [kɔft], [simd], [maʊntəd]

3. [dɪˈzɜvɪŋ], [ɹɪˈmaɪndə], [dɪˈlaɪtfʊl], [ɹɪˈstɔə], [dɪˈvoʊʃən], [dɪˈsɪst], [pɹɪˈfɜ], [ɹɪˈzɪst], [pɹɪˈpeɪ], [ɹɪˈsiv], [ɹɪˈtɜn], [diˈmoʊtəveɪt], [diˈbʌg], [diˈkoʊd], [ɹɪˈmɛmbə], [dɪˈzaɪə], [dɪˈsaɪfə], [diˈfɹɑst], [ɹɪˈdʒɔɪs], [dɪˈspaɪt], [pɹiæmbəl], [pɹɪˈzɛnt], [dɪˈlɪbəɹət], [ɹɪˈvɪə], [pɹiˈdeɪt], [dɪˈsɪʒən], [ɹɪˈsplɛndənt], [pɹɪˈdɪkt], [dɪˈspɛə], [pɹɪˈvɛnt], [dɪˈstɹɔɪ]

4. [bɪˈlɪtəl], [sɪˈkluʒən], [ɪgˈzæmpəl], [bɪˈnaɪn], [ɪkˈstætɪk], [bɪˈnoʊnst], [ɪkˈskɹɪt], [ɪˈkwɪp], [sɪˈkjʊə], [ɪˈlɛkt], [sɪˈɹin], [ɛkwətəbəl], [sɪˈvɪə], [ɛgzət], [ɪˈlæstɪk], [sɪˈmæntɪks], [ɛkskɹəmənt], [ɪˈlæbəɹət], [ɪgˈzɔltəd], [sɪˈkwɛstə], [ɛksplətəv], [ɪˈveɪd], [bɪˈgɪn], [ɛgzaɪl], [bɪˈheɪvjə], [ɪgˈzæktətjud], [bɪˈliv], [ˈɛksˌpæt] [bɪˈspik], [bɪˈsaɪd], [ɪˈvɛntʃuəl], [bɪˈkɔz], [bɪˈfɔə], [bɪˈtwin], [ɪˈbʊljənt], [sɪˈkɹiʃən], [ɪgˈzɪst], [ɛkstəsɪ], [sɪɹɪz]

5. could be, sweet dreams, great triumph, drop down, gladness, keep peace, help proudly, take courage, walk quickly, invoke crime, bad thoughts, good luck, glad tidings, big girl, dog growls, fond dreams

Chapter 15: The Structure of German

1. The following abbreviations will be used in this section: prefix (p), root stem (rs), suffix (s), verbal ending (ve).

un (p) **vergess** (rs) lich (s), zer (p) **brech** (rs) lich (s), un (p) aus (p) **weich** (rs) lich (s), be (p) ein (p) **fluss** (rs) en (ve), ver (p) **geb** (rs) en (ve) s (s), ge (p) **broch** (rs) en (ve), ver (p) **wend** (rs) bar (s), un (p) be (p) **wohn** (rs) bar (s), durch (p) **dring** (rs) en (ve), un (p) **ruh** (rs) ig (s), **lang** (rs) sam (s), ver (p) **sinn** (rs) lich (s) en (ve), un (p) **glaub** (rs) lich (s), ver (p) **führ** (rs) er (ve) isch (s), un (p) ge (p) **zwung** (rs) en (ve), un (p) er (p) **reich** (rs) bar (s), außer (preposition) ge (p) **wöhn** (rs) lich (s), vor (p) ent (p) **halt** (rs) en (ve), be (p) **end** (rs) en (ve), aus (p) **länd** (rs) isch (s)

2. abmachen, darbieten, fortpflanzen, einladen, ausbreiten, dastehen, aufklären, durchlesen, nachbestellen, niederputzen, zurückkehren, hergeben, wegziehen, mitnehmen, umbauen, anhören, einkaufen, vorbereiten, weitermachen, hinfahren

Chapter 16: Characteristic German Phonemes

1. [tsɛçɐ], [kuːχən], [byːçlaen], [zʊχt], [zuːχən], [faelçən], [bɛçlaen], [gəˈbraoχən], [mɛçtɪç], [gəˈdɪçt], [hoːχ], [mœçtə], [laoχ], [dʊrçzɪçtɪç], [nɛçstə], [ˌjeːˈdɔχ], [ʃmaːχ], [flʏçtlɪŋ], [naːχzɪçtɪç], [ɔfənˈzɪçtlɪç], [naχtlɪçt], [naːχtrɛːklɪç], [naːχbaːrʃaftlɪçl], [zaχlɪçkaet], [naχthɛmtçən]

2. [eːvɪklɪç], [luːtvɪç], [bəˈlaedɪçt], [mɪnɪklɪç], [frɔødɪçst], [køːnɪklɪç], [fɪrtsɪçstə], [køːnɪkraeç], [bəˈfriːdɪçt], [vɔnɪklɪç], [hɛrtsɪçstə], [hɔfəntlɪç], [fɛɐˈgɛslɪçkaet], [ɪnɪklɪç], [bəˈzɛnftɪçt], [vɪçtɪçstəm], [gəˈrɛçtɪçkaet]

3. [flʏstɐrn], [bɪtɐ], [daːˈfoːɐ], [foːɐˈheːrgeːən], [mʊtɐ], [mʏtɐrn], [roːɐ], [meːɐ], [ɔfənbaːɐ], [iːrən], [fɔrdərstə], [vɪrən], [zaoɐ], [ʃvɪrən], [klaːɐ], [ʃveːrɐ], [miːɐ], [ʃaodɐrn], [mʊstɐ], [viːdɐ], [bəˈryːrən], [trɛfən], [roːt], [meːrərə], [ʊntərɪçt], [yːbərˈgeːən], [viːdərzeːən], [ɛɐˈzeːən], [fɛɐˈʃtɪmən]

4. [mɛçtɪç], [maχt], [nɔχ], [laχən], [lɛçərlɪç], [veːnɪçstəns], [hantyːçɐ], [hantuːχ], [leːdɪklɪç], [hoːχ], [gəˈʃprɔχən], [gəˈʃprɛːçə], [høːçstə], [dʊrç], [tɔχtɐ], [byːçɐ], [zaχə], [aχ], [rɛçtsbʏndɪç], [zeːlɪçkaet]

Chapter 17: Vowels

1. [kɪndɐ], [ruˈiːnə], [ʃtɪlə], [miːɐ], [paranoˈiːt], [ɪnərhalp], [iːrətveːgən], [diːɐ], [liːfɐrn], [ɛɐˈʃaenən], [blɪk], [kaːpiːrən], [ʃiːbən], [gəˈʃvɪstɐ], [fɪŋɐ], [bəˈdiːnən], [ʃmɪŋkən], [bəˈfiːlt], [zɪnə], [ɪst], [fɪrtseːn], [fiːɐ]

2. [ɛːnəlt], [aofheːbən], [hɛmt], [trɛːnən], [mɛːən], [ʃɛŋkən], [neːbəl], [blɛːzɐ], [fɛstɐ], [eːdəlʃtaen], [meːɐ], [mɛːtçən], [tɛːtɪç], [eːrlɪç], [bɛːɐ], [zeːfaːrɐ], [lɛçərlɪç], [klɛmpnɐ], [muːˈzeːən], [trɛnʊŋ], [ʃpɛːtɐ], [mɛnʃ], [fɛɐˈkeːɐ], [krɛːə], [vɛçtɐ], [vɛːrə]

3. [gasən], [taːgəstsaetʊŋ], [amtlɪç], [voːnvaːgən], [gast], [aːnən], [aːl], [aŋəln], [fraːgəstsaeçən], [draːt], [andərə], [ʃtraːlən], [baŋə], [aosvaːl], [astərn], [klamərn], [bʊndəsʃtaːt], [zamlʊŋ], [eːəpaːɐ], [tanənbaom]

4. [hɔkɐ], [oːbən], [ʃtɔlpərn], [zɔnə], [broːt], [teleˈfoːn], [vɔnə], [oːɐ], [hoːə], [vɔlkən], [ʃtroːhalm], [tsɛˈrɔnən], [zɪç loːnən], [moːɐ], [lɔkɐ], [tsoː], [vɔlən], [kroːnə], [pɔst], [frɔm]

5. [ʊntɐ], [ruːdɐ], [bʊnt], [uːfɐ], [ʃʊltɐ], [aenluːt], [fɛɐˈʊnzɪçərn], [juːdən], [ʃtʊm], [tuːn], [truːə], [mʊnt], [ʃuː], [kʊnst], [ruːɪç], [buːlə], [ʃʊlt], [lʊft], [uːrən], [ʃlʊmɐ], [fluːχən]

6. [kœstlɪç], [trøːdəlmarkt], [œrtlɪç], [byːgəl|aezən], [kœnən], [tøːtlɪç], [ɛˈgyptən], [mœçtə], [yːbərˈfalən], [ɛmˈpøːrən], [røːtlɪç], [gəˈbyːɐ], [tœpfə], [pflykən], [høːlə], [kyːlʃraŋk], [anoˈnyːm], [røːrə], [glykl], [anʃpryçə], [vœrtçən], [føːgəl], [hœlə], [ameˈtyst], [dyr]

7. [ʃlaeçən], [kaoən], [graozaːm], [zɪç frɔøən], [frɔølaen], [fɛɐˈmaedən], [hɔøtə], [laonɪʃ], [fɛɐˈglaeçən], [aofʃteːən], [haosfrao], [ʃtaonən], [maelant], [bəˈtrɔøən], [baeɐ], [maːləˈrae], [tsɔøknɪs], [tsɔønə]

Chapter 18: Consonants

1. [rɛmbrant], [tɛːklɪç], [gɛrn], [aosbɪldən], [tastaˈtuːɐ], [naχtɪgal], [buːχ], [zabərn], [agrɛˈsiːf], [tiːɐ], [krɪbəln], [bəˈflagən], [puːblikʊm], [daːmaːls], [biblioˈteːk], [kɪrçə], [gəˈpɛk], [kʊplʊŋ], [klaen], [teːma], [ʃlɛpən], [keːlə], [laop], [spœtɪʃ], [tsuːk], [drykən], [paˈpiːrkɔrp], [aosdrʊk], [rɪtɐ], [deˈtsɛmbɐ], [ʃtɛːtə], [vɪkəln]

2. [ʒyːri], [vɔlkən], [aosvaes], [ʃeːrə], [voːnən], [vɛnˈtiːl], [ʃyːlɐ], [festhaltən], [kʊrvə], [ʃpʊkən], [faent], [kysən], [ʃpiˈoːn], [fɔrɛlə], [trɛfən], [ʃtɔf], [mɛsɐ], [foːˈryːbɐ], [apsɛrviːrən], [leːzən], [haːzə], [ʃpas], [fɛɐ'boːtən], [ak'tiːf], [ʃteːlən], [fan'toːm], [hɛlftə], [zyːsɪçkaetən], [faːze], [haelen], [ʒe'liːrən], [ʃtreːbən]

3. [vaŋən], [nɪmɐ], [fɛɐ'nɪçtət], [klɪŋəln], [ɪnɪç], [vɪŋkən], [mɛnʃ], [raŋ], [mɪlç], [baːdəvanə], [ʃpaŋə], [anɛːərn], [lam], [rɛnən], [markt], [naen], [bʊməln], [tɔnə], [nʊmɐ], [maŋəl], [taŋkʃtɛlə], [fʏlʊŋ], [yːbər'ʃvɛmʊŋ]

4. [ɛkɪç], [baχ], [tsuːgɪç], [taoχən], [tsakɪç], [zuːχən], [kraːnɪç], [aoχ], [ʃprʏçə], [baoχ], [tyːçtɪç], [laeçt], [dʊrç], [rɔøçərn], [ʃpraːχst], [ɔøç], [naːχbaːɐ], [çe'miː], [braoχst], [çi'rʊrk], [maχən], [çi'neːzə], [flʊχt], [mançmaːl], [aχtʊŋ], [mɔøsçən], [hɛrtsçən], [buːχ], [rɪçtən], [raχə]

5. [deːɐ|art], [fraehaet], [raʃ], [haetɐ], [arbaetən], [ɛɐ'kɛnən], [karə], [ʃraebən], [ɪrə], [foːɐbəraetən], [fɛɐ'glaeçən], [rœntgən], [ɛɐ'ʃaenʊŋ], [bruːdɐ], [eːɐ], [deːɐ'zɛlbə], [vaetərhɪn], [kɛrl], [bə'ryːrən], [tsvɪrn], [rɛtʊŋ], [ɛɐ'tsɛːlən], [veːrdən]

6. [eːbnən], [yːblɐ], [gɔldnə], [handlə], [vandrɐ], [andrɐ], [ʊnzrɐ], [reːgnərɪʃ], [bɪldnɐ], [reːdnɐ], [ɔrdnʊŋ], [wandlə], [oːbrɐ], [lɔøgnən], [friːdrɪç], [laebnɪts], [eːvgən], [frɔødgə], [ɔørɐ], [aegnə], [vaːgnɐ]

Chapter 19: Advanced Concepts in Diction

1. [apbaoən], [apbɪndən], [apbrɛçən], [anfɛrpbaːɐ], [antraepbaːɐ], [aofheːpbaːɐ], [taopblɪnt], [ɛrpbəzɪts], [farpbɪltʃɪrm], [ʃraepbədarf], [halpbədɛkt], [gɛlpbeːrən], [laopbaχ], [ʃaepbant], [fɛɐ'|ɛrpbaːɐ]

2. [bɪltdaːrʃtɛlʊŋ], [ɛntdaːtən], [eːrtdrʊk], [fɛltdiːnst], [gɔltdraːt], [mɔrtdroːʊŋ], [nɔrtdɔøtʃlant], [zantdɔrf], [ɛntael], [ʃɪltdryːzə], [zyːtdɔøtʃ], [blɪntdarm], [ɛntɛrmiːn], [grʊntariːf], [gɛltaʃə], [grʊnteːma], [lantaːk], [liːtɛkst], [aːbəntdɛmərʊŋ]

3. [bɛrkgɪpfəl], [bʊrkgraːbən], [fluːkgəzɛlʃaft], [vɛkgəbraχt], [tsuːkgʊrt], [vɛkgeːbən], [vɛkgəlasən], [vɛkgənɔmən]

Bibliography

Adams, David. *A Handbook of Diction for Singers: Italian, German, French, 2nd ed.* New York: Oxford University Press, 2008.

Barber, Charles. *The English Language: A Historical Introduction.* Cambridge: Cambridge University Press, 1993.

Cox, Richard G. *The Singer's Manual of German and French Diction.* New York: Schirmer Books, 1970.

Davenport, Mike, and S.J. Hannahs. *Introducing Phonetics & Phonology.* London: Arnold Publishers, 1998.

Duden. Die deutsche Rechtschreibung, 25. Auflage. Mannheim: Dudenverlag, Bibliographisches Institut AG, 2009.

Freeborn, Dennis. *From Old English to Standard English, 2nd ed.* Ottawa: University of Ottawa Press, 1998.

Handbook of the International Phonetic Association. Cambridge: Cambridge University Press, 1999.

Hey, Julius. *Der kleine Hey: Die Kunst des Sprechens.* Mainz: Schott Music GmbH & Co., 1997.

Hirschfeld, Ursula, et al. *Phonetik intensiv—Aussprachetraining.* Berlin: Langenscheidt KG, 2007.

Jones, Daniel. *An Outline of English Phonetics, 9th ed.* Cambridge: W. Heffer & Sons, Ltd, 1962.

———. *Cambridge English Pronouncing Dictionary, 17th ed.* Cambridge: Cambridge University Press, 2006.

Kenyon, John S., and Thomas A. Knott. *A Pronouncing Dictionary of American English.* Springfield: Merriam-Webster, Inc., 1953.

LaBouff, Kathryn. *Singing and Communicating in English.* New York: Oxford University Press, 2008.

Ladefoged, Peter. *Vowels and Consonants, 2nd ed.* Oxford: Blackwell Publishing, 2005.

Levitin, Daniel J. *This Is Your Brain on Music: The Science of a Human Obsession.* New York: Dutton, 2006.

Mangold, Max, ed. *Duden Aussprachwörterbuch, 6. Auflage.* Mannheim: Dudenverlag, Bibliographisches Institut & F. A. Brockhaus AG, 2005.

Marshall, Madeleine. *The Singer's Manual of English Diction.* New York: G. Schirmer, 1953.

Moriarty, John. *Diction.* Boston: E. C. Schirmer Music Company, 1975.

Odom, William, and Benno Schollum. *German for Singers, 2nd ed.* New York: Schirmer Books, 1997.

Parkin, Ken. *Anthology of British Tongue-Twisters.* London: Samuel French Ltd., 1969.

Paton, John Glenn. *Gateway to German Diction.* Van Nuys, CA: Alfred Publishing Co., Inc., 1999.

Pfautsch, Lloyd. *English Diction for the Singer.* New York: Lawson-Gould Music Publishers, Inc., 1971.

Pinker, Stephen. *The Language Instinct.* New York: HarperCollins Publishing, 1994.

Pompino-Marschall, Bernd. *Einführung in die Phonetik, 2. Auflage.* Berlin: Walter de Gruyter GmbH & Co., 2003.

Pullum, Geoffrey K., and William A. Ladusaw. *Phonetic Symbol Guide.* Chicago: University of Chicago Press, 1986.

Schmidt, Wilhelm. *Geschichte der deutschen Sprache, 10. Auflage.* Stuttgart: S. Hirzel Verlag, 2007.

Schollum, Benno. *Sprechen für Sänger.* Published by author as course material for study of speech at the Universität für Musik und Darstellende Kunst Wien (Vienna, Austria), 1993.

Siebs, Theodor. *Deutsche Aussprache, 19. Auflage.* Berlin: Walter de Gruyter & Co., 1969.

Uris, Dorothy. *To Sing in English.* New York: Boosey and Hawkes, 1971.

Venezky, Richard L. *The Structure of English Orthography.* The Hague: Mouton & Co., 1970.

Wall, Joan. *International Phonetic Alphabet for Singers.* Dallas: Pst...Inc., 1989.

Wall, Joan, et al. *Diction.* Dallas: Pst...Inc., 1990.

Woods, Howard B. *Syllable Stress & Unstress, 2nd ed.* Ottawa: Public Service Commission of Canada, 1987.

Wynn, Dr. J.B. *An English Pronunciation Dictionary: A Concise Dictionary of Received Pronunciation.* Douglas, Isle of Man: Domino Books, Ltd., 1987.

Removable Flashcard (please cut out and laminate)

Front side: English

Monophthongs

[ɑ]	father [fɑðə]	[oʊ]	wrote [ɹoʊt]	[m]	summer [sʌmə]
[æ]	lamb [læm]	[ɔɪ]	joint [dʒɔɪnt]	[n]	neptune [nɛptjun]
[e]*	vacation [veˈkeɪʃən]	[ɔə]	floor [flɔə]	[ŋ]	minx [mɪŋks]
[ɛ]	meant [mɛnt]	[ʊə]	tour [tʊə]	[ɲ]	onion [ʌɲən]
[ə]	above [əˈbʌv]			[p]	maple [meɪpəl]
	altar [ɔltɚ]	**Triphthongs**		[ɹ]	narrow [næɹoʊ]
[ɜ]	early [ɜlɪ]	[aʊə]	hourly [aʊəlɪ]	[s]	cease [sis]
[i]	niece [nis]	[aɪə]	aspire [əˈspaɪə]	[ʃ]	shout [ʃaʊt]
[ɪ]	victim [vɪktɪm]			[ʒ]	vision [vɪʒən]
[o]*	obey [oˈbeɪ]	**Consonants**		[t]	attempt [əˈtɛmpt]
[ɔ]	cause [kɔz]	[b]	grab [gɹæb]	[ts]	warts [wɔəts]
[u]	gloom [glum]	[d]	plodding [plɑdɪŋ]	[tʃ]	chance [tʃæns]
[ʊ]	should [ʃʊd]	[f]	flavor [fleɪvə]	[θ]	thrifty [θɹɪftɪ]
		[g]	gaggle [gægəl]	[ð]	clothes [kloʊðz]
Diphthongs		[dʒ]	German [dʒɜmen]	[ʌ]	love [lʌv]
[aʊ]	clown [klaʊn]	[gz]	exit [ɛgzɪt]	[v]	vein [veɪn]
[aɪ]	tide [taɪd]	[h]	house [haʊs]	[w]	winter [wɪntə]
[eɪ]	dazed [deɪzd]	[j]	fuse [fjuz]	[ʍ]	whether [ʍɛðə]
[ɛə]	chair [tʃɛə]	[k]	coarse [kɔəs]	[z]	puzzle [pʌzəl]
[ɪə]	leer [lɪə]	[ks]	oxen [ɑksən]		
		[l]	lily [lɪlɪ]		

*unstressed

Monophthongs

[aː]	sagen [zaːgən]
[a]	der Bach [baχ]
[æ]	das Feuer [fɔøæ]
[eː]	das Beet [beːt]
[e]*	die Melodie [meloˈdiː]
[ə]	die Mühe [myːə]
[ɛ]	hätten [hɛtən]
[ɛː]	später [ʃpɛːtɐ]
[iː]	ihre [iːɐə]
[ɪ]	immer [ɪmɐ]
[oː]	die Botschaft [boːtʃaft]
[o]*	die Apotheke [apoˈteːka]
[ɔ]	voll [fɔl]
[øː]	die Söhne [zøːnə]
[œ]	die Götter [gœtɐ]
[uː]	die Mut [muːt]
[ʊ]	das Bund [bʊnt]
[yː]	die Bühne [byːnə]

[ʏ]	künstlerisch [kʏnstlərɪʃ]

Diphthongs

[ae]	zwei [tsvae]
[ao]	der Baum [baom]
[ɔø]	teuer [tɔøɐ]

Consonants

[b]	bang [baŋ]
[ç]	echt [ɛçt]
[d]	der Widder [vɪdɐ]
[f]	der Lauf [laof]
[g]	die Flagge [flagə]
[ʒ]	das Journal [ʒʊrˈnaːl]
[h]	die Hoheit [hoːhaet]
[j]	jagen [jaːgən]
[k]	das Kind [kɪnt]
[ks]	der Tag [taːk]
[ks]	die Hexe [hɛksə]
[kv]	die Quelle [kvɛla]
[l]	füllen [fʏlən]

[m]	der Mann [man]
[n]	erneuern [ɛɐˈnɔøɐn]
[ŋ]	danke [daŋka]
[p]	die Rippen [rɪpən]
	hinab [hɪˈnap]
[r]	die Ehre [eːrə]
[s]	der Fuß [fuːs]
[ʃ]	die Schwester [ʃvɛstɐ]
[t]	treu [trɔø]
	das Land [lant]
[ts]	nichts [nɪçts]
[tʃ]	der Kitsch [kɪtʃ]
[v]	weinen [vaenən]
[χ]	der Lauch [laoχ]
[z]	sehr [zeːɐ]

*loan words

Reverse side: German

Index

"Abendempfindung" (Mozart/
Campe), 220
affricates, 15, 20, 23, 29, 34–35,
38, 113–14, 197
"An die Nachtigall" (Brahms/
Hölty), 148
Anglo-Saxon conquest, 243–44. *See
also* England
articulators: as active, 128, 213–14;
articulation process, 103–4,
106–8; and consonants, 96–97,
186, 191; in lyric diction, 235;
as passive, 128. *See also* points
of articulation
assimilation: as contextual, 42; as
historical, 42
"Auf dem Wasser zu singen"
(Schubert/Graf zu Stolberg),
205
Das Aussprachewörterbuch (Duden),
134

Barber, Charles, 241
Bentley, Richard, 246
"The Blessed Virgin's Expostula-

tion" (Purcell/Tate), 91
Brahms, Johannes, 227–28
British Broadcasting Corporation
(BBC), 43
British Received Pronunciation
(RP), 12–13, 22, 43, 66, 80,
94, 133, 158
Britten, Benjamin, 66
Bühnendeutsch, 133, 158. *See also*
Stage German

*Cambridge English Pronouncing Dic-
tionary*, 43
Canada, 43, 133
Cardinal Vowels, 4; back vowels, 5;
front vowels, 5. *See also* vowels
cognates, 99–103, 105, 113,
188, 190–91; articulation process, 106; as continuants, 104;
as fricatives, 103–6, 192–94;
implosion/explosion, 118;
omissions in, 239–40; as sibilants, 106–7; as stop consonants, 102; substitutions in,
239–40. *See also* consonants

287

About the Author

Canadian collaborative pianist **Amanda Johnston** is Assistant Professor of Music at the University of Mississippi, where she is Head Coach for the Opera Theatre, professor of advanced diction, collaborative piano, and song literature classes, and coach for students at the undergraduate and graduate level. She also serves on the faculty at *Lied Austria*, an intensive international summer program for singers in Leibnitz, Austria. Since 2004, she has been Artistic Director of "In Recital", a recital series held at the Heliconian Hall in Toronto, designed to showcase Canadian singers and cultivate the art song. An avid polyglot and etymology enthusiast, her area of research is comparative diction. In addition to the "standard" languages, she is also adept at coaching Czech and Russian literature.

Amanda Johnston has held positions at the University of Toronto, Royal Conservatory of Music, and York University. An active recitalist, she has performed in Canada, the United States, Germany, France, Austria, and Scotland, and has been broadcast on CBC Radio 2. She has received numerous grants to work with masters in the field of collaborative piano, most notably Malcolm Martineau, Rudolf Jansen, Martin Isepp, Dalton Baldwin, Elly Ameling, Wolfgang Holzmair, and Helmut Deutsch. She was educated at Queen's University at Kingston, the Hochschule für Musik "Franz Liszt" in Weimar, Germany, and the Janáček Academy of Music in Brno, Czech Republic.